*This memoir is dedicated to my wife, Kay, and my
siblings who have stood with me
in sickness and health and worked tirelessly
to make this a better read.*

© Jerry and Kay Hall. 2016.

ISBN: 978-0-9972856-2-8 (print)
    978-0-9972856-3-5 (ebook)

Some names and identifying details have been changed to protect the privacy of individuals.

Cover and logo design by Lori Hollifield.

We Gotta Get Out Of This Place
Words and Music by Barry Mann and Cynthia Weil
© 1965 (Renewed 1993) SCREEN GEMS-EMI MUSIC INC.
All Rights Reserved International Copyright Secured Used by Permission
Reprinted by Permission of Hal Leonard Corporation

Crystal Blue Persuasion
Words and Music by Tommy James, Ed Gray and Mike Vale
Copyright © 1969 EMI Longitude Music
Copyright Renewed
All Rights Administered by Sony/ATV Music Publishing LLC, 424 Church Street, Suite 1200, Nashville, TN 37219
International Copyright Secured   All Rights Reserved
Reprinted by Permission of Hal Leonard Corporation

Run Through the Jungle
Words and Music by John Fogerty
Copyright © 1970 Jondora Music
Copyright Renewed
International Copyright Secured   All Rights Reserved
Reprinted by Permission of Hal Leonard Corporation

Early Mornin' Rain
Words and Music by GORDON LIGHTFOOOT
© 1965 (Renewed) WB MUSIC CORP.
All Rights Reserved
Used By Permission of ALFRED MUSIC

though
YES SIR, YES SIR, 3 BAGS FULL!
VOLUME II

Flying, Friendship, and Trying to Make Sense of a Senseless War

JERRY HALL

Praise for *Yes Sir, Yes Sir, 3 Bags Full!*

Yes Sir, Yes Sir, 3 Bags Full! is a deeply rich and personal account of a man's lived experiences in the context of war. Jerry brings us closer to the realities of war through his relationships with those whom he fought side by side with and against. Jerry's book teaches us the power and nature of all relationships. For clinicians, the indications are to invest not only in evidence-based therapies, but also in the healing possibilities of therapeutic and non-therapeutic relationships. Taking this cue from Jerry, as his therapist, the possibilities appeared to be limitless.

—Taryn M. Jaramillo, LCSW

Trauma Therapist

Yes Sir, Yes Sir, 3 Bags Full! captures what living through Viet Nam as a pilot was like with an incredible degree of detail and accuracy—the emotional highs and lows, the boredom and bedlam we all experienced. In reading Jerry's book, I relived the craziness of our performance and ultimate survival.

—Bill Healey (Father William)

Jerry Hall's vivid descriptions of life in the military during war brings understanding to anyone whose loved one served during a time of crisis. Jerry's incredible journey is one of survival, coping, and trying to make sense of the inhumanity of war. Yes Sir, Yes Sir, 3 Bags Full! is an important look at history and how war impacts those we ask to risk their lives as they struggle with the morality of taking the lives of others.

—Patti Frazee,

author of *Cirkus* and *Out of Harmony*

Table of Contents

Part 1: The Victims

Chapter 1　　Nightdreams 3

Chapter 2　　Killing Time 35

Part 2: The Vacuum

Chapter 1　　The Visitation 65

Chapter 2　　Change 77

Chapter 3　　War Stories 99

Chapter 4　　Something Is Missing 129

Chapter 5　　Back to Normal 159

Chapter 6　　A Beer and a Broad 179

Chapter 7　　Another Cluster Fuck 199

Chapter 8　　My Friend Jack 211

Part 3: The Verdict

Chapter 1　　Fini Flight 225

Chapter 2　　Memories 239

Epilogue 255
Map of U.S. Air Force Bases, Viet Nam 256
Glossary 257
About the Author 261

Jerry Hall's gripping memoir of his service in Viet Nam continues

In *Yes Sir, Yes Sir, 3 Bags Full! Volume I*, Jerry Hall described his climb into "the Vortex." Viet Nam was calling and Jerry answered. As a pilot, he saw the war from a bird's-eye view and felt the anguish of battle with every comrade he had to say goodbye to.

Volume II continues after Jerry has found out several of his best friends, men he'd trained with, had been shot down and killed. His spiral into the vortex has him holding on for dear life.

Note: A glossary of acronyms used in the text is provided at the back of this book.

Part 1

The Victims

Chapter 1
NIGHTDREAMS

I felt sober enough to fly the next morning. I spotted several gooks in the middle of a stream in a free-fire zone. No clearance was needed. They were not supposed to be there. If they were, they were V.C. I wanted to kill them, but it didn't seem right. It made no sense. Why were they out in the open? I scoured the countryside every day looking for them, and now they were standing in the middle of a stream. Why were they there? What were they doing? I could see no weapons. Was it possible they were a family that just wandered into the free-fire zone, unaware of the consequences? Were they fishing?

Quit thinking, just kill them! A couple of gooks. *What the fuck? They're nothing!* Even if I killed them, I would still have nine hundred and ninety-nine thousand, nine hundred and ninety-four gooks to go to avenge Billy's death. But it didn't feel right. It was too easy. What if I made a low pass over them? If they broke for the banks, I could break off the pass, order up some air, and kill them. If they didn't move, I could get a good look at what they were doing in the middle of a stream in a free-fire zone. I rolled the airplane up on its side, pulled my throttles back, and headed down the chute. I was jinking, rolling the bird back and forth from left to right, just in case anyone down there had my airplane in their gun sights. I leveled off, two maybe three feet off the water, and brought my power back in. My best visibility was out my left window, so I planned and executed my plan so they would be on my left. They never looked up. They never moved as I passed beside them at nearly eye level. I decided they were innocent, confused peasants as I started my pull up and crossed the other side of the bank. It was then that the ground fire started. It was then that I was wishing I had an afterburner on my little Cessna airplane as it struggled to gain altitude.

"Come on baby. Climb. Goddammit climb!" I shouted. I pulled and jerked the airplane left and up to move away from the ground fire.

"Goddammit, Billy, I'm not ready to join you."

The overloaded and underpowered airplane slogged upward as one propeller strained to grab air while clawing its way forward, and the other propeller pushed like the airplane was stuck in sludge. Upward we chugged like *the-little-engine-that-could*, and when we reached 1,500 feet and I was sure I was out of small arms range, I rolled wings level and inhaled air until my empty lungs were filled to capacity, and then I inhaled some more. And then I started to shake. I squeezed the yoke with both my hands and all of my strength.

I knew better. What was I doing? I had injected morality into warfare. And I let the dinks sucker me. I wanted to give the pricks the benefit of the doubt when I should have crushed them with 500-pound bombs and cooked their bodies to well done with a few napalms. I should have hit them or ignored them. I checked all my instruments and control surfaces and looked for holes. They should have been able to turn my airplane into a colander, but I could see no damage. My courage returned. I decided to order up a couple of airstrikes or at least pound the area with artillery. It was a free-fire zone and I needed to make them pay. I encoded the coordinates and transmitted them to *Smoky* forty. All was quiet.

Bizz-ezz-et! I jumped up, my ass separated from my seat. If I hadn't been strapped in, I would have jumped right out of the airplane. It's just noise from the radio, I told myself, but I was still terrified. I couldn't stop shaking. The enemy missed my airplane but they hit my nerve center.

"*Smoky* four-four, *Smoky* four-zero."

"Four-zero, go."

"Clearance is denied. Province chief says there are friendlies in the area."

"You gotta be shitting me."

How could I avenge Billy when I couldn't even get clearance to kill a couple of gooks lollygagging in a free fire-zone?

"Say again, *Smoky* four-four."

"I guess they were just out on a picnic."

"*Smoky* four-four. Are you talking to *Smoky* four-zero?"

I did not answer. Everyone was faking it. The bad guys were pretending that they were just innocent bystanders. The province chief was pretending that he was on our side. I was pretending that I was a tough guy who was not scared.

"Ah, Roger. *Smoky* four-zero copies."

And *Smoky* four-zero was pretending that he understood it all.

I rechecked my instruments and studied the underside of my wings. How could it be? How could they have missed me? I turned my attention back to the landscape. The gooks were gone. Then I turned my attention back to Billy...

"What the fuck were you doing, Billy? You had a death wish, didn't you, you son of a bitch? You've always had a death wish, always fucking around, always pushing the envelope, whether in an automobile or airplane. You had a draft-deferred job. What the fuck were you thinking when you volunteered to come over here, you asshole? You motherfucker! What were you doing flying in shitty weather? Fucking around, right?"

That night I rolled violently in my bunk. I could feel it, even though I knew I was still asleep. When I stopped rolling, Billy was sitting at a table with his head down. Moondoggie was with him...

"Tell him, Doggie," I said. "Tell that hick-ass coal miner he deserved to die. Tell him!"

There was silence. Billy raised his head. I began to cry.

"I can't help you anymore, Billy," I said. "I have two sons who need me."

My body pivoted just below my stomach and the top half of me snapped up like a spring in my back had broken. I was sweating. I was shaking. My bunk was shaking. My eyes were slow to open. I looked at the clock and read the hands: 9:18. I looked into the bunk below me; no Captain Puff. Had he joined the procession? No, that was days ago. My head hurt. My tongue was stuck to the roof of my mouth. I was awake. I was in Viet Nam. I eased my way down to the floor. I walked to the john. On the way, my mind replayed a scene...

I watched as Billy was getting thrown into the "solo" tank beside a searing airstrip, in the middle of a West Texas desert. A dust devil danced in front of rattlesnakes. I was laughing. Moondoggie was laughing. Billy was laughing. Thumper was laughing. The last of the fantastic four had soloed. We were pilots.

I walked up to a sink. I splashed water in my eyes, on the back of my neck, and then threw it at my face. Jefferson entered, followed by Joey.

"Sorry to hear about your friend," Jefferson said.

"It's the shits, mate," Joey said as he laid a hand on my shoulder. The mamasans cackled in the corner.

"Shut the fuck up!" I yelled.

Two nights later I was again lying awake, when I heard the outside hootch door slam. Then I heard a hissing sound and smelled something. What was it? Sulfur? I jumped down, my poncho liner in hand, and held it against my face and nose.

"Get up!" I yelled at Captain Puff.

There was a commotion outside our door, voices shouting and feet scurrying. Captain Puff stirred.

"Get something over your face!" I yelled as I opened the door.

I could see the hallway light, but it was faint, obscured by a white smoke.

"What the fuck?" someone in the hall said.

"Pick it up! Throw it out the door!" another yelled.

"I got it! Open the door!"

"Kiwi, open the fucking door!"

"It's bloody fucking open."

I heard the outside door open and close. I saw someone fanning the smoke by opening and closing the door. I moved to the bar area. Visibility was better in there. Men from both sides of the hootch were gathering. When the air cleared, we could see white markings—like cops at a murder scene made around a corpse—on the floor where the canister had landed. A *Nugget* FAC brought the empty can back inside, and we examined it. It was a smoke canister used by the ground troops, mostly, or by a pilot in an aircraft that had no smoke rockets to mark a position, either ours or the enemy's.

"They are sending a message," a *Daredevil* FAC stated. "It's a warning, for Christ's sake!"

Staff-weenies drifted in.

"This is the result of you assholes busting the guys on the flight line," another FAC said.

"You don't get it, do you? We have been telling you to get off their backs. Now, it's fucking serious, maybe you will listen." The FACs sounded like a lynching party in an old Western movie.

"Yeah, yeah!"

"Better do something about this!"

"Yeah, yeah!"

"Listen to what?" the commander asked.

"Listen to us!" an OV-10 driver yelled. "There is a pattern to this. First a smoke bomb. No results? Here's some C.S. gas. You know what that is? That's the shit our grunts throw down Cong tunnels. And when the dinks come out coughing, gagging, puking, and rubbing their eyes, we can shoot them one at a time. Still don't get the message, you fucking lifer motherfuckers? Well, we are done talking. Here's a grenade. It's been nice knowing you. This hootch is going to get gassed and then *fragged*!"

"What are you talking about? This is just a prank," the commander said.

"Prank, my ass! They smoke you, they gas you, and then they frag you! What fucking world are you living in, colonel?"

"Ah, it's nothing, just a bunch of disgruntled troops playing a little joke. We need to tighten up the discipline. Now, go back to bed," the commander said. He turned and walked out and the weenies followed. The FACs milled and murmured.

"I'm getting the fuck out of here just as fast as I can, Joey," I said. "We are going to get hit."

"You think, mate?"

"Absolutely. Smoke, C.S. gas, and then a grenade. I'm moving. This hootch is going to get blown up."

"Your own men will try to kill you? I don't get it, mate."

"I'll try to find a place for both of us."

I headed back to my room. Captain Puff was standing in the door. His eyes and nose were oozing liquids. I spun him slightly as I passed. He said nothing.

"Maybe you can find a way to turn this into a medal," I said.

His eyes suddenly cleared.

Captain Puff had now turned his attention to figuring out ways to get out of flying missions when all he had to do was ask. We didn't mind. He was short. He earned it. We would let him stay in his room, opening and closing his locker door and studying the manuals to see if he qualified for medals. He had put his time in. He should be thinking about packing.

There was one flight, however, he could not get out of. His night currency—he had not flown a night strike mission in thirty days—had run out. He needed to fly with someone who was current to reestablish his currency. I was that someone. I had not flown with him since my training flights. At that time, I was the observer; this time, he would be. I liked to launch a little before sundown to get a good fix on the target. I would triangulate using some prominent landmarks that might still be visible after the black of night engulfed the sky and the jungle. Once I had the target fixed in my mind, I exited the area so as not to alert the bad guys that an airstrike was coming.

We launched, and on climb-out I turned directly into the setting sun, a signal that the day killers were winding down while the night killers were gearing up. Most of the sun's rays bounced off, but some filtered through the white smoke rising from the red fires on the green jungle floor. Bomb craters filled with lime-colored slime were punched into the ground at different intervals. Black shadows of palm fronds dangled in the clearings, their frayed ends looking like legs of a giant spider moving for cover before darkness encroached the earth. Two-hundred-feet-tall jungle trees, recently sprayed with toxicants, were rust in color; those dead were gunmetal grey. Healthy jungle trees lit by the setting sun created what seemed like an illusion, for they were not green but copper and crimson in color, like autumn in the north woods. Or perhaps it was my mind wishing I was hunting deer back home instead of humans here. Human vampires that were now crawling out of their underground hiding places, vampires needing to spill the blood of American GIs in order to survive. My never-ending dread of nighttime flying surfaced with a shiver.

An RF-4 blew past our nose, missing us by less than fifty feet. I watched as his strobe light blinked every second, indicating that he was on a photo-recon mission.

"Bien Hoa, *Smoky* forty-four. What is that RF-4 doing at our altitude?"

"Oh, he is on a recon run. He is due to exit the area in one to five minutes."

"We just missed each other. Next time advise of all activities taking place in our A.O."

"Roger forty-four."

His answer was devoid of emotion, like yeah, yeah, no big deal, get over it. But, for me, it was a big deal. In my mind I could see in slow motion the cockpit of the RF-4 as it folded up my cockpit like an accordion playing a screeching note, the sound of metal scrunching metal. I instinctively crossed my arms in front of my face in a futile attempt to fend off an airplane traveling in excess of 400 miles an hour. I could smell the jet fuel as it emptied from the wings just before the fireball consumed me. And I continued to fly my mission.

We were scheduled to fly for two and a half hours. We had been airborne for a short time and were already into our first argument. He was an instructor pilot, in-country longer, and he was my boss. I was in the pilot-in-command seat because I was current, and he was not.

"Burn the auxiliary tanks dry," *Smoky* forty-one ordered.

"There is no reason to burn the aux tanks. We are scheduled to fly for no more than a couple of hours," I argued. "We have plenty of fuel."

"Well, I say do it," he replied.

"All right. But my experience is that I will get busy and forget they're on aux feed, and then the engines will flame out at a critical time, typically in a rocket pass."

He did not answer. I reluctantly complied, as I did too often. But I decided this was not a life-or-death situation. Actually, "Pick your battles" were the words that were rolling around in my brain, followed by, *Shoot him when we get back on the ground.*

We drove around to kill some time before the fighters would check in. The only light now came from an occasional fire on the ground, the winking evening star Venus—red, yellow, then green, an enticing jewel. I wondered if it was blinking a message in Morse code from Moondoggie and Billy, "Come to me. Join us here in the heavens where everything is beautiful and peaceful."

I pointed the airplane back into the target area. The front engine sputtered and then quit. The aux tanks had burned dry. I shot a look at Captain Puff. The fire in my eyes should have lit the cockpit. I rotated the fuel selector switches to main tanks. I hit the boost pump located under the yoke and between my legs, and the engine restarted.

"*Smoky* forty-four, *Smoky* forty."

"Forty-four here. Go ahead."

"Be advised that *Shadow* will be late for the rendezvous."

Shadow, an AC-119 gunship with a gigantic spotlight.

"I suggest we cancel the first set of fighters rather than work with flares. It's only a training mission. No sense taking any chances. We can still get you current with the second set of fighters."

"Use the flares," Captain Puff replied. And again I capitulated.

The fighters checked in, and I briefed them. I drove over the target and released my flare. Then I began a roll to my left for my rocket pass, when *Smoky* forty-one shouted, "No, no. I've got the airplane," and he snapped the plane back to the right.

"What are you doing?" I screamed.

"Right there. That's the target," he said.

"I don't think so. But if you have the target, put in a rocket before the flare runs out."

He took the airplane and squeezed off a rocket.

"I don't have the fighters. Do you?" I asked.

"I've got them," he replied. And he cleared the first F-100 in hot. I cranked my neck in every direction, trying to pick up the fighter bomber's lights. Suddenly, a long flame filled our windscreen. I felt the heat generated by the F-100's exhaust as it passed our airplane with a whoosh and then a roar.

"I thought you had the fighters," I shouted.

"I did. He just ran in on the wrong heading."

"Bullshit . . . Listen, two people can't fly one airplane. You got it. I'm just going to sit back and take a nap."

I slid my seat back so I could no longer reach the rudder pedals. I wanted it perfectly clear that he was in charge and responsible for flying the airplane. He lined up for another flare drop, and I scanned the horizon. I was sure we had missed the target, and by a lot too. I knew there were no friendlies in the area, so I didn't give a fuck, and I let him proceed. He rolled in for the rocket launch, and the front engine sputtered and died.

"Fly the airplane," I hollered and I slid my seat up and hit the boost pumps.

"I cannot get a relight," I yelled. "You fly the airplane; I have the radios."

"*Saber* one-eight, *Smoky* four-four. We have lost an engine. Salvo bombs on this pass. You are cleared hot."

"One copies."

"Two copies."

I turned my attention back to the airplane's gauges.

"What the fuck are you doing? I've got the airplane!" I yelled as I wrestled control of the aircraft from Captain Puff.

We were at 650 feet and the airspeed indicator read 71 knots and dropping. We were about to fall out of the sky, crash and burn in the bad guy's backyard. I dropped the nose and reached up to hit the panic button, which would jettison our rockets and lighten our load.

"Don't do that," he said. "If you do, we will have to file an incident report."

I punched off the load.

"Don't touch another fucking thing on this airplane or I will shoot you dead," I said.

I *feathered* the front prop. It froze in the best wind-resistant position, causing the least amount of drag on the airplane. Then I tried to stabilize our altitude and airspeed. I managed to get to and hold 78 knots. I could not gain any altitude but I was no longer losing any either. We would be alright if I could just hold what I had.

"Bien Hoa tower, *Smoky* four-four declaring an emergency."

"Roger, *Smoky*. State your position."

"We are thirty miles off the end of the runway and lined up for a straight-in approach."

"Roger *Smoky*, continue your approach."

With everything stabilized, I reviewed the entire engine-out emergency procedures to make sure I had not missed anything. I had lots of extra runway, so my plan was to land long. I would not chop the power until I was over the runway. Only one problem now: With the loss of the front engine, we also lost hydraulic power. There were two ways to get the landing gear down: Either release the front prop and let it *windmill* to build up hydraulic pressure or use a hand pump. I looked over at Captain Puff who was sitting with his hands folded like a kid in a theater watching the climatic last scene of a Saturday afternoon serial, or maybe he was praying. I didn't know but I suspected he hadn't even considered our hydraulic problem.

"Everything look all right to you?" I asked.

"Everything looks good," he replied.

"Can you think of any problems we might encounter?"

"Negative . . . negative. Everything looks good."

"What about the landing gear?"

"What about it?"

I did not answer. I unfeathered the front engine and as it windmilled, I watched the hydraulic pressure build and when the needle hit the green, I placed the gear handle down.

"Oh, the gear. Yeah," he said.

"*Smoky* forty-four, Bien Hoa tower. You are cleared to land."

I watched until the lights indicated all gear down and locked. Then I again feathered the front prop. I was over the runway. I had it made. I lowered my nose and two feet above the asphalt, I started my flare, and when I did, the tip of my right wing dropped, and suddenly the airplane was nose high and at a 45 degree angle to the runway. I feared we were going to cartwheel over the tip of my wing. I added power and snapped the yoke hard left while kicking full left rudder, and the airplane slowly stabilized with wings nearly level. I nursed it down and onto the runway. My instincts had saved me . . . no, check that—my instincts had saved us.

What the fuck was that all about? I wondered.

I looked up at the fuel selector switches. The left main was mistakenly on *crossfeed*, which burned the fuel in the left wing tanks dry. All remaining fuel was in the right wing, causing a weight imbalance. And when I slowed the airplane for landing, the right wing dropped.

"Why did that wing drop like that on landing?"

"I don't know," Captain Puff replied nervously.

I taxied the airplane perpendicular to the revetment and shut it down. The crew chief and one other helper would roll the airplane into the revetment when it was refueled and rearmed. I caught up to Captain Puff, grabbed him around the bicep, and spun him around.

"Don't ever ask me to fly with you again!" I said.

"Well, that suits me just fine," he replied.

"Let me finish. You're short. Stay out of the air. We will cover all flights for you. Stay in the hootch so you can get out of this miserable fucking shithole of a place alive."

"We have to file an incident report."

"I'm going to the club."

"No, you have to come with me. We have to meet with the flying safety officer. You were the one who was flying the airplane. You have to be there to sign the papers."

I looked at him for a long time thinking about what I should say or what I might say or what I might do to him.

"I'm going to get a beer," I said. I turned and walked away.

I dropped off my chute, survival vest, and firearm and started my walk to the club. He drove the jeep alongside of me, slowing it to keep pace with my walking.

"Get in," he said.

He didn't listen much, so I used sign language and raised my middle finger. I heard him grind the gears as he tried to shift.

I was into my fourth beer when the flying safety officer walked over to my booth. I looked up.

"Did I miss choir practice?" I said.

"What the fuck happened up there?"

"What did he tell you?"

"He said you fucked up and had the fuel selector switch on crossfeed."

I looked at him and shook my head. I wondered how many beers it would take to suppress my anger. I wondered how many years I would get in Leavenworth if I just shot Captain Puff dead, or might they rule it justifiable homicide. I wondered how Captain Puff, an extremely religious man, could rationalize shoving the blame on me, when I actually saved his life even though my only intention was to save my ass.

"Well, I guess that's right, I screwed up."

He tapped a cigarette on the table and stared at me.

"That doesn't sound like something you would do."

"What difference does it make? He will go on to be a full colonel like his daddy and guys like you and I will keep taking the blame for fucking jerks like him."

"You know, I don't like doing this," he said.

"I know. But guys like you always do. The order came down from up high, didn't it?"

He did not answer.

"They got you by the balls, don't they?"

He did not answer.

"You might as well defrock me now. Strip me of my wings and officer's bars. Take away the uniform that I love."

He did not answer.

I signed the report. He stood and I gave him a half-assed salute. Not the salute I practiced in the mirror, a salute that was snappy and tilted perfectly across my brow, but one that was nonchalant and disrespectful like I didn't care. But I really did.

"Three bags full, major."

He turned and walked away. I ordered another beer. The motherfuckers in the bunk below me were still trying to kill me.

That next night, Buddha stopped by.

"Gums got it today."

"Goddamn it, Buddha. How can you stand it? I am up to my eyeballs in hate."

"Fucking tough, man; it is fucking tough. They keep sending me younger kids. They are brave, but their judgment is clouded. I am not sure how much longer I can keep sending them into battle."

Once again, I could not sleep. My mind swirled, like the needle on an instrument receiving a bad homing signal it would not lock on. I thought about how war punishes complacency. How it exposes inadequacy. How it ignores morality. How it jangles nerves. How it stifles emotion. How it fosters hate. I thought about how there were days when I shook with fear and then there were days when I felt immortal, invincible, and indestructible. Nothing could kill me, which led right back to complacency.

The arms of a woman might have helped heal my soul; they might have revitalized my confidence and refilled my cup of courage. But with the absence of cradling arms, music would have to fill that void. I needed a U.S.O. show at the O club. Jefferson, Carlos, and Joey joined me.

It was a night that passed too quickly. The band was wrapping it up, and the crowd was again in a frenzy. I was numb. I felt alone. I changed the words. I substituted "I" for "we."

> *I gotta get out of this place.*
> *If it's last thing I ever do.*

> *I gotta get out of this place,*
> *Girl, there's a better life for me and you.*

I wanted it to be true. I wanted a guarantee that if I stayed, lived, and sacrificed a year of my life in this shithole, my life would be returned, intact, and just as it was prior to my deployment. I wanted to be assured that my girl and our children would be there with open arms, waiting for me. I needed to know for certain that my country would honor my service. It was not a lot to ask for, was it?

And then it ended. Quiet, sullen men now lumbering around, lost and drained. They may have been coming down from the evening's entertainment, but I was drained from combat, and losses, and lack of sleep. There was a moment when I was singing, when I was home and entwined with my loved ones. But the music stopped and I was still here, in this shithole. I shuffled toward the door.

When I got outside, everyone I knew was gone except one *Daredevil* FAC who was revving a jeep at the front door.

"Get in," he said. "They've all left."

I climbed aboard.

He was weaving all over, on and off the road, not with laughter like teenagers on a joy ride, but with rage because he was drunk. He took a strange route, one I had not been on.

"Where are we going?" I asked.

"Shortcut," he replied. "We are cutting through the Viet Namese side."

I nodded.

We approached a Viet Namese checkpoint.

"What the fuck is this?" the *Daredevil* FAC said. "They are usually just lying on top of the conex boxes and they wave us through."

"Halt!" a gomer guard ordered as he jumped in front of our jeep.

"Why you little motherfucker," the *Daredevil* FAC said as he started to get out of the jeep. The Viet Namese leveled his M-16.

"Easy," I said as I jumped out my side in an effort to get to the *Daredevil* before he got to the gomer guard.

I landed on the ground. An M-16 rifle was shoved in my gut and the Viet Namese guard, who was supposed to be on our side, chambered a round. Click, click. My heartbeat accelerated but my breathing stopped. I could feel the bullet ripping its way through me. I slowly raised my arms. My voice dropped to a whisper.

"It's okay. It's okay," I said.

I moved my head slightly to my left.

"Get back into the jeep and do it very slowly," I said to the drunken *Daredevil*.

He backed up and slid his butt back onto the seat of the jeep.

"Put your hands on the steering wheel where they can see them."

He complied.

"It's okay," I said gently again as I made eye contact with the man who could end my life. *My God, what's happening?* I thought. *One mistake, one slip of the finger and a bullet...*

"Tick, tick, tick..."

We stood connected, my stomach, a weapon of death, and a Viet Namese hand.

"Tick, tick, tick..."

He backed his rifle out of my gut, but the barrel end was still touching my fatigue jacket.

"Tick, tick, tick..."

Slowly and methodically, he moved the rifle off to the side just past my elbow, and we waited again.

"Tick, tick, tick..."

Then, with his head, he motioned for me to get back into the jeep.

"Drive away very slowly."

When we cleared the area, the *Daredevil* FAC ground the gears.

"That smiling son of a bitch, I'd like to kill him," he said.

"Me too, man. But he had the gun."

When we got back to the hootch, tough guy couldn't wait to talk.

"Fucking gooks! I should have killed them."

"Yeah, how come you didn't kill them?" a *Nugget* FAC asked, looking at me.

"I was at a slight disadvantage," I replied. "I had a loaded M-16 barrel jammed in my gut."

This was followed by a long discussion about how we should have killed them. I shook my head and kept my mouth shut; it was dry. I noticed my hand shook ever so slightly as I wrapped it around a glass of bourbon. I shook a cigarette loose from my pack to disguise the tremor and placed it between my lips. Miss Sam lit it. Her eyes focused on my hands. Then she watched me throughout the entire I-would-have-cut-their-balls-off-if-I-would-have-been-there discussion. I remember thinking, I hope she spares me when she leads the V.C. charge overrunning this hootch.

Carlos came in and whispered in my ear.

"I just heard. One of our guards killed a South Viet Namese soldier at our checkpoint earlier tonight. That's why they were so hyper."

I nodded.

How will I be able to sleep when I can still feel that gun barrel sticking in my gut? I wondered.

"Miss Sam, I need another beer, please."

While in my airplane, I could climb to mitigate the South Viet Namese heat, but I was never able to outrun that smell. It seemed to be attached to my skin. When the front prop was spinning, it would slice the air, forcing some of it back into the cockpit through a small triangular-shaped window, like the ones featured in automobiles up until the late '60s. This air would then flow through the interior of the airplane and exit via a small square-shaped window at the rear. This rear window also served to cool and dissipate the heat generated by the extra radio equipment stacked against the back cockpit wall. Both windows were left open during flight. The downside of this primitive air-conditioning system was that it also sucked up the smell of the country, which varied from awful to horrific, depending on where and when I was flying. Since my standard mission was flown from noon until 1600 hours, when the sun was at its garbage-baking zenith, I was able to experience the pinnacle of Viet Nam's heat and odor.

I was flying south to put in an airstrike against a bunker complex, which always made me smile since it was never a single bunker, or a bunker with a psychosis or neurosis, but always a bunker with a complex. Both the airplane and I were humming along at about 1,200 feet when I heard whosh-whosh-whosh, a strange sound coming from the rear of the aircraft. I turned to see maps fluttering, half in and half out, of my rear window. I watched as two more maps got sucked out of my map case. I disengaged the seat buckle and slipped loose of my parachute straps. I had to retrieve the maps because I did not want the classified information written on them to get into the hands of the enemy. I brought my feet up to the seat and sat crouched Viet Namese-style. Then I swung one leg over the throttle, fuel mixture, and prop synchronization levers, followed by the other leg, and moved to the back of the airplane.

When I got there, the airplane pitched violently straight up, like I was on the losing end of a teeter-totter and I was tossed against the radios. I felt immediate fear knowing this cockpit would be my coffin if one of the wings lost lift or if the aircraft stalled—which could happen at any second, since the aircraft was slowing down because of its nose-high attitude. I needed to get to the yoke. I stretched out on the cockpit floor, in the center of the airplane, and inched my way forward. When able, I grabbed the back of my seat and pulled myself up until I could lean over it and push the yoke forward, which dropped the nose. Then I swung my legs over and sat back down. Breathing was difficult because of fear, not exertion. My heart and head thumped long enough for me to drive out of my A.O.

When I recovered, I felt stupid. Not because of losing the maps, but because I should have anticipated that my body weight would change the center of gravity of the aircraft as soon as I moved past halfway. But the beauty of flying solo was that I didn't have to admit my stupidity to any other human being; Sky King could just carry on as though nothing had happened. A smile crossed my face as I strapped back in, and then I started to shake as I relived my fuck-up and realized how close I had been to death. Spin, crash, and burn. It did not seem funny when I said these words this time. Then there was a period of time where I just shook, realizing how close I had been to death. I am unsure how long any of these feelings lasted. I only knew that they were intense, and I needed to get over them immediately since I had several hours of flying before I could land.

When I landed, I deliberated: Should I talk about it so another pilot may learn from my mistakes, or should I jam it in the "what-the-fuck, who-would-believe-it-anyhow" file? It ended up where so many things in Viet Nam did. It ended up in the "I-just-want-to-forget-this-ever-happened" bin, and it stayed there until I tried to go to sleep that night.

I had adopted Jefferson's propensity of killing the jeep's engine and coasting into my destination. I was now comparing M.P.H. with distance to be traveled to various locations around the base. If I reached 40 miles per hour and killed the jeep's engine just as I passed the BX, the base exchange, I would coast to within a few feet of my mailbox. Of course, spectators thought I was crazy when they spotted the jeep creeping along.

"Having some trouble there, lieutenant?" they would yell.

"No, just practicing," I would yell back.

But what the hell, I was crazy, wasn't I? I was a tactical, trained killer. *How do I kill? I kill with rockets, bombs, and bullets. How do I kill the jeep? I choke the engine to death.* I was still giggling at my crazy thoughts and actions as I hopped out of the jeep and walked to my mailbox. Box! Another name for the pussy, or hair-pie, or . . . My crazy mind was off again rummaging through the nomenclature for a specific female body part. As I entered the combination: right, stop—beaver; left, stop—bearded clam; right, stop—poongtang, I noticed a menacing shadow crossing mine. I opened the mailbox door, pulled out a letter, closed the door and spun the dial, then turned to face Colonel Buzz Cut.

"You are getting a new reputation, colonel," I said. "The troops are calling you the hatcheck colonel. No fighter squadron, huh?"

"Well no, not yet. There are just too many lieutenant colonels over here."

"You're telling me?"

I saw little pools of sadness in his eyes, and I wondered if he would be sadder if he got his squadron and spent his time writing letters home to mothers and fathers and wives of dead pilots instead of harassing young men struggling to get through a day, so that a day could add up to a week, then a month, and after twelve, they could go home and spend the rest of their lives trying to forget about assholes like him who made the most miserable year of their life worse, when he could have made it better. The smell from living in this shithole will someday wash off, weight will be regained, but the loss of dignity will smolder, forever.

"I don't even own a hat anymore, so don't even ask me," I said. "And I have no intention of getting a haircut either." The bottom of his square jaw dropped, like the hinge holding it broke. He stammered while driving his right fist into the palm of his left hand. Then his words became barely intelligible, and illogical.

"We need to set an example," he pleaded, "perform to a higher standard. Remember, this is not our country. We are visitors here."

Now it was my turn to stammer. I swished my letter against an empty palm, while glancing down to read the address. The letter was from the wife. I shoved it in my pocket.

"Well, look, I will let it go this time," he said. "It's just very important that officers set a good example. We are tightening up on the discipline around here. It will increase the morale. Have you seen how black guys can now grow beards? It's disgraceful."

"Have you seen what Admiral Zumwalt has said?"

He gave me that dumbshit look.

"He said: 'There is no correlation between length of hair and bravery.'"

Colonel Buzz Cut tilted his head sideways, with his chin exposed, and squinted even though the sun was on his back, and I wondered if anything ever penetrated his bristled scalp. I turned and walked away.

"I want to see you wearing a hat next time."

"Yeah, sure. Three bags full!"

I jumped into the jeep and sat, watched, and listened to him.

"Hey you, airman. Get a haircut!"

"Sergeant, I want you shaved by tomorrow!"

"Tuck that shirt in, over there!"

"Hey, lieutenant, you got a cap?"

"Yes, indeed," I said to myself as I started the jeep. "The amount of bullshit is directly proportional to the distance from combat."

I drove to the hootch, sat on my stool in the corner, and opened my letter.

"You need beer?" Miss Sam asked.

I gave her my that's-a-stupid-question look, then followed it up with a smart-ass comment just to see her scrunch up her lips and display her tightly clenched, beautiful white teeth.

"What the fuck do you think?"

"*Numbah* ten, you speak *numbah* ten every time," she said as she scurried down to the other end of the bar to fetch me a can.

"You speak to wife like that?" she hollered.

"Only when I'm pissed off."

I smiled as she popped a can open and placed it before me.

"You fall for that every time," I said.

She tilted her head to one side, like a bird might before decapitating an unsuspecting worm. She walked to the back wall and with a grease pencil made a vertical mark next to my name. It was easy to see. I was leading the whole hootch in beers purchased this month. I took a cigarette from my pack, lit it, and read the first line of my letter.

Our son is going blind.

"What the fuck?" I yelled.

"Is this a fucking joke?" I checked the envelope, then the letter, turning each over several times. It was my wife's handwriting.

I noticed he was knocking things over when he reached for them, so I took him to the base doctor. The doctor sent him to a specialist. The specialist said he is legally blind but he thinks he can help him get better.

"Motherfucker." I said it softly.

I ground out my cigarette and lit another.

"Two years old and he is going blind, and I'm stuck in this shithole and can't do one damn thing to help him."

Tears started to form. I didn't think I had any left. I thought I had used them up for my lifetime, but they were there, just a few drops. And then I shut them off.

"Goddamn this fucking place! Goddamn this stupid fucking war!

Goddamn the stupid fucking people I have to deal with every day . . . *Goddammit, goddammit, goddammit . . .*"

I stopped screaming for a second, and I realized I sounded exactly like the pilot in the bunk below me, the one who wanted to kill me on my first day in-country.

"Give me a jug, Sam."

She moved slowly. She placed it on the bar and I grabbed it, but she hung on. I knew what she was trying to do, and maybe if I could just let her rock me for hours, I wouldn't need it. But she couldn't rock me, my wife couldn't rock me, I was too old for my mother to rock me . . . so I tore the bottle out of her hands and walked out of the hootch. I knew what I was looking for. I was looking for a bar that was so dark no one knew who was sitting next to them. No one knew or cared what drug anyone else was using. I found it on my sixth try, after my thirteenth pull on the bottle, after falling down twice.

I sat at the bar beside a man who was in his seventies. He had white hair and an unusually large nose and bulging eyes, both jutting from a rutted ghoulish-grey face crisscrossed with little red lines. He wore civilian clothes, a stained pullover shirt, and Bermuda shorts. Unpolished and unlaced combat boots covered his feet. What was he doing here? I wondered. I said nothing, but I couldn't resist several more looks at his skinny arms and nicotine-stained fingers and distended belly. Finally, I couldn't help but ask.

"What are you doing here?"

"I'm in the service."

"What?"

He stared straight ahead.

"How old are you?" I asked.

"Why don't you just fuck off!"

He stood, and then half-stumbled outside to take a piss.

"He's a master sergeant. He's forty-three years old," said the young troop bartending. "A quart of booze every night for eleven months will do that to you. His wife ran off with his brother."

The man returned. He threw his military I.D. on the bar. I looked around for a shaft of light and tilted the card until I could read the date of his birth. He was forty-three. The photo was of a healthy man.

I returned his I.D. and said nothing to him during the remainder of my stay, but I continued to throw drinks down with this withered human. First he'd buy, and then I'd buy. With each swallow, I thought about a boy who was starting life with an outstanding smile but failing eyesight while his papa, half a world away, was unable to help so he got drunk instead while sitting alongside a man who wanted to spend the rest of his life pickled inside a bottle. I wondered if that man had any children, but I never asked.

"Are you two having a contest?" the bartender asked.

I rose slowly from my stool and headed for the door. Halfway, I turned and went back for my bottle of whisky. There was an inch or two left. Once outside, I felt the need to piss and eventually I got a stream. I watched as the urine ran downhill; then I put it on autopilot and took a long swig from my bottle. My leg buckled, and I pissed the side of my pants. I laughed. "Nearly shot myself down there," I said.

I started back to my hootch. It was a long walk, mostly because I fell several times. When down, I'd cross my legs Indian-style; then I'd laugh, struggle to my feet, and stagger on. I spotted my hootch and teetered toward the barroom door, but I overshot by at least ten feet and crashed into the building and fell to the ground.

"Must be a strong crosswind," I mumbled.

Rain began to fall. I put my hand out, palm up, to make sure. I stood and walked back to begin another approach. I wet my index finger and held it up in the air. It was an old Boy Scout trick to see which way the wind was blowing. Of course, it doesn't work when it's raining.

"Who gives a shit?"

I laughed.

"Sky King's got it this time."

I missed left, so I decided the wind must be blowing from the right. "Head upwind, you dumbshit," I said to myself. "Let the wind drift you into the door!"

I lined up, arms outstretched; right arm down, left arm up. It was looking good. I was playing the drift perfectly. But then the wind must have picked up, and again I crashed into the hootch and fell to the ground. I sat and laughed. "All right, you son of a bitch, this time I'll give it right aileron and left rudder." I circled and headed back in again, my arms stretched out, reacting to the expected drift.

"More rudder, more rudder," I yelled, and again I crashed against the building some ten feet downwind of the door.

"Get a run at it . . . get there fast before the wind has a chance to blow you off course."

I moved back, took a big first step, and lunged forward.

"More power! More power!"

Again, I bounced off the hootch and fell to the ground. I tried to lift my head, but I could not, and I realized I was never going to get in that door on this night. I crawled around looking for a place to spend the night. I found a nice indentation in the ground, long and narrow like my body. I felt the rain against my face. How long had it been raining? I wondered.

"Who gives a shit!"

I stretched out, belly down, arms at my side, and nestled into the mud, a perfectly contoured bed. "ZzzzzzzzzzzzzzzzzzzzzzzzzZZ."

Something startled me. I swung my legs over the side and jumped. But it was from a bottom bunk, not the top height I was used to, so I crash-landed butt first with head following. And that's when I noticed the pain. I checked my watch. Could I make my flight? I wondered.

"Aspirin and some food," I mumbled, "then I'll decide."

I was covered with mud.

"Nice landing, peasant." Father William's feet were inches from my eyes; his ass was stationary in a chair, his mouth running.

"Would you like last rites?" he asked.

I looked up.

"Oh Jesus, it's you? I must be in hell already. Just heal me."

"You are unhealable, Humpty Dumpty."

"I couldn't get into my hootch. Strong crosswinds."

"You are lucky I happened along. You would have drowned."

"What do you mean?"

"I mean the ditch you were lying in filled with rainwater. I just happened to hear someone gurgling . . . and that was you. I couldn't even wake you up. But it sure was fun slapping your face about ten times, heathen."

"Drowning: it's just a different way to die in Viet Nam. Who gives a shit? Throw me a fucking pillow."

"No chance. Get your ass over to your own hootch. Now that I know you are alive, I need to get some sleep. Shove off, fossdick."

I struggled to my feet and walked out of his room and hootch. The hot sun, now the color of my eyeballs, blinded me. My hands held my head in place until I was able to see again. I thought about my son and how he could not see. It was not of his own making, mine was. My blindness was also temporary, his . . . well, we did not know for sure. I walked to my hootch, opened the door, and entered. Carlos was there to meet me. He led me to his room.

"Miss Sam told me about your son. I've got your flight covered. You can sleep in my bed until I get back. I put you in for an emergency MARS call. They will come and get you when the phone patch goes through."

I slumped onto his bunk, and I vaguely remember my feet being lifted onto the bed. Here I slumbered, indefinitely.

"Lieutenant, your call has gone through. Come with me."

I stood. All I knew about a MARS call was that it was some sort of a telephone patch through Ham radio operators who volunteered their time and equipment so that in-country GIs could communicate directly with family back home. Carlos had used it. I had not. I believed it would be so emotionally difficult to hear my wife and oldest son's voice that I would lose my edge and do something stupid that might get me killed or thrown in jail.

"You need to say 'over' when you are done talking," the airman said while driving me to the MARS station. "That way, the other party will know it is their turn to talk."

I nodded.

He stopped the jeep. We walked in, and he showed me where to sit.

"Hello," I said.

"Say '*over*,'" the airman said.

"*Over*," I said.

"Hello, *over*," came the reply from some 10,000 miles away.

"Is that you?" I asked.

"Say 'over,'" the airman said.

"*Over*," I said.

She told me what the doctors on the base said about my son's condition. I liked that word "condition" instead of "sightless." I told her she needed to immediately drive him to see my uncle who was an E.N.T. doctor. Then she asked if I would like to talk to my son.

"Yes, *over*," I said.

"Hi Daddy," he said. And in the background I heard my wife say, "Say '*over*' when you are done talking."

"*Over*," he said, and I laughed for the first time during the call, for indeed he was his daddy's son; *over*, I thought.

"Daddy, when are you coming home. I miss you." Say "*over*" she said and he did.

How should I answer him? I wondered.

"Daddy misses you too . . . a whole bunch, *over*."

"Daddy, I have nightdreams when you are not here," he said. And my wife added the "*over*."

"Trust your mother, son. You are safe, and everything will be alright, *over*." I tried to say it with conviction, even though in my heart I was not certain anything would ever again be alright. I knew that I was dying inside. I could only hope that I would not die on the outside and that someday I could hold him in my arms and protect *him* instead of thousands of people I did not know, people who probably hated me. How could this be? I wondered.

"Are you crying, Daddy?" he asked.

"Yes," I answered, "crying for joy because I get to hear your voice and tell you that I love you and your brother and your mother, *over and out.*"

My head still hurt the next day. The phone was ringing. Captain Puff did not answer it. He was not in the room. I jumped down and picked up the handset.

"This is *Smoky* forty-four."

"Forty-four, forty. We got a TIC!"

"Roger that. I'm out the door."

I jumped into the jeep, backed out, and raced for Personal Equipment. Storm clouds were moving in, treacherous black clouds spitting streaks of white lighting; clouds so dark they forced me to turn my headlights on, clouds that dipped as low as the rooftops. Charlie loved to launch attacks in weather like this. He knew the battle would be on a horizontal plane, which evened the odds because our air supremacy was negated. My insides began to churn.

"How dare you attack Americans in bad weather, you little motherfuckers! Do you think Sky King is going to be a *hanger queen*?"

It just poured out of me because I was so mad. Actually, hanger queen was the wrong label. Hanger queen referred to an airplane that was always undergoing maintenance, never airworthy. *Fair-weather* pilot was the correct label. I was mad. I was mad because good friends had died. I was mad because I couldn't be home to help my son. I was mad because Captain Puff was never around when trouble was brewing. I was mad because I was tired. I was mad because I had to fly in shitty weather. And I was going to take it all out on Charlie because he woke me from my first actual slumber in weeks. My heart pounded blood to my extremities. I could feel it, and I could hear it. Adrenaline sharpened my focus, expanded my thinking, and alerted all parts of my body that a fight was imminent. I was nervous, but only because I did not want to forget something or make a wrong decision, costing an American life. I was also calm: thinking, plotting, and preparing a plan.

What's the weather in the target area? Will I be able to use air? I was looking at ceilings of 200 feet, maybe less. Would I even be able to launch? Hopefully, the weather would be more favorable in the target area. I grabbed my chute, weapon, and map bag, then drove to the flight line, jammed on the brakes, and ran to my airplane.

"Is that bird preflighted?" I yelled to the chief.

"Yes sir, all set to go."

"Pull the pins. I got a TIC."

"Are you going to fly in this weather?"

I didn't answer. I opened the door, slid over the copilot's seat and into the pilot's seat, and strapped in. The crew chief showed me the streamers as I spun my index finger. He nodded, and I started the front engine.

"Bien Hoa tower, *Smoky* four-four taxi, takeoff."

"*Smoky* four-four, Bien Hoa tower. Field is presently closed due to low ceilings."

"*Smoky* four-four copies. I have a troops-in-contact. Find a way to open it."

"*Smoky* four-four, Bien Hoa tower. We copy. You are cleared to taxi."

"*Smoky* four-zero, *Smoky* four-four."

"Four-four, four-zero. Go."

"What is the weather like in the target area?"

"They say it's lousy."

"What the hell does that mean? Ask them to estimate the distance from the ground to the clouds. And give me coordinates and call signs. Are they using artillery and, if not, is there a battery that can reach them?"

"Roger."

I taxied to the middle of the runway, performed the rest of my pre-takeoff checklist items, and copied down all information passed on by four-zero. I watched clouds rumbling down the runway as I waited for a drenched airman to pull the pins arming my rockets. Where was my clearance to take off? The airman stepped back, showed me the pins, and gave me a crisp salute. And when I returned the salute, he followed with a thumbs-up. Mutual respect, it felt good: One man standing alone all day in the weather, bored and tired; another man also working alone in the weather, spring-loaded, preparing for battle. Each man acknowledging the sacrifice and work of the other, each man hopeful that their sacrifice might result in the saving of an American soldier's life, even if it meant killing another man. Today, however, it wasn't hope that drove me to attempt a launch in this weather. It was anger and foolish arrogance.

"*Smoky* four-four, Bien Hoa tower. The field is still officially closed. Altimeter: two, niner, eight four."

"*Smoky* copies, 2984. And I am going to launch."

I reset my altimeter, pushed my throttles forward, turned onto the runway, checked my instruments—"everything in the green"—hit rotation speed, lifted off, and disappeared into the churning storm. I pulled the gear handle up while struggling to control the airplane as it began pitching and yawing, and I listened to rain as it tried to hammer its way into my cockpit.

The airplane bounced, jumped, and shook, forcing me up against the web belt that secured me to the seat.

"*Smoky* four-four, four-zero."

"Four-zero, go."

"*Buster* guesses the ceiling is about 100 feet."

"I copy."

"*Buster* three-three, *Smoky* four-four."

"God, even in this rain, Viet Nam smells worse than normal," I mumbled to myself.

"*Buster* three-three, *Smoky* four-four. How copy?"

I checked my gauges. "Jesus, what's going on? My gear is not up!" I recycled the handle, first down and then back. An odor, like tires burning, filled my cockpit. Dark grey smoke billowed from under my instrument panel, and I heard the gear struggling to retract. Finally, I heard the gear doors slam shut, and my instruments told me my gear was up and locked. I followed the emergency procedures for *Fire in Cockpit* by turning off all nonessential electrical equipment, saving my radios for last.

"*Smoky* four-zero, *Smoky* four-four. I have got a problem. Tell *Buster* to order up artillery. I will be going off air."

I was in the soup, both inside the cockpit and out. I began fanning the smoke so I could see what my instruments—the ones I had chosen to leave on—were telling me. I started a shallow climb. I looked at my whisky compass to try to figure out where I might be.

"I must be south of the field. But where?"

The compass indicated I was heading WNW.

"That doesn't make any sense."

I fanned more smoke.

"No flames. That's good."

I started a gradual turn back to the south. At 2,500 feet, I broke free of the clouds.

"Where's a hole? Where's a hole?"

I needed to find a hole where I could see the ground and punch back down through the clouds.

"Fuck! The whole world is socked in."

I switched hands on the yoke.

"Has the smoke lessened? I can't tell for sure. Looks like it has, though."

I continued looking for a hole. No luck.

I needed to switch on one piece of equipment at a time, then wait to see if the smoke increased, working my way through all electrical equipment to see if I could isolate the cause of the fire. When I turned on my U.H.F., radio I heard someone say: "Viet Nam fucking sucks!"

"Precisely what I'm thinking," I mumbled back.

"*Smoky* four-zero, *Smoky* four-four. Back up freq."

"Good to hear your voice four-four. *Buster* advises artillery broke the contact. You are free to R.T.B."

"I have an electrical fire. I cannot determine the origin. Contact tower and tell them I may be coming in with my radio out. I'm going off the air again."

"Four-zero copies"

I decided to try to take her in V.F.R., using visual flight rules as opposed to turning on my instruments and risking an increase in the fire. This meant I had to take her down on deck. I eased the nose over and watched as the altimeter unwound down, waiting to break out . . . 600 feet . . . 400 feet . . . 200 feet . . . and I was still in the soup. My muscles tensed. My temples throbbed; my jaw was squeezed taut. I was expecting impact at any second: *Will it be a tree? Will it be a building? How about a giant statue of Ho Chi Minh?*

I broke free of the clouds. I was flying over terrain I did not recognize. Then the clouds began to dip down, whiffs at first, then puffs. Downdrafts and updrafts bounced and twisted my aircraft. I figured I was west and south of the airfield. I switched a radio on.

"Bien Hoa tower, *Smoky* four-four."

"Roger, four-four. This is Bien Hoa tower."

"*Smoky* four-four is south and west of the airfield requesting an emergency landing."

"Roger, *Smoky* four-four. Visibility is below minimums. The runway is closed at this time. However, there is no traffic in the area. You are cleared for a right-hand base leg."

I drove and drove. The terrain was getting higher, but was still unfamiliar. Occasionally I had to turn sharply to avoid obstacles. Still no strip in sight.

"*Smoky* four-four, Bien Hoa tower. State position."

Between broken clouds, I spotted the airstrip off to my right.

"Goddamn, finally a break. Thank you," I said to nobody, or perhaps I said it to Moondoggie and Billy, and to myself, and maybe to my maker.

"*Smoky* four-four is turning base."

"*Smoky* four-four, Bien Hoa tower. We do not have you in sight. Are you turning right or left base?"

"I am turning a right base."

And then I noticed. I was turning base alright, but at an entirely different airstrip. I did not recognize it. What the hell was happening? *Should I land here? No. Bien Hoa must be nearby somewhere.*

"*Smoky* four-four, Bien Hoa. We still do not have a visual."

"Stand by, Bien Hoa. I'm having problems."

"Roger, *Smoky* four-four. Can we be of assistance?"

"That's a negative."

I had to take a chance and switch on my TACAN to verify my position. I turned the instrument on and the needle continued to swing. I was too low; it would not lock on. I had to climb. I pointed the nose of the airplane up and back into the tumbling rain-driven clouds. When the needle finally stuck, I was thirty-eight miles west northwest of Bien Hoa. I had become disoriented while trying to handle my emergency.

"Bien Hoa, *Smoky* four-four. I'm west northwest of strip. How copy?"

"Roger, we have negative *tally-ho*. Can you see the airstrip?"

I was now back riding that bucking bronco. I turned to center the needle and drove to the airstrip. When the TACAN read five miles, I dropped back down through the soup. I broke out at 150 feet and spotted the runway. I checked the numbers at the end of the runway; it was Bien Hoa. I eased my grip on the yoke and wiped sweat from my brow. I would be on the ground in seconds.

"Bien Hoa tower, *Smoky* four-four is downwind."

"Roger, four-four. We have you in sight."

"Gear handle down," I said as I drove the airplane parallel to the runway.

I could hear the doors open, and the gear seemed to be on the move. But it was sluggish . . . not cooperating . . . I could feel my lips pull tight against my teeth. I recycled the gear handle.

"There was no indication that my gear is *down and locked*. Dammit!"

I turned on base leg and shook the airplane up and down and from side to side as I descended. The lights would not come. My gear was most likely not down and locked.

"Bien Hoa, *Smoky* four-four. Put the glasses on me. Can you see if my gear is down and locked?"

"Negative, *Smoky*. It is hanging, but does not appear locked."

"Roger."

I looked down the runway. I could see black clouds dispensing walls of rain rolling toward me. I would lose visual contact with the runway very soon. Should I go around, climb back into the soup, and make another approach? The smell was back, and so was the smoke.

"*Smoky* four-four, Bien Hoa tower. Your gear appears to be about three-fourths of the way down. Do you request we foam the runway?"

"Negative. I've got to get this bird on the ground. Request fire trucks. I will land in the dirt between runways."

"Roger. Bien Hoa is launching Pedro for helicopter rescue. Fire trucks are on their way. Bien Hoa tower is standing by."

I recycled the gear handle one more time and violently shook the airplane up and down in an effort to shake the gear down. I dropped the flaps.

"Bring her in slow, Sky King. Wings level, twenty feet, airspeed good."

I took my hand off the throttle and pushed down hard on the gear lever. Something broke loose. I heard the gear lock in place and then the gear down-and-locked lights flashed green. I dipped my right wing.

"Bien Hoa tower, change of plans. I will be landing on the right runway."

"Roger, *Smoky* four-four."

I touched down, and when the gear held, I exhaled. I stopped the bird straight ahead on the runway, shut it down, and got the hell out of it. Pedro circled overhead. A fire truck raced up beside me; we were both doing about twenty miles an hour. Two medics got out and, during the chase, they convinced me to stop running. A fireman pinned my rockets while two firemen sprayed foam on the gear. Major Personovitch, the squadron flying safety officer, approached. I was quite sure he wasn't there to ask me why I wasn't at choir practice last Sunday.

"What happened?"

"I don't know. I've got gear . . . hydraulic . . . electrical problems . . . I just don't know."

A fireman approached. He held up a bent gear pin.

"It was still in," he said.

Personovitch and I looked at each other. We both thought we knew what had happened. The pin was there to prevent the gear from collapsing when the bird was on the ground. It is removed on preflight inspection. A long red streamer is attached to the pin and hangs down from it. This makes it easy to see if the gear pin is in or out. In this case, the red streamer was pulled off, and the gear pin remained in place. When I raised the gear handle, the pin restricted the gear from retracting. More pressure was needed. Therefore, more fluid was forced through the line. The line overheated and ruptured, and the fluid caught fire . . .

"Goddammit! I told you somebody was going to get killed if you staff-weenies didn't lighten up on the guys working the flight line."

"Jumping to conclusions again, my friend," he said as he wrote notes on a clipboard resting on his knee, which was bent at a 90 degree angle, since his boot was resting on the bumper of the jeep.

I thought for a minute. Maybe he was right. They wouldn't sabotage my bird, would they? Hell, I'm the loosest officer on the base. Maybe it was an accident.

"Lots of bad weather," he said.

I studied his face.

"Lots of rushing to make something happen."

I studied his face.

"When we rush, mistakes happen," he said.

I studied his face.

"The field was closed."

I studied his face.

"Most pilots would use better judgment. They would not be flying in weather like this."

I studied his face.

"It's the pilot's responsibility to do a thorough preflight inspection before he starts engines."

I studied his face.

"I'll tell you what I want," I said. "I will eat this one too, but I want permission to pull a crew chief off the line at any time and take them up with me."

"You will have to check with the boss on that one," he said.

We walked to his jeep. He drove while I pondered. When we arrived at the DASC, he motioned for me to get out. Inside, we sat silently for a long time, waiting for the commander to take a piss, or sharpen his grease pencil, or finish writing Captain Puff's citation for bravery, or finish chewing out an enlisted man whose sideburns were too long, or whatever else commanders do when no one is flying. He had no big-titted secretary that I knew of, unless he was hiding her in some back office. The door opened. We entered. Fly-safe, or Major Personovitch, or his real name—whichever you prefer—explained what happened. I studied the colonel's face.

"He has a request, commander."

"What's that?"

"He wants permission to take a crew chief off the line and have him fly a mission with him."

Now the commander pondered. I hated his indecision. I felt my hand wrap around the pistol grip of my loaded .38. I could see the headlines: *Pilot who used to fly T-38s shoots commander with his .38.*

"It is the only way we can make sure our birds aren't sabotaged," I said.

He pondered again.

"Okay, you've got it."

We saluted and turned to walk away. I stopped when I reached the door and turned back toward him.

"And tell all the staff-weenies to lighten up on the guys working on our birds, sir."

"I wish you would quit calling us weenies," he replied.

"Would you like to move to a different room?" the commander asked the Kiwi right after the rocket destroyed his room.

"No way," he said, "they never hit in the same bloody place twice."

"I would move if I was you, Kiwi," Carlos said.

For a man that positive—"they never hit in the same bloody place twice"—he acted as though he wasn't positive. He had moved his flak vest and steel pot closer to his bunk. There were rumors that he was sleeping in them, but no one knew that for a fact. He could be seen, however, wearing them while he sat at his desk for endless hours with books on rocketry. He plotted and calculated, re-plotted and re-calculated until he was sure he knew the exact launching place of that rocket. He finished calculating about the same time as the Viet Namese carpenters finished repairing his room.

Father William stopped by to check out his new décor. The gomers had packed up and were walking out just as we walked in. Father William pointed at them.

"They giveth and they taketh away, huh Kiwi?"

The Kiwi said nothing.

"Looks good," I said. "Are you going to have a housewarming party?"

He tipped his steel pot back so I could see his eyes; then he turned and said, "Fuck off, I'm busy."

The next morning the dinks launched another round of rockets, and it was obvious they were from the same tubes. Once again Kiwi's walls and ceiling came tumbling down, and once again we dug him out of the rubble. This time he was wearing his flak vest.

"Aha," Joey said. "You do sleep in it."

The Kiwi waved the palm of his hand beside his ear. A pilot will use this hand signal when flying to indicate to his wingman that his radio is out and he is not receiving any transmissions.

"Can't hear a bloody fucking thing," the Kiwi yelled entirely too loud. "Me ears been ringing since the first blast."

Short-timers don't talk much anyway, and the Kiwi was getting short. He was nervous, and it was understandable. He also was not smiling very much. Most of the time he sat at the bar with his steel pot and flak vest on, a cigarette in one hand and a beer in the other. Come to think of it, most of us had a beer in one hand and a cigarette in the other. We just didn't wear the vest and pot. He was still plotting though, even at the bar.

"Why don't you give up, Kiwi?" a *Nugget* FAC asked.

"It's got to be right here." He pointed to a point on the map.

"Is it jungle?"

"Yes, of course it's the jungle, you twit. This is Viet Nam, isn't it?"

"You can't possibly find it in the jungle," the *Nugget* FAC said as he walked out.

"You can't possible find it in the jungle," the Kiwi repeated in a nasal voice.

Our Kiwi was struggling. I decided I would fly with him, help him find that vine in the jungle, the one the gooks where using to sling rockets at him.

The next day I strapped into the backseat of his OV-10 (OV). This was a real airplane, specifically designed for close air support. It had lots of power and was extremely maneuverable. We were not vine hunting, however. The Kiwi was flying cover over a fire support base—circling it while on the deck, hard left turn then right turn, climbing while changing direction—when a white phosphorous projectile, obviously fired by our guys since Charlie had no such weaponry, exploded directly on line but slightly below us. By slightly, I mean it missed us by less than ten feet.

"Bloody hell," the Kiwi yelled as he banked the airplane sharply and started a climb.

Damn, I thought. *The Kiwi really is a magnet ass. Hot lead is attracted to him as hot chicks are attracted to Fast Freddie, Fighter Pilot. Maybe I should get him a pair of Captain Puff's magic underwear.*

"Who the fuck fired that thing?" he was asking over the radios.

He was correct in trying to figure out where it came from, since no airspace felt safe now. There were several more explosions, but they were below us. I felt helpless because I could only sit, watch, and trust his decisions. I did not feel nervous at the time because I had many months to go before I was *short*. I figured eventually something or someone was going to cut my life short. But at this time in my tour, it did not matter to me how I died. That was what I told myself.

That night, as I lay in bed, I couldn't help thinking about a story I had heard. A FAC, driving an O-2, was directing fire from the *USS New Jersey*, a battleship that fired shells sixteen inches in diameter. The ship and everyone else lost *commo* with the FAC. He just disappeared. There was no trace of him or his airplane. Speculation was that he had taken a direct hit from one of those monster shells.

I thought about our close call today and some other ways I could die over here and never know what hit me, or where it came from, or why I was chosen for a seemingly random stroke of bad luck. Death could be delivered by the enemy, an ally, or a fellow American. It could happen when I was lying in my bed, or standing at the bar, or sitting on the crapper.

That night, I saw Billy and Doggie in their flight suits . . .

They were walking away from me. They were walking into white streaks of smoke emanating from the pulsating center of white mass, a white pinwheel spinning in a pool of blood. A pinwheel lit to celebrate our bloody beginning. The prophets were wrong. It was not dust to dust, but rather blood to blood that we shall return. Periodically, Billy and Doggie would stop, look over their shoulder, and motion for me to join them. "Come on," they said. "We miss you. Come join us." And then the pinwheel stopped. And they disappeared.

In the morning, I sat at our desk and wrote a letter home, a letter that would cover the last two weeks in the shortest month of the year.

> *Hi,*
> *Have you heard about Billy? He's dead.*
> *I nearly joined him.*
> *I've had a couple of mid-air close calls.*
> *Capt. Puff tried to kill me on a night flight.*
> *A gook jammed a loaded M-16 into my gut.*
> *I also thought I was going to die chasing maps*
> *flying out the back window of my airplane.*
> *Crew chiefs are sabotaging our planes,*
> *and we are about to get fragged.*
> *I damned near drowned when I heard*
> *about our son's blindness.*
> *Bullets, rockets, mortars and artillery shells; some theirs,*
> *Some ours, just missed me,*
> *and I miss you all.*

I crumpled it and tossed it.

> *Hi,*
> *Billy got it, but I am safe.*
> *Lots of funny things happening here.*

Please update me on our son's blindness.
Life is quite boring. Lots of drinking,
and not much to write home about.
All my Love,
Sky King

Chapter 2
KILLING TIME

The clouds had departed, and the wind was still sleeping when I arrived at the airplane. I watched as the crew chief and his helper rolled the bird out of the revetment and pointed it toward the runway. It used to be that crew chief and pilot maintained and flew one aircraft. Both their names were stenciled on the side of the bird. Pilot and crew chief both familiar with the idiosyncrasies of their aircraft. There was competition between crew chiefs as to which aircraft had the fewest write-ups and which aircraft looked the best. But that was in the past. Some genius upstairs decided that crew chiefs, pilots, and airplanes ought to be as interchangeable as spare parts. There would be no pride of ownership.

"How's it going, Sarge?"

"Hot as hell," he replied.

He handed me the maintenance forms. I scanned the sheets. Only minor problems. I signed my name at the bottom of the report.

"Is the bird ready to go?" I asked.

"Yes, sir."

I stared at the airplane. Then I studied the crew chief's face.

"Pull the pins. I'll be right back."

I returned to P.E. and checked out an additional survival vest, headset, and parachute.

"Need an extra sidearm, lieutenant?"

I shook my head no, picked up the gear, and walked back to the airplane.

"The bird is ready to fly, correct?"

"Yes, sir."

"Let's go," I said as I held out the survival vest for him to slip into.

"What's this?"

"You are going along."

"I can't do that."

"What rank am I?"

"You're a lieutenant."

"That's correct. First lieutenant! So slip this vest and chute on, and get in after me."

"But I can't. I have to—"

"Sergeant, I hate pulling rank. Don't make me pull rank."

He moved slowly into the vest—one arm, then the other—and zipped it up. I did not preflight the airplane; I would assume he had. I tossed his parachute on his seat and then climbed over it and into mine. I cranked the front engine and motioned for him to get in. He tried to protest once more.

"Put that parachute on or you might wish you had." The words and tone just happened. I was not sure what I was trying to convey.

Did I mean you will be in big trouble if you do not follow my order, or did I mean we may have to use our parachutes to ease our fall to earth at sometime during the flight? I wasn't sure how he interpreted it, but he immediately put his arms through the parachute straps, grabbed the straps from under his thighs, connected them to the chute, and cinched them tight; same with the chest strap. Together we bounced along the taxiway to the main runway.

"I depend on you every day," I said.

He did not reply. He seemed nervous. Was he nervous about the state of the airplane, or was he nervous about the flight? I could not tell.

"If you get sick," I said, "you will be the pilot. I guarantee you, I will bail out."

It was a useless threat since my only escape was out through his door. There was a red handle on his door, the only door. The handle separated the hinges from the airplane, allowing the entire door to fall away. In the event of any bailout, he would have to go first, unless I could slide out between him and the instrument panel. Fat chance! I never thought about bailing out of this airplane before. Why was that? I wondered. Was it because I believed my skills were so honed that I could land it anywhere? Was it because I was too focused on the mission? Was it because I suffered from *it-could-never-happen-to-me disease*? I couldn't answer. And why, I wondered, had the powers-that-be never put a door on my side of the aircraft? Money, I suspected. The answer was money. Hey, and why not? Why spend a couple of hundred dollars to save a pilot who cost a million dollars to train? Maybe I should talk to Major Personovitch, the flying safety officer, about that. Ah, fuck it!

"*Smoky* four-four, Bien Hoa tower. You are cleared for takeoff."

"Roger, four-four copies and I'm rolling."

We lifted off, and I must admit I was a tad nervous as I raised the gear handle. I heard the gear retract, lock in place, and the doors close. So far, so good. I flew across our A.O. and showed him the landmarks—Casper's Head, the Dog Bone—and told him the story behind the Thumbtack. I put in a set of F-4s against a suspected V.C. base camp. Hell, everything over here was a suspected V.C. base camp! Whenever he felt sick, I made him fly the airplane. I even let him try to land the aircraft, but I had to take control before we drove off the runway. He taxied back to the revetment. And when I shut the engines down, I noticed a big smile on his face.

"That was great, lieutenant. Thanks."

I returned his smile, took my glove off, and offered my hand. And we shook. And I hoped we now understood each other and he realized that I was not his enemy.

The ring of a telephone at any time, but especially in a combat zone, is a horrible way to be awakened. It had been ringing in my room and also across the hall in Jefferson's room. We had played this game before. Whoever answered the first call would have to answer the following calls. Jefferson excelled in out-waiting me. This morning, I did not want to answer it. Experience taught me that he was able to ignore rings forever, like he never even heard them, whereas I could not. I looked at the clock: 9:00 a.m. I could sleep for two more hours if I could just get him to pick up.

Ring!

"Eight," I whispered.

Ring!

"Nine."

I pulled my poncho liner over my head. *Smoky* forty-two seldom capitulated. Even if he had a full bladder, he had perfected different positions and bragged that he could put off nature's call for hours, whereas my experiments all ended in failures.

Ring!

"Fourteen goddamn rings."

I swung my legs over the side of the bunk and sat there. The phone rang two more times. And then it stopped. I had won. I returned my pillow to its proper position, over my head, and I laid back down facing the wall, determined to celebrate my victory with a couple more hours of succumbing to *Ralph, the Rack Monster*, when the door burst open and the overhead light flashed on and off, then remained on. I sensed the presence of *Smoky* forty-two, and I heard my tape deck click on, followed by my amplifier.

"*I can't get no, satisfaction . . .*"

The Rolling Stones for an alarm clock? Even I couldn't tolerate that, but I didn't move. This wasn't supposed to be happening; I had won. Then I heard a familiar voice.

"This is your captain, Captain Jefferson from the flight deck, bringing you tunes for your listening pleasure. And so all of you in the cheap seats, you know the ones in the back of the airplane, get the stewardesses off of your laps and start dancing in the aisle while I turn up the volume to serenade you with music for your sing-along with Mick Jagger."

"*I can't get no . . .*"

"*fucking sleep.*" I sang it to myself, as I didn't want Jefferson to know I was awake.

He walked over to my bunk, put his combat boot up on it, and started keeping time to the music. His foot bounced with each beat, and when I didn't turn my head to look at him, he increased the pressure until my bunk was shaking like a V.C. prisoner in the presence of South Korean soldiers. I had won the phone game, just like we were winning the battle here in Viet Nam, but I lost the war. Jefferson had changed the unwritten R.O.E., rules of engagement, for sleeping in. I rolled my head back and looked at him.

"What the fuck are you doing?" I asked.

"It was for you," he replied.

"What was for me?"

"The phone," he said as he started singing again.

"Ah, bullshit. Come on. Get the fuck out of here!"

"No, listen," he said. "I just couldn't sleep, and being it's such a nice day, I was wondering if you would like to have breakfast with me?"

"What the fuck? A guy can't win around here." I jumped down and into my flight suit.

"Who was on the line?" I asked.

"Personovich. He needed a sign-off on a form."

"He woke me up because of a signature on a form? Fuck! I'd sign it Mickey Mouse."

We headed outside. It was pouring rain. No one would be flying today. Not even me. It was the start of the monsoon season.

The next day, at the end of my flight, Jefferson jumped me just over the Dog Bone. When I saw him, it was too late. He rolled out of a bank of clouds and was in my six o'clock before I could react. Of course he had an advantage. I was looking at the ground, looking for signs of Charlie moving goods up the river and into Saigon. And of course he had another advantage: he was twice the pilot I was. We bent our airplanes around, over, and through a bank of clouds, then I took him down on the deck but I couldn't shake him off my ass. It was fun. I didn't mind losing. I considered it an honor to be in the same sky with him; Lieutenant Jefferson, *Smoky* forty-two, my mentor, a man who only talked to me about two subjects: pointers on how to live through a tour in the Nam, and rock and roll. He was my mother hen, I was his chick. He was my teacher, I was his student. A mother hen/chick arrangement is a much better wartime connection than big brother/little brother or friend/friend. By design, emotion is not a part of the mother hen/chick relationship. He would tolerate me and lecture me until it was time for him to leave Viet Nam. Then he would board a freedom bird and fly back to the world, never to know if I made it out, got maimed, or got killed unless my name popped up in idle conversation, unless I happened to make the newspapers, hopefully not on the obit page.

Still, Jefferson crossed the line when he allowed music to become a part of our conversation. Now we knew about each other's love of melody, tempo, lyrics . . . The armor was off when we listened to music, and spoken and unspoken feelings surfaced.

"Captain Puff: What's the deal with him?" I asked.

"A career soldier," Jefferson answered. "Gets his combat ticket punched, goes home, and with his papa pushing in the background, he might make full colonel someday."

"Scary thought."

Jefferson shrugged his shoulders while I elaborated.

"He's only interested in getting a few medals . . . without risking bodily harm . . . at least his bodily harm . . ." Jefferson laughed, and I continued. "He only worries about keeping his nose clean while catering to the whims of the assholes above him . . . and getting home to whatever it is he keeps hidden in his locker."

"Sounds like you've got him pegged. Why'd you ask?"

"Don't know . . . And you?" I asked. "What about you?"

"I just want to fly for the airlines. It is all I ever wanted to do since I was a little kid . . . I'm just here to get flying hours and hopefully pick up an assignment flying transports back in the world until I can get out of the military and fly some friendly skies, with clipboard on one knee and a stewardess on the other."

"Hmmmm. Sounds nice."

"And you, Sky King?" he asked.

"Where did you hear that name?" I asked with a flash of anger.

"Hmmm . . . Not sure . . . Maybe Father William. What's it all about anyway?"

"The TV show . . . And we fly the *Skymaster* . . . It just seemed to go together."

His head moved up and down.

"Sky King? It works for me," he finally said. "You fly a good airplane, but you take this war much too personally . . . I admire your courage and commitment, but if you keep looking for a fight, you are going to get yourself killed . . . And for what? How is your death going to change the course of this war? It has been going on for five years now. We take some ground one day, and give it back the next . . . Your friends are dead . . . they are not coming back."

He looked at me. I said nothing.

"How is your death going to help your two young sons?" he asked.

I did not answer. I could not answer.

"You have got to live to tell them to avoid all wars in the future; otherwise, they will be filled with the same hate and anger you have, and they will also want to go to war."

We sat in silence for what seemed to be a long time.

"I've heard Captain Puff's replacement is coming in next week," Jefferson said. "And Carlos has a staff-weenie working on getting us rooms in a different hootch . . . hopefully before we get fragged . . . and the 19th TASS is now going to become home to FACs flying in support of U.S. forces. And all FACs flying for Arvin forces, and that is you," he said as he pointed a finger at me, "will be assigned to the 22nd TASS . . . And, here's the good part, the Viet Namese are going to take over all of the fighting . . . *Vietnamization*, they are calling it."

"*Vietnamization*? You gotta be shitting me. How come it takes us five years to train a South Viet Namese to fight when Charlie and the North Viet Namese can do it in two weeks?"

"Good question."

"And you are getting short too," I said, changing the subject.

"Shhhh . . . don't jinx me," Jefferson replied.

Two days later, I was sitting at the bar in our main officers club having a beer—or two, or three, or six, or eight—when a major sat down beside me. We did not speak. He drank a beer; I drank a beer. He ordered another beer.

"And get the lieutenant one," he said to the bartender.

When the beer arrived, I raised the can and nodded to him.

"My name is Davis." He held out his hand. I did not shake it.

"What's your name?" he asked.

"They call me Sky King."

"Sky King, really? They call you that for any specific reason?"

"No. It just kind of happened."

"I watched the TV show as a kid. It was one of the main reasons I wanted to fly," he said.

I did not reply.

"Are you a FAC?" he asked.

I nodded.

"Me too. OV-10s. I just got in-country."

I nodded again, this time more slowly.

"I volunteered."

"You volunteered?"

"Yeah. The Air Force has been my meal ticket for fourteen years. I figured it was time to pay them back."

"By volunteering for Viet Nam?"

"Yeah."

I thought about what he had said, about how the Air Force has been his meal ticket for fourteen years and I also thought about the Air Force's *up or out* policy for officers: Get passed over for your next promotion three times and they throw you out just before you put in twenty years and qualify for retirement pay. My guess was that he had been passed over for Lieutenant Colonel twice and was panicking. All those years invested for nothing. *Maybe, I bet he thought, if I have a combat tour on my record . . . earn some medals . . . they won't throw me out.*

"Got any kids?" I asked.

My bloodshot eyes noticed that his eyes lit up.

"Yeah, four kids. One of them will be in college soon."

I jumped down from my stool.

"Good luck to you," I said. "Don't take this war personally. It is not worth it. Your job is to live through your tour and get back to your kids."

I walked away. I could feel his head swing from right to left as he watched me walk out of the bar. Three days later some gomer offed him. I tried to visualize the day his wife was told . . .

Two men in military dress uniforms walked to the front door of the major's house.

Ding-dong.

"Mrs. Davis?"

"Yes."

"Sorry, your husband is D.O.A. compliments of the D.O.D. or Dead on Arrival compliments of the Department of Defense."

"Don't you mean K.I.A. or killed in action?"

"Yes, ma'am. That too."

"But who will tell the children?"

"Sorry, ma'am: That's not our problem."

Captain Puff's replacement arrived.

"Name's Earl," he said as he stuck his hand out. I shook it. He looked like a miniature version of Colonel Buzz Cut. He liked to grin a lot. He had Bucky Beaver teeth, pearly white, the size of piano keys. Every time I looked at him, I expected him to break out in a song. Actually, it was a jingle. "Brusha, Brusha, Brusha, New Ipana toothpaste. Hiya, folks! I'm Bucky Beaver."

That night Earl hung around our bar. He didn't say much, and better yet, he seemed to be listening. I liked that. After all, what does an F.N.G. know? Nothing! Not a fucking thing! F.N.G.s should shut up, if they are interested in getting out of here alive.

That night my nightdreams reappeared in cinemascope . . .

They were all there: Moondoggie, Billy, Lucky Larry, Mike in the Jungle, Banjo, Mehoff, Gums, and two new faces: Major Davis and Camptown. Strange, I thought, I hadn't heard that Camptown had died. Yet there he was, in my group of dead faces. Last I heard he was paralyzed, but living . . .

Sleep was elusive. It was work just to get a few hours. It seemed the sun had to rise before I could fall into a deep slumber.

Jefferson had once again outlasted me. I picked up the phone.

"Hello, hello. Bien Hoa sector, *Smoky* FACs."

"Forty-four, forty. The whole southern region has exploded again. You have got to launch. Forty-one and the new boss are down there working now."

"Roger that." I slipped into my flight suit and headed for the jeep. Within minutes I was airborne.

"*Smoky* four-zero, forty-four is airborne. Give me a brief."

"Roger, forty-one. Be advised. The old *Smoky* forty-one and the new *Smoky* forty-one are working a contact ten klicks to November Echo of your target. Your coordinates are . . . I shackle: papa, lima, foxtrot, x-ray . . ."

I smiled—Captain Puff and Earl in the same airplane—as I wrote all information on my side window. Then I decoded the coordinates and the frequency for ground troops. Call sign: *Shaker*. I contacted them while flying toward their location. I knew the area well. It was a bad area, particularly for choppers. We lost a couple of Buddha's boys there.

"*Shaker*, *Smoky* four-four, over."

"*Smoky* four-four, *Shaker*. Get me some TAC air ASAP."

"Roger *Shaker*, it is on the way. Hang tough."

"Fuck you, hang tough! You are not getting shot at. I've got gobs of gooks everywhere!"

"Understand."

"*Smoky* four-four, *Smoky* four-zero. Two sets of F-100s are airborne."

"Four-four copies."

I was switching my fox mike radio to order up artillery when suddenly every radio in my bird went dead. I couldn't believe it. The fighters had launched, the boys on the ground were getting hit, and suddenly I was helpless. I threw switches and rechecked all radios. It made no sense that all three radios would fail simultaneously, but they had. All other indications looked normal. I would have to return to base and get a new aircraft. Everyone would surely be wondering what had happened to me, probably suspecting that I was shot down. I switched to guard frequency and transmitted blindly. Maybe I could transmit but not receive. I decided to join on *Smoky* four-one and give him the hand signals for radio out. He could call and inform *Smoky* control and Bien Hoa tower of my problem. Flying formation in an 0-2 was forbidden by Air Force regulations, but this was an emergency.

I spotted *Smoky* four-one's bird and advanced my throttle. I had closed to within fifty feet and he had not spotted me. If I had been a gomer in a MiG, he would have been dead. Fortunately, we did not have to worry about any enemy aircraft lurking over III Corps. Air superiority allowed us to concentrate on the three million other things we were trying to control. I continued my transmissions on guard channel.

"*Smoky* four-one, *Smoky* four-four. If you read, rock your wings."

His bird remained wings level. Airspeed was steady. Finally, he spotted me and broke down and away. I couldn't believe it. I banked and pulled my nose around to follow him, frantically waving my hand back and forth over my ears, indicating my radio was *in-op*. I could see Earl. He was pointing at me. He kept looking at me and then back to Captain Puff.

It had turned into an unwanted dog fight. Finally I just decided, *the hell with it*, and headed for Bien Hoa. Once there, I rocked my wings on downwind and base leg, again standard *radio out* procedure, until I got a green light signaling me that it was okay to land.

I jumped out of one O-2 and into another. When airborne I again contacted *Shaker*. I was concerned that he would be so pissed off at me, he might try to shoot me down. Fortunately, I had something that he wanted. No, I had something that he needed in order to live another day. I had air power.

"Sorry, *Shaker*, I had radio problems. I will have bombs on target in seconds. Pop smoke."

Two and one-half hours of many airstrikes, and lots of help from the Buddha's helicopters, the dinks finally broke contact. Today's mission was supposed to be nice, peaceful, and easy: A day of leisurely flying, after which I would divert into Vung Tau to meet Joey at a seaside resort for a few beers. Instead, I remained over the target area until all wounded troops were medevaced, and then I relayed all the numbers: B.D.A. (bomb damage assessment), K.B.A. (killed by air), amount and type of ordinance expended, T.O.T. (time on target), and on and on for the pencil-pushers in Saigon. Because of the contact, my day at the beach would be: CANCELED!

"*Smoky* four-four, *Shaker*."

"*Shaker*, four-four. Go ahead."

"I owe you, brother. Good job. And thank your fighter jocks also. I'll buy you a beer sometime."

"I'd like that *Shaker*. *Smoky* four-four out."

When I landed, Earl, the new *Smoky* four-one, was waiting for me.

"Captain Puff was sure you were trying to get him in trouble," Earl said. "I told him your radios were out twenty times before he finally believed me. When it sunk in, we called Bien Hoa tower and told them to expect you. Then we called forty and he made sure a new bird was ready for you."

"Stupid fucking Captain Puff," I said. "Did you know his father is a full colonel?"

The next day I jumped into an Oscar Deuce and immediately headed for the beach. I did not pass GO and I did not collect $200, but I did have $200 worth of M.P.C.s on me since I would R.O.N. (remain overnight) and fly the early morning mission from there. I was anxious to get out of Bien Hoa and away from Captain Puff for a night, and get into Viet Nam's in-country R & R site. I was thankful to land in an airplane that didn't have any holes in it, but I was landing on a runway that had lots of holes. It was referred to as P.S.P. (pierced steel planking), and it always felt like I was landing on ice.

I skidded over to where Joey was sitting in the back of a jeep. I nodded to the Australian driver, threw my gear in back, and then jumped in the front right seat.

"We will get a pint of beer," Joey said, "and then I've got a mate I want you to meet."

The driver dropped us off at the Australian officers club, where Joey ordered up a beer for each of us and a couple of six packs to go. We moved out to the front porch and sat in silence until a jeep screeched to a halt in front of us. The jeep was spit-shined and customized with .50 cal. machine guns, both fore and aft. An Australian lieutenant jumped out.

"Trader Tom," Joey said.

I shook his hand.

"Anything I can do for you, mate?" I thought for a while, while looking at Joey. The Australians had been fighting in the tropics for a long time and their flight suits reflected that. They were lightweight and made from a material that let your skin breathe.

"How about a couple of Australian *zoom bags*?" I said, trying to show off my knowledge of the Australian language.

"Can do! Hop in. Bring your beers along."

Trader Tom drove us to a huge warehouse. We entered and we walked along a row of lockers.

"Let's see, what size? Oh, yeah, this should be it."

He reached in, grabbed a couple, and threw them to me.

"What do you need in return?" Joey asked Trader Tom.

"How 'bout one of those tinnies, mate?"

Joey popped the top off a beer and handed it to him, then looked at me and said, "Now, that's a bloody good trade, eh?"

I nodded.

We walked around the warehouse: refrigerators, air conditioners, boots, AK-47s, jeeps. You name it, he had it. I walked over to some large crates.

"What the hell is this?" I asked.

"That is a brand-new Cobra helicopter. I'd let her go for, say, ten air conditioners and five refrigerators."

"No shit. I figured maybe you'd keep something like that for yourself."

"What for, mate? I've got two choppers of my own now. Listen, if that's it, I've got to be off. Business calling."

Two American grunts walked up to him.

"Whatcha got?"

"9 mm Chin-Com pistols."

"Whatcha need?"

On the way out, we were nearly run over by a forklift with pallets of beer.

"Trader's got a nice little business going," I said to Joey.

"I'm working on a trip to Malaysia, mate," he replied.

Our chauffer drove us back to the Australian officers club.

"My shout," I said as I reached for my wallet.

"It's on the house tonight," the bartender replied. "Trader Tom's got the tab."

A couple of Joey's pilot friends entered, and they exchanged greetings.

"Hey, any news from Grady?" Joey asked.

"Yes. I was up to Phan Rang when he came in to study for his exams. He's driving a U.S. F-4. We're all standing on the ramp waiting to greet him. He taxied in and parked. The front canopy opened"—the pilot used his hands to demonstrate the canopy opening—"and Grady popped out. Then the back canopy opened, and a Viet Namese bird popped out. She's carrying all his books, all wobbly"— the pilot staggered around, like a man trying to spin plates balanced on a stick—"while she tippy-toed behind him." Everyone laughed.

"Notice, she walked behind him, eh?" a second pilot observed. "The fucking war hasn't liberated her."

"I've seen gook women walking in front of men," another bloke said.

"Yeah, when?"

"When they are walking through a minefield, eh." Everyone laughed again.

"What do you expect?" another Aussie said. "They are only ten days out of a tree."

More laughter.

"Joey, Trader Tom mentioned you might be interested in a C-130 ride down to Malaysia."

Joey looked at me. "How about it, mate?"

"Fucking A," I said. "Red China, anywhere, just to get out of this shithole."

"Ain't bad duty here, mate."

I nodded and smiled. And then several Aussies started to back into me, pressing me up against the bar. Soon, two Aussies were arguing.

"No, you can't," one said.

"Yes, I can," the other replied.

Back and forth, like a couple of kids on a playground.

"What do you think, Yank?"

I shrugged my shoulders.

"What?" I answered.

"This bloke says he can lift three men. I say he can't."

Then others at the bar joined in, yelling back and forth. Then the biggest pilot opened his wallet and threw money on the bar. Four other pilots matched him.

"Bloody hell, I'll take that bet," one yelled.

I tried to turn my back to them, ignore them, but they kept backing into me, pinning me up against the bar.

"Come on Yank. Get in on this."

"Me?"

"Yeah, you." I reached for my wallet.

"No, you can be one of the three, eh?"

"Yeah, pick two others," the big man said, indicating he was going to be third. "Any two!"

I tried to protest. I was feeling a bit nervous, but Joey gave me the nod, so I chose two portly pilots.

Soon they had me lying down on the ground. I was on the outside with the two burly Aussies beside me. The lifter took off his shirt and flexed his muscles and paraded around the barroom while howling. Each time he circled us, the howl got louder.

"Come on. Get on with it!" a man shouted.

"Nick off, mate!" the lifter shouted back. The lifter walked around us. He squatted over the man in the middle and tried to lift. Nothing happened. He walked around us again several times, studying the situation. He moved us closer together, then squatted to lift once again, and again nothing happened.

"No, it's not right," he said.

He moved me to the other side so that there was a new man in the middle and he proceeded to psych himself up with new and higher-pitched chants. The crowd grew restless. Eventually, he stood over the middle man and the room went silent. The lifter stooped with his ass in the middleman's face, his hands around the man's hips, and attempted another lift. Again nothing happened.

Now the bets and the shouting increased. Script was slapped on the bar, and when the money was counted, the lifter chugged a beer, moved me to the middle, and began his ritual of stomping and chanting. Finally, he stood over me. My arms were under the necks of two men on either side of me. We were tucked in tight. Again the room went silent. The lifter crouched over me, stooped, and opened my pants. Two other Aussies dumped ice water on my Johnson and balls, shrinking them to the size of cherry pits. The entire bar crowd was roaring with laughter, and I hoped it wasn't at the size of my balls. I had to laugh too. Not because the ice had shriveled my dick to the size of a gherkin and my nuts were now so small a hungry squirrel would ignore them, but because I was so impressed by the production. Only Aussies would work so hard to play a prank on a Yank, just to have a good laugh. I was exhausted, but I still laughed. When they turned me loose, I stood and shook the remainder of the ice out of my pants. The entire bar crowd slapped my back and again Aussie laughter was contagious.

The lifter put a friendly bear hug on me. He leaned back and squeezed, and my feet dangled two feet off the cement floor. He set me down gently and then slapped me on the back hard enough so that if I had anything stuck in my throat, it would have sailed over the bar and bounced off the far wall.

"My shout," the lifter said.

Joey stood. "Alright mates," he said. "It's killing time in Viet Nam. What will it be tonight? Let's see, we have napalm and high drags, pistols and cannons, mortars and artillery, Budweiser and Victoria Bitters, and then there's telling jokes."

"Let's tell jokes," an Aussie shouted.

"*Did you hear about the Polmey who entered a masturbation contest?*" Joey paused and looked at us.

We all looked at each other and shook our heads no.

"*He took first and third.*"

Hee, hee! Hee, hee, hee!

We all joined him in laughter. The Aussies beat their beer cans and fists on the bar and hollered, "Yeah, yeah, yeah. Killing time in the Viet Nam!"

Another Aussie stood and raised his hands and when the mob quieted, he said:

I broke down oot in the outback one dark night. In me good fortune, I spotted a light on in a ranch house. I walked up to it and knocked and a toothless bastard opened the door. He was as pissed as a newt.

"Come in," he said, "stay the night." His ugly wife with a canker on her snout stood behind him.

"Tell you what, mate," the old bastard said, "let's see if you can bugger me daughter tonight more times than I can do the old lady here."

Well, I was shivering in me boots, thinking, my gawd, his daughter must be an ugly wench. But no, she was a real beaut. So we jumped into the farter and I immediately got it away and I reached up and with me grease pencil scratched a big I on the wall.

Then about 3 a.m. I did her again and put a second II on the wall.

Just before dawn, I thought one more to beat the old bugger, so I knocked her off a third time and put another mark on the wall. III eh?

He looked at us and we all shook our heads, yes.

Just then the rooster crowed and sun rose. The door flew open and that old bugger asked. "Well, sonny, how did you do?" He looked up at the wall, saw the three lines, and was gob smacked. "Gawddamn laddie, one hundred and eleven—you beat me by three!"

Bang! Bang! Bang!
"Killing time in Viet Nam!"
Then Joey held his hands up, asking for quiet.
"*I was out of work*," he began, "*roaming the streets of Sydney and pervin' on the birds when I saw a sign in a bar window that said: Piano Player Wanted.*
"*I opened the door.*"

Joey acted out opening an imaginary door and stepped in, then shut the door behind him, then paused to make certain he had everyone's attention.

"*I'm here to apply for the piano job.*"
"*Can you play Waltzing Matilda?*" *the manager asked.*
"*No, I only play me own songs.*"
So I walked over to the piano and began to bang out me most favorite song.
"*That's terrific,*" *the manager said.* "*What's the name of that song?*"
"*I call it, 'The Fucking Doggie Style Waltz.'*"
"*Well, I can't have that,*" *the manager said.*
"*Here's another,*" *I replied.*

And Joey cracked his knuckles, and then like a game of charades, he played an imaginary piano. "Plink, plink," he said now, playing with one hand and encouraging the crowd with his other. And when he was finished, he stood and bowed to the listeners who were now cheering and clapping mightily.

"*Wonderful,*" *the manager said.* "*And what might be the name of that tune?*"
"*I call it, 'Her Cunt Was as Wet as a Billabong.'*"
"*Oh my,*" *the manager exclaimed.* "*I will hire you, but you can never tell any of me customers the names of your songs.*"
Saturday night I was performing to a packed house, and the crowd was pounding the suds and going wild over me music. I took a break, for I had to drain me one-eyed trouser snake. When I returned to me piano, a poofter walked up to me and whispered, "*Do you know your zipper is down and your dick is hanging out?*"
"*Know it?*" *I said,* "*I wrote it.*"

Hee, hee! Hee, hee, hee!

Joey was joined in laughter by all the men in the barroom.

Bang! Bang! Bang.

"Killing time in Viet Nam!" we all shouted.

An Aussie stood.

Two deaf and dumb twins were separated at birth. Many years later they met up again.

"Howdy," one said. The other signed back.

"You can speak."

And the storyteller worked his hands up and down, side to side, pointing to his mouth and then his ears, and then he crossed his hands over his heart.

"Yes," the talking twin replied. "A very long, painful operation. I do not recommend it."

"No, I want it! I want it! I want to be able to talk just like you!"

"Okay."

Two weeks later, after putting down a large sum of money, the deaf and dumb twin stood before the doctor, who told him to strip and bend over. And when he bent over, the doctor stuck an auger in the twin's ort and began to hand crank it. The storyteller bent over, and he cranked an imaginary auger, his hand rotating in a circle. *The dumb man was silent. The doctor cranked again, this time longer and more vigorously, and still all was quiet. The doctor gritted his teeth and cranked a third time with a vicious rotation.*

"Ah!" the twin screamed.

"Okay," the doc said. "Come back tomorrow and we will work on the Bs."

Bang! Bang! Bang!

"Killing time in Viet Nam!"

Then the barroom went silent, and when I looked up there were a host of Aussie eyeballs peering back at me.

"Ahem," I said.

A rich man was impressed by the genitalia of another man.

"My God, man, where did you get such a large cock?"

"Oh," the endowed man said. "There is a doctor in China, but the operation is very expensive and painful and I do not recommend it."

"Nonsense, give me the doctor's name."

The rich man went to China and met Dr. One Hung Lo. I waited but no one laughed.

"Would you like the deluxe treatment?" the doctor asked.

"Absolutely!" the man replied.

He recovered and decided to return to America by cruise ship. He was walking the promenade. I stood and strutted with my arms swinging at my side as I turned a corner. Then I stopped abruptly and opened my arms, eyeballs, and mouth.

"My God, man, you have a large cock!" the astonished seafarer said.

"Ah, that's nothing," the rich man answered. "My balls are coming on another ship."

There was complete silence in the barroom. I looked from side to side. Once, twice, three times. *Oh Jesus*, I thought to myself. *The ugly American has made an ass of himself in front of the entire Australian Air Force.* I wanted to dissolve into a puddle of piss. I wanted to walk out the door without opening it.

Hee, hee! Hee, hee hee!

Bang! Bang! Bang!

"Killing time in Viet Nam," the barroom yelled. Joey patted me on my back. The Digger ruffled my hair and another Aussie shoved a beer in my hand. A smile crossed my face and then evolved into a boisterous laugh, and I couldn't stop banging my beer can on the bar.

Joey drove me to the *Smoky* FAC hootch where I would be staying. He would stay with the Aussies. It was like the end of a perfect first date.

I walked away. I did not look back until I heard him drive off. Then I stopped and stared as he disappeared down the road, and I wondered if I would have done the same for him.

I walked into the Vung Tau *Smoky* bar. It was dark, with the exception of a rotating flashing red light, the kind you might see on a tow truck or on the top of a cop car. As kids we used to call them *gumball machines*.

"It's our hate light," the major said. He was their *Smoky* ALO, air liaison officer, and *Miffwick* or Motherfucker What's in Charge. "The boys turn it on when they need to burn off some steam."

"Did something happen?" I asked.

"One of our crew chiefs got drunk last night and was taxiing a bird around the flight line when he decided he wanted to fly. He knew just enough to get himself in trouble. He got it airborne, but he couldn't get it back on the ground. One of our guys launched. He joined on the crew chief's wing and began to talk him down. They were coming down final together. It looked like he was going to make it, but the crew chief panicked and he augered it in." The major held his hand out, palm down, and then he rolled it over and bashed his fingers in the bar.

"We went out and found the airplane. The crew chief was dead. We pumped a couple of holes in the airplane, and I wrote it up like he was killed in action. The body was shipped home this morning."

I should have learned by now what to say when this subject arose, but I hadn't. So I always said nothing. I just stared straight ahead.

"How you doing with Captain Puff?" he asked.

"Oh, it's okay. He's short now, so he has mellowed. His replacement seems alright. Guess what he pulled on me today?" And I related the radio-out episode.

"Jesus," he said. "What an asshole. You can fly down here with me anytime you want. I'd love to have you. Just say the word."

I thought about his offer for a while. It would mean leaving Father William; that might be a good thing, I reasoned. It would also mean abandoning Jefferson and Carlos, even though they would be heading back to the world soon. And Joey, I couldn't leave Joey after he had extended his tour to stay with me.

"Yeah, well. You all have such a soft life here, I probably wouldn't even want to rotate home when my time was up."

The light was making me feel dizzy. A couple of the FACs smashed glasses against a plaster wall behind me.

"Got to spin in, major. I've got the early one in the morning."

"Hey, hold it the fuck down!" the bartender yelled. "I've got a phone call. Who the hell is *Smoky* forty-four?"

I took the receiver, identified myself, listened, grunted yes, and hung up.

"What's that all about?" the major asked.

"They have decided to defoliate the area where all our contacts have been happening. First time we will be using Agent Orange, and I get to put it in."

"Lucky you," he said.

"I need to be in the target area before dawn."

The major showed me an empty bunk and then pointed to an alarm clock. I set it, and then I collapsed on top of the bunk. I figured I could sleep longer if I didn't take off my combat boots. I heard the door close, and then I heard the alarm go off. I sat up. My head throbbed. I shook it like I was trying to dislodge water from my inner ear. My nuts hurt, but I smiled when I discovered my dick was still there and in one piece. There were no piss-hards for me that night, even though I was carrying enough urine to mark a one-acre perimeter. I "drained the dragon," as Joey would call it, and headed out to the flight line.

It was dark: black as coal dark, ghosts and goblins dark. And there was no discernible difference in degrees of blackness between earth and sky. I pointed my airplane into the darkness above and climbed until I could see the first rays of sunshine.

"*Smoky* forty, *Smoky* forty-four airborne out of Vung Tau."

"Good morning *Smoky* forty-four. Ready to go to work?"

"No, but whatcha got?"

"Got *Ranch Hands*. We are going to spray the jungle."

"You mean *spay* the jungle, right."

"I guess."

"Good morning, Viet Nam! Time to kill some gooks!" It was a wakeup call on guard channel for all early morning flyers. Our troops were awake airborne and testy. I turned up the volume to enjoy the show that was certain to follow.

"Fuck you, with your good morning Viet Nam crap, must be some kind of Air Force puke."

"Hey, who is that morbid fuck who said, 'Good morning, Viet Nam'?"

"Hey, fuck you, and the horse you rode in on, and the colonel who sent you!"

"Get off guard channel, you cretins! Don't you know it's only for emergencies?"

"Who you calling a cretin, you moron. I will shoot your ass out of the sky."

"Must be a strap hanger."

"Damn! Viet Nam sure smells worse than usual today."

"Roger that."

"*Bearcat arty* with a commo check on guard."

"I've got you five by."

"Me too, *Bearcat*."

"Commo check guard, too loud and too often."

"I've got you loud and clear, *Bearcat*."

"I've got you *lima charles*."

"I've got you *lickitly clit*."

"I've got you *livacious clitoris*."

"All right guys, you've had your fun. Now knock it off and let's get to work."

"Must be that colonel who rode in on a horse."

"Yeah, fuck you, colonel, and the horse you rode in on!"

"And don't forget, three bags full," I mumbled to myself.

But inside, I knew he was the voice of reason, an older man who understood. He had let the kiddies play as they did every morning and then said, *Enough*. And what amazed me was that it always worked. Even I turned my attention back to the mission at hand. I switched frequencies to Bien Hoa tower.

"*Ranch Hand*, *Smoky* forty-four on tower frequency."

"Roger, *Smoky*. What is the weather like in the target area?"

"It's clear in a million."

"And the wind. What is the direction and velocity?"

"Roger, standby."

How the fuck was I going to answer that? I wondered. I didn't have any wind instruments. I guess I could wet my finger and stick it out the window, or I could give it a WAG (wild ass guess). Ah, the Air Force way: measure with a micrometer, then cut it with an axe. Hmmm. Maybe I could give them something a little more accurate. I spotted a road and dropped down on the deck and started S turns over it, to get some idea of wind direction and velocity.

"Looks like the wind is out of the southeast at no more than a couple of miles per hour."

"Okay, *Smoky*. We will launch. Break, break. Bien Hoa tower. *Ranch Hand* twelve, flight of four 123s taxi, takeoff from the corral."

Jesus, they were going to disperse yellow death on my wind assessment. What a fucked-up war.

They arrived over the target area. It was the same area where Charlie continued to knock our helicopters out of the air. Our strategy now was to kill everything that was down there, destroy everything that was green and alive, spare nothing, just kill, kill, kill!

I would fly slightly off to one side and a little below the spray birds. If they took ground fire, I would roll in and mark the target. The C-123s would fly into the wind and on the deck so the chemicals would not be blown out of the box. Right! I would also be on the receiving end of the spray. It would be sucked into my front triangular window. But dioxin couldn't possibly be hazardous to humans. Our government wouldn't allow that, would they?

"All right, cowboys, let's saddle up and take her down," the spray bird commander ordered, and the four airplanes with mounted spray bars nosed over.

I visualized the pilots with their starched fatigues, purple scarves, and cowboy hats and boots. I remembered staying in their hootch my first couple of weeks in-country, and how my classmate had bitched about all this gung-ho nonsense about being cowboys. It seemed so long ago. I was a kid then, a lot like the troops playing verbal grab-ass on the guard channel this morning; a kid doing a man's job. But these cowboys were grown men playing kids' games with chemicals that could kill jungle growth that had survived for hundreds of years.

"Take that, tree! Breathe it in," I said as I saw the mist heading for the jungle floor. "I will watch as your leaves turn brown, as brown as the rust on a piece of farm equipment left out in the elements. And your limbs will turn ghoulish-grey, as grey as a bloated battlefield corpse. And then you and the lush green jungle around you will turn white, as white as a cemetery headstone."

Joey was waiting for me when I landed back at Bien Hoa. I slid onto the jeep seat.

"Ever thought about getting out of the Air Force?" I asked.

"What would I do, drive a taxi in Sydney?"

I laughed. I imagined the fright on his passenger's face after a shot ride with him at the controls, and if another cab tried to get in Joey's six o'clock, the passenger would be puking for sure.

"Let's go to the O club tonight, mate," he said. "I've heard there is a new base commander and he is allowing *beaver shows* back in the club."

"Hey, that's good old Air Force rationale," I replied. "We have got to wear hats in the heat, but gomer girls can bare their boxes in public. But, hey, who gives a shit what the reason is, let's go!"

That night Joey led us into the club. The place was packed. A Filipino band opened, and the crowd booed every note.

"Where are the girls?" someone shouted.

"Get off the stage and bring on the ladies."

"Boo! Boo! Boo!"

The band tried to play the song "I Want to Go Home," but the troops substituted their own lyrics.

"I want to get laid." Then louder, "I want to get laid!" Then drowning the band out with: "OH, HOW I WANT TO GET LAID."

Eventually, in order to avert a potential riot, they brought the ladies onstage. They were gomer, zip, slope . . . gook girls . . . but they were women with tits, hips, and furry muffs. God, they were beautiful. I guess I had now been in Nam long enough to appreciate their beauty.

"Is their pussy slanted?" Father William wanted to know as he put his hand on my shoulder to try to get a better look. "Goddammit! I've got to piss like a racehorse," he said. "Try and get them to hold up the show until I get back."

"How the fuck am I going to get them to do that?"

"I don't fucking know! Start a riot or something!"

They were still performing when he returned.

"Listen to this," he said.

"There was one lone Army major sitting in the bar. I walked over to him and said: 'What the fuck are you doing sitting in here? There are naked Filipino girls out there . . . with curried little muffs.'"

"'I'm a chaplain!' the major responded as he pointed to the cross on his uniform."

Hee, hee! Hee, hee, hee!

"I'm a chaplain!" Joey repeated. He kept repeating it, at least ten more times, each time laughing louder.

"Like the nun in the story," Father William said.

"What nun in what story?" I asked.

"Like the nun who got kicked out of the convent for doing push-ups in the cucumber patch."

"Yeah," Joey said. "*Like the time Sister Matilda and Sister Mary Margaret were driving in the rain and a glowing red Devil appeared on the hood of their car. He started throwing lightning bolts at them. "What shall I do?" Sister Mary Margaret asked.*

"*Show him your cross!" Sister Matilda answered. So Sister Mary Margaret rolled down the window and shouted: "Get off the fucking hood of our car."*

"Jesus," I said, shaking my head, "you two have got to be the only guys on the planet who can go from talking about curried muffs to nun jokes. But I'm glad to be here with you." And we clanked beer cans.

"To curried muffs," Father William shouted.

"To bearded clams," Joey offered.

"To hair pies," I yelled.

On the way back to our hootch, Joey told us he had heard about an incident up north.

"An Australian bird with a beautiful face and body, dressed in a skimpy, little mini-skirt . . ." he tried to shake his ass while driving the jeep because he could not tell a story without acting it out.

"Yeah, yeah. We get it," we said. He continued.

"She was an escape artist with a USO show and she was performing at a Marine base. She brought a Marine captain up on the stage where she had a bunch of ropes and chains and handcuffs, shit like that, and she invited him to tie her up, which he did. And when he was done, he pulled her skirt down and proceeded to eat her out, right on the stage, to a massive amount of cheering by a roomful of horny Marines." Joey looked into the backseat while laughing and clapping his hands over his head. He would have gone off the road if I had not straightened the wheel.

"What did she do?" someone asked.

"I guess she couldn't do anything but smile," Joey said. "The Marine was a hero. He drank free in every bar he set foot in until he disappeared. Word was the brass sent him to their northernmost fire support base."

"I don't believe that story," a FAC said.

"I've heard that story," another pilot said. "And I have also heard that's why there are no round-eye U.S.O. performers."

"Except in the Bob Hope show," someone replied.

"Yeah, well, who gets to see that? We sure as hell don't!"

"An American TV audience, that's who!" Father William said.

"Do you believe that story?" a *Daredevil* FAC asked me.

"Yeah, I believe anything can happen over here. I didn't believe U.S. soldiers massacred more than five hundred old men, women, and children in My Lai when I first heard it; but that turned out to be true."

Nothing further was said. When the jeep stopped, we got out in silence and walked our separate ways. I walked to the john, rolled up my sleeves, and soaped-scrubbed my hands and face. Then I rinsed my hands, arms, and face; once, twice, three times.

The next day, I asked Carlos to get me a *short-timer's calendar*—one with the drawing of the naked lady divided into 180 squares with squares 3, 2, and 1, two teats and a pussy. I had now been in-country longer than six months. After six months, I could put in for my two R & Rs, which I immediately did, since I wanted to make sure I got them in before something bad happened to me. I wondered if I could put in for Moondoggie's and Billy's too, since they never had a chance to use theirs.

> That night I wrote a letter.
> *Hi honey, thinking of you a lot.*
> *Get ready for our trip to Hawaii.*
> *I will send you the dates when I*
> *get them. The war is winding down.*
> *Viet Namation, they are calling it.*
> *I might be heading to Malaysia with*
> *Joey. That should be fun. I am doing fine.*
> *Kiss the kids for me.*
> *Sky King*

The next morning, I swung my legs over the side of my bunk. But before jumping to the floor, I thought about how I had lived in this shithole for a long time, so long that I could no longer visualize sleeping in my own bed back in the world. I thought about how, in an effort to coexist with Captain Puff, I had expanded my outreach. I had played cards in a fighter hootch, but that ended with the death of Lucky Larry. I drank with Buddha's helicopters boys, but paid dearly when his brave young men died or became paralyzed. I hid out in Father William's room when he was flying. Hell, I even spent time with the *Ranch Hands*, the arrogant Agent Orange dispensers. I thought about how Thumper, Moondoggie, and Billy were becoming distant memories, as distant and as artificial as the cowboy actors I watched as a child on Saturdays in a beaten-down movie theater called the Roxy. And I hated the fact that Thumper, Moondoggie, and Billy no longer seemed real. I jumped down. Joey was barfing in the john. I locked the far door and positioned the mamasans.

Joey was my salvation now, my mate. We were raised on different sides of the earth, yet when I stood beside him, I felt alive, protected, and sane. He understood me, and I him. I smiled as I thought about how he terrorized senior officers and got away with it. We weren't crazy, they were.

"*Wa-ooch!*"

I watched as he wretched, but he had nothing left inside to puke up. I understood that too, as there were days I felt empty inside.

"That's behavior we expect from crazy Aussies," the brass would say. But they were wrong; instead they should have said, "That's crazy behavior we expect from troops that have been in combat."

I washed my face and then studied it in the mirror. I could see the hate. I had tried to not hate Captain Puff, but the hate had seeped into my soul. Those who looked at me could see it, and I could see they approached me cautiously. Every morning—half awake, half asleep—I walked into the shower-sink-shitter room, smelled nouc mam, a dead fish sauce that the gooks ate even though it actually smelt a lot worse than anything Joey could bring up, and listened to the mamasans cackle back and forth until I could no longer tolerate it.

"Shut the fuck up!" I yelled. Joey turned and looked at me.

I shook my head.

"Everyone who lives in the Nam pays a price," I whispered to myself.

"Do you think it is possible we could go to Malaysia?" I asked Joey.

He wiped his face with a towel.

"I will piss in someone's pocket to get it done, mate," he said.

Two days later, Joey handed me the orders.

"We are headed down to Malaysia for a couple of days, mate."

"God, that's great. How the hell did you pull that off?"

"I promised the old man that we would not get thrown in jail."

"Wow! He must have figured you would need someone to watch over you, someone with good judgment, someone who would stay sober so there would not be any international incidents, someone like me," I said.

"You must be joking," Joey said. "Come on. I can't wait to see Puff's face when I tell him we are going."

Captain Puff was peering into his locker when I opened the door to our room, and we walked in. He slammed his locker door shut. Joey laid our orders on his desk, and then sat—with his legs extended and arms and ankles crossed—on Captain Puff's bunk. Captain Puff locked his locker, picked up the orders, and began to read them. He looked up. "How come no one ever asks me to go on any trips?" he asked.

"Because you are such an asshole, that's why!" Joey replied emphatically. Joey stood, and we walked out.

We would be leaving in ten days. The timing could not have been better, for Captain Puff would be on his way to the States before we returned. Also, I would be going on *basket leave*. Staff would cut my leave orders and throw them in a basket. If something happened to me while in Malaysia, I was covered. If I managed to make it back, they would tear the orders up so the time gone would not count against my allotment. "Hot damn! What a sweet deal." Someone was watching over me.

Three days before we were scheduled to depart, I was standing at the bar when Doc, our flight surgeon, walked up and started running his finger along my chest.

"How long have you had these?" he asked.

"Had what?" I replied.

"These busted blood vessels."

"Fuck, I don't know. I was probably born with them."

"It might be serious. It's a sign your kidneys may be failing."

"What you talking about?"

"Maybe you had better lay off the booze."

"What?"

"I'm serious. I want to run some tests on you. "

The doc walked out, and I ordered another beer.

He reappeared with a syringe, which he immediately stuck in my arm.

"Ouch, goddammit! How about asking, for Christ's sake?"

He laughed and removed the needle.

"Stay off that booze," he said. "It will be ten days before I get the results."

Stay off booze in Nam? Man, that's like saying don't sweat, or don't shit. What else is there? We drink for medicinal reasons; the other option is insanity.

"I'm going to Malaysia with Joey."

"When?"

"In a couple of days."

"There is no way I can get the results that fast. Stay off the booze down there."

"I'll give it a good test once I get there," I laughed as I said it, but noticed that no one else was laughing. I tried again: "Hey, maybe I can bring back some special strain of VD for you to work on."

"Listen, you want some rubbers?" he said. "I've got lots of rubbers." He said it with a straight face.

"Will you stop, Doc? You're going to need a shrink before you get out of the Nam."

"Can you get us special shrink rates, Doc?" a FAC asked.

"Yeah, how about some group rates?"

Now everybody was laughing.

"I've heard," another FAC said, "that some grunt units have contests to see who gets the worst strain of VD. They throw a bunch of money in a pot, and the one who needs the most ccs of penicillin to knock it out wins the money."

"That's not funny," Doc replied.

A man, Joey said, *walks into an American doctor's office.*

"Doctor," he sez. "Me toe hurts."

"Why does it hurt?" the doctor asks.

"Because me dick keeps dripping on it," the man answers.

"Let me see," sez the doctor. So the man drops his trou and the doctor takes a look.

Joey cupped his hands, like he was holding a pair of balls. He studied first one hand, and then the other, and then he looked up with his eyes open wide, eyebrows raised.

"Why of course," the doctor sez. "You have the Hong Kong Dong."

"Is that serious?" the man asks.

"Yes, very serious."

"Can it be cured?"

"Yes," the doc answers. "But we will have to cut it off."

"My dick?"

"Yes."

"Yikes!"

The man pulls up his britches and walks next door to see the Viet Namese doctor.

He drops his trou. The Viet Namese doctor examines him.

"Ah, you have Hong Kong Dong," the Viet Namese doctor sez.

"I know. What do we do?"

"We do nothing," the Viet Namese doctor sez.

"Do nothing? The American doctor says we have to cut it off."

"Ah, American doctors. All they want to do is cut, cut, cut. You wait three days, it fall off."

Hee, hee! Hee, hee, hee!

"That's funny!" a FAC said.

"Funny, ha, ha," the doc replied. "I am serious. Stop drinking for ten days!" And he walked away.

The next day, I was scheduled to put in four airstrikes. *Recon by bomb*, I called it. I was given coordinates of a suspected V.C. base camp. Because there were no friendlies in the area, I could play around with the bombs, place a few, then have the fighters hold high and dry while I dropped down to have a look-see for bunkers, trails, spider holes, anything that might indicate the enemy was operating in the area. Then I would repeat the process, over and over again.

It was a typical day in the Nam. What air that was available for breathing was heavy and musty, and painful to pull through my mouth and nose and into my lungs. To assist my breathing, I tugged at my parachute straps, with hands covered by fire-resistant Nomex gloves. I smiled. Of course they were fire-resistant; they were soaked with sweat. Periodically, I raised my sun visor to mop the perspiration from my forehead. I counted the drips—ten, eleven, twelve—as they rolled down my ribs from their origin, my armpits, but I could do nothing with the pools of sweat that had formed in my crotch. My balls had best learn to float, or they would drown. Through it all, I found nothing of interest on the ground, and I didn't know if that was good or bad. After three sets of fighters, I was exhausted and exasperated. Now, all I could think about was getting the fuck out of here and down to alcohol-flowing, laugh-inducing Malaysia.

I pulled back on the yoke and pushed my throttles full forward to climb toward the heavens. I pointed my overloaded Cessna into a grouping of puffy, white clouds. I watched my altimeter needles rotate—*five thousand, six thousand, seven thousand feet*—and I was now able to suck in cool fresh air as I ascended, yanked and banked, and descended in between and in and out of the Oxydol white clouds against the Rinso Blue sky. My airspeed tumbled and soared, but my spirit only soared as I maneuvered my airplane to enter another billowing patch of cotton-white fluff.

VArooom!

I saw the underbelly of an oncoming F-100 as it passed just above me and so close that it consumed my entire windshield. It seemed to happen in slow motion: So slow that I could count the rivets on its fuselage as they passed by. The fighter bomber parted my airplane perfectly—dare I say dead center—for, had it not, it would have clipped one or both of my twin horizontal stabilizers. The pilot in the fighter never saw me, for his aircraft did not deviate from course or altitude. Nor would he be looking for me since I was operating in his airspace without permission. The roar of his engines penetrated each of my ears, then banged against my drums and the insides of my skull as it tried to find a way to escape. My eyes seemed to bulge from pressure created by his closure velocity. I felt the heat from his engines, heat so hot that it steamed my visor and warmed my skin inside my fire-resistant flight suit material. My stomach rolled. I must have stopped breathing, as I remember gulping air when it was over. And then I began to shake. My aircraft shook with me because I had a death-grip on the yoke. I descended slowly, using clearing turns, and I leveled out at 1,200 feet over the smoldering bomb craters I had created. I welcomed the hot jungle air and the safety it now provided. I keyed my mike.

"*Smoky* four-zero, *Smoky* four-four."

"Roger, go ahead four-four."

"Cancel my last set of fighters. I will be returning to base, and have four-three scratch me from the schedule tomorrow."

"Roger, is there anything wrong?"

"That's a negative."

No, nothing wrong, I thought. Nothing, except I just want to live. I just want to live long enough to leave this shithole of a country even if it is only for a short time. And I want to hold my wife and my sons in my arms. That's not asking for too much, is it?

They say each of us has a cup of courage somewhere inside our body; mine was now empty. Perhaps I would be able to refill it in Malaysia.

Part 2

The Vacuum

Chapter 1
THE VISITATION

Captain Puff was packing. Hell, he had been packing for the last month. Besides packing, he spent his days poring over *Awards and Decorations* booklets to see how many medals he could put himself in for. If there was a medal for looking for medals, he would have received the highest order with many oak leaf clusters. I found his search disgusting, but because he was leaving my agitation was tempered.

We were now assigned to the 22nd TASS, having been moved from the 19th Tactical Air Support Squadron, which only meant that our squadron commander would change. The Viet Namese would finally be taking over the majority of the fighting; therefore, the reasoning went, they would use their own FACs. The O-1 Birddog—the O denoting *Observation*, but it could have just as well stood for oldest airplane in inventory—would now be flown by VNAF (Viet Namese Air Force) personnel with American flyers being phased out.

Captain Puff leaving, a new squadron commander coming on board, and the Viet Namese taking over the fighting was a perfect trifecta for me. At least on paper it looked good. I said good-bye to Captain Puff, and a sore that had festered inside me for nearly the entire time I had been in-country. He would take his magic underwear and be gone by the time I returned from Malaysia. *Hallelujah!* He gave me a shitty O.E.R., officer efficiency report, average grades in all categories. But in the comment section, the man had written about me: "*The most honest I have ever met, and that candidness sometimes gets him in trouble.*" I wondered what it all meant. Could I have done more? If I pressed a little more, could I have saved another American life; or was my own life at the top of my priority list?

Joey and I sat on straps in the cargo area of the Australian C-130. We were heading south, following the winding coast down to Malaysia.

"So Tarzan says to Jane," Joey hollered over the roar of the engines, "'Me, Tarzan. What your name?'

"'Me, Jane.'

"'Whole name?'

"'Cunt.'"

Hee, hee! Hee, hee, hee!

He could not stop laughing. And the more he laughed, the more I laughed, and soon everyone in the airplane, even those who could not have heard the joke, were laughing. They were laughing because we were laughing. Joey's laughter was absolutely infectious.

God, what a great feeling to put Nam in my rearview mirror, even if it was only for a few days. And the thought that Captain Puff would be gone when I returned increased the pleasure.

After level off, Joey motioned me to follow him forward and into the cockpit. I looked forward out the cockpit window. It was a perfect day to fly, with the blue ocean blending into the blue sky. I could feel my skin relax as Viet Nam disappeared on the horizon, and the tension from my spring-loaded nerves seemed to dissipate into the cockpit air. I swatted at them while smiling. Little imaginary tensions floated out of and around my body like pesky black flies on a Canadian canoe trail. I tried to catch them, and when I did, I threw them against the bulkhead. Joey raised his eyebrows but said nothing. Eventually, I settled in and maybe slept a little until the pilot nudged me and pointed out the window. "Penang Island," he said, "beautiful, eh?"

I gave him a thumbs-up.

We landed and I followed Joey as he checked us into the Australian officer's quarters. I dropped my small bag on the white tiled floor. A sitting area with table and chairs, a desk with stationery on it, and a dresser, all made from rattan, were neatly arranged on the right side of the room. Two swirling fans pulled air from the louvered windows and door. The air was cool since the room was protected from the sun by a roof extended along the colonnade. A large bed was centered on the back wall of the room. White mosquito netting, which looked like it was made of linen, hung gracefully from a hook on the ceiling and draped around the bed except where it was tied back to provide an opening for entry. I gasped.

"This is your room," Joey said. "I'm just 'round the corner. Meet you in the mess, mate, in twenty minutes."

I showered and then had a horrible time deciding which shirt I would wear that day; I had two to choose from. It felt great to be dressed in civilian clothes, even though they had been scrubbed clean by stones and carried a faint smell of *nouc mam*. I finished dressing and met Joey for lunch. A porcelain plate and sterling silver utensils sat upon a white tablecloth. The waiter approached wearing a starched white uniform. I felt dirty.

"Would you like soup or salad, sir?"

"What did he say?" I asked Joey.

"Soup or salad," he replied.

I tried to remember what salad tasted like, but I could only recall that it was good.

"Salad, please."

"Oh, yes, and the largest glass of milk you have," I added.

"And you, sir?" the waiter said to Joey.

We finished eating, grabbed a couple of beers, and headed downtown in a rickshaw built for two. No guns, no bunkers, no barbed wire. It was scary beautiful. We disembarked and wandered in and out of the shops and bars.

"The prices are still good," Joey said. "But when the Yanks on R & R hit Singapore, the prices doubled."

"Yeah, we are the last of the big spenders, huh?"

Then it was back to the base to meet Joey's mates. We gathered in the casual bar of the officers club. As evening arrived, so did several Australian birds, mini-skirted and braless—a fad that I heard was happening in the States but waited for me to leave before it started—and the hinges that held my jaw in place strained and gave way. I grabbed Joey's arm for strength.

"What's this?" I asked.

"Australian birds. Nurses!" he replied. He called one over.

"How about walking in front of us for a while so we can perv on your legs?" he said. The nurse smiled and swung her ass as she departed. He poked me with an elbow.

"She's no scrubber, eh?" he said to me.

"I'll say!" I said, even though I had never heard the word "scrubber" before.

Then, Aussie fighter jocks started to file in. They flew the Mirage, a shit-hot French-built fighter. They greeted Joey, and he introduced them to me one by one and I ordered a round of drinks for all.

"My shout," I shouted, showing them that I indeed spoke Australian.

"I was flying the Mirage before I was twenty-one," Joey said. "Me and me mates flew on the Australian acrobatic team for several years."

I was jealous.

"I'd like to strap one on," I said.

"The birds or the airplane?" a flight lieutenant asked.

"Both."

"I can only help you with the airplane."

"Is that possible?" I asked.

"Absolutely," he said. "We only have single-seaters, so if you think you can handle it, then let's have a go. Flight line, Monday morning at 0600 hours."

"Can do," I replied, and we shook hands.

"Shit-hot!" I yelled as he walked away.

A bird walked by, winked at Joey's worm, and he was gone. I ordered another beer and thought about flying a Mirage, and I could feel my heart as it ramped up its beating. The booze told me I could do it, and instantly I became the classic arrogant and obnoxious Yank.

"Solo a Mirage, why not? Just give me a few airspeeds for takeoff and landing. Piece of cake," I boasted. Several Aussies laughed and all broke ranks and left. I was standing by myself when Joey returned.

"Was that guy blowing smoke?" I asked Joey.

"About what?"

"About flying the Mirage?"

"No."

"They will let me solo a Mirage?"

"Yes, why not? You're a pilot, aren't you?" he said, like I was crazy for asking.

"That could never happen in the U.S. Air Force."

"For fucksakes, it's just an airplane. You get in trouble, you bang out. More beer, here," he motioned with his arm, then looked at me and continued. "Why would you want to fly when you are on holiday?"

"It's a *Mirage*!" I replied.

"Our acrobatic team was doing a show in Darwin," he said. "Miss Australia was the guest of honor. She was watching our show with the base commander in a yacht just off the coast. When we finished our demonstration I wanted to win her over, so I flew low over the yacht, gear and flaps hanging, and then I came back around and tried to drop me drag chute on the yacht. I plopped it on the front of the yacht and damn overshot the runway when I tried to land without me chute. That night there was a presentation and seated at the head table with Miss Australia was the base commander and all his cronies.

She refused to attend unless the acrobatic team was allowed to sit with her at the head table. The colonel was fuming that he had to replace his men with a bunch of young lieutenants. But we weren't done yet. A British parachute team also participated in the festivities. Me mates and I decided the night wouldn't be complete until we played a joke on the pommies, or prisoners of Mother England. I bribed a steward. I put on his uniform, filled a wash bucket with gasoline, and then I proceeded to swab floors.

"'Excuse me, mate. Excuse me,' until I managed to get the jump team in a circle. Then one of me mates torched the gasoline. Another couple of mates stood by with fire extinguishers and doused the British gentlemen. A donnybrook may have ensued except a thatched roof over the bar caught fire and it damn near took the whole club with it. We had to pay for repairs. It was money well spent."

We ordered more beers. The bar was now packed with Aussie officers dressed in their tropic uniforms, which featured short trousers. The base commander walked in, turned down the music, and said, "Gentlemen, there will be no short trousers allowed in the club after 1900 hours."

"What's that?" The leader of the fighter jocks asked, cupping his ear with one hand and a nurse with the other.

And the base commander repeated his order.

"What's that, *cunt* hear you?" the officer replied and everyone laughed but the base commander.

The fighter jock jumped up on the bar.

"Gather round, mates," he said. "There are no short trousers allowed in the club after 1900 hours. Now, we don't want to be in breach of the rules, do we?"

"No-o-o-o!"

He then opened his belt and dropped his trousers, and all of his men followed suit.

"There, now we are legal."

Everyone laughed and cheered, and then they raised their beers in the direction of the colonel, who turned and walked out.

I felt like I was representing the entire United States. I felt compelled to show the Aussies I could drink as much and more as any of them and I could fight the whole lot of them if I had to. The more I drank, the bigger jerk I became. I became the asshole that I hate: a loud, foul-mouth, know-it-all, bad-ass-projecting, money-splurging American. Aussies were avoiding me. They were talking to Joey about me. I knew it, but I could not stop. I was transmitting only, and never on receive. I just shouted louder, drank faster, swore more, and tried to grope any passing nurses.

"Are all Yanks assholes?" an Aussie said to me.

"What the hell does that mean?" I asked with a snarl.

Joey had my six o'clock. He grabbed me, then a couple of beers, and led me out of the club. He hailed a cab and we headed downtown. It was dark. When had the sun gone? I wondered. The streets were deserted. The cab stopped in front of a building that looked like a saloon in the Wild West. Joey pulled me out of the cab and stood me up while he settled the fare. We walked inside. The place was rocking. I collapsed in the first chair available. Joey disappeared into the crowd. I could feel my head bobbing. A woman appeared with a beer and sat on my lap. Her blouse was open. She was not wearing a bra. She placed the beer in my right hand and a magnificent breast in my left hand.

"You like?" she asked.

A beer and a breast. I had never seen that on any menu. Was this a late-night special? Was it à la carte? Would it be a full course? She was beautiful. She stood, grabbed my hand, and pulled me to my feet. She laughed as I stumbled up the stairs.

"Where's my friend?"

"No worry," she said.

At the top of the stairs, there was a large man sitting on a stool. I waved as she led me down a hallway. Not a muscle moved on the man. I decided that a passive giant was better than a returned wave, and I continued following her down the hallway. She stopped and pointed to a door.

"No worry," she said again. "Your friend here."

She opened the next door. There was a vaulted ceiling. The side walls stopped halfway up. The guard on the stool could have looked over them and into the adjoining rooms. There was a large bed, which she gently pushed me down on, and then she began to remove my clothes. When I was naked, she undressed and then began to sniff. She sniffed rapidly but moved slowly, starting just behind the lobe of my right ear, down to my Adam's apple, and for a minute I thought she was going to take a bite of the apple, then continued sniffing up to and behind the lobe of my left ear. Two large, unbalanced fans whirled above us, and in Joey's room I could hear Joey over the whoosh of the wobbly, rotating blades. It had been months since I had heard the noises that emanated from his room, but I was fairly certain I knew what was going on in there. In a short time, it was my turn to make the very same noises.

When sunlight lit the room, I tried to sneak out. I was down on the floor searching for my shoe when she grabbed my ankle and pulled me back onto the bed, and then on top of her. She still looked beautiful in the morning, a rare phenomenon, and she was very strong. I heard Joey laughing in the next room, and then he went back to making those noises again. She squeezed me with powerful legs and arms, and even though she could qualify as a whore, I believed she cared for me, and I her in a strange sort of way only warriors may know. I wanted her to protect me, cradle me, and piece me back together. I wanted her to wring out all the evil that had taken possession of my soul. What had happened to me? I wondered. The strongest words my mother spoke were, "Fie on you." My father punctuated his speech with only an occasional *hell* or *damn*, and he did so only at work. I never swore, drank, or smoked until after high school, yet I had turned into this monster that killed for sport, revenge, and glory. I inserted a swear word in nearly every sentence, and was damn proud of it, and now I was sleeping with a prostitute; and I felt cherished, loved even. Hold me! Save me! Let me stay nestled in your arms, forever.

It was hunger that drove me from my nest. I tried to give her some money.

"No worry," she said. "You have very good friend."

I met Joey downstairs. His face looked like it had been ironed; it was pulled tight with no wrinkles anywhere and I wondered if maybe he spent the night with "No Worry's" sister. We giggled all through a breakfast of bacon and eggs and in the cab on the ride back to the base. We were like little kids, deliriously happy, as if we had somehow ironically reclaimed our innocence. It was as though we had just peeked through a hole in the wall of a women's locker room, only this was more serious; but we chose to ignore it, to laugh it off, to drink it away; to put on our *fuck-it* act so that nobody would know we were trembling inside. We walked to my room.

"See you at six in the stag bar," Joey said.

I nodded, opened my door, and listened as he began to whistle "Waltzing Matilda," which echoed down the colonnade. I closed the door, stretched out on my white sheets, and fell asleep.

I slept like a dog chasing a cat in his dreams. I awoke agitated and with a massive hangover. I needed a drink. I walked to the club and ordered a Fosters and waited for Joey. Several Aussies came and went. They whispered and pointed at me when they thought I wasn't watching. Even the bartender stood at the other end of the empty bar. With each beer I cranked up my courage for my Mirage flight tomorrow morning. I ordered a shot of bitters on the side. Mr. Big Shot needed several shots to conquer his fears.

At five Joey arrived with another Aussie. He was a helicopter pilot and he was to be my host for the evening as Joey was meeting with some of his friends. We shook hands and drank several more beers and shots, and when the bar got crowded we left.

"I got a bike, mate," he said. "You get on the back and we will head downtown."

"Roger that."

I was dressed in sandals, shorts, and a pullover shirt, not exactly your prototype Hells Angels attire. "Helmets are something you wear while flying," he said as he jumped up in the air and stomped the engine into a start.

BA room!

It roared with vibrato in both the high and the low registers as he rotated the throttle.

"You've been on a hog, mate, haven't you?"

"Hell, yeah!" I replied.

It was assumed that all pilots drove motorcycles. We were adrenaline junkies who loved speed: airplanes, sports cars, motorcycles, fast women. Mr. Big Shot had lied. I had never been on a motorcycle and I drove a Pontiac station wagon.

I jumped on behind him. I could not find a secure place for my hands, and I damn sure wasn't going to wrap my arms around him like some kind of chick, so I grabbed the edges of the padded seat, and when he launched, I damn near fell off the back. We raced down the straightaway. He leaned left to make a turn. I felt the rear wheel was going to skid out, so I leaned right, and the motorcycle began to fishtail. The front wheel hit the curb. The motorcycle tried to do a somersault, and as it did, I sailed through the air, flying in a perfect arc until the left side of my forehead, shoulder, elbow, and hand struck the pavement in the oncoming lane, leaving skin, blood, and cloth at the point of impact. Cars skidded to a halt. I got to my knees, blood dripping from the side of my head, shoulder, elbow. I could see where the skin had peeled off my hand, which was blood red like the leg of a skinned chicken before it is cooked.

"Got to get you to a hospital, mate. Christ, Joey is going to be pissed at me."

He put me in a cab and followed on his bike. The nurses tried to get me on a stretcher, but I protested and we compromised and they rolled me down the hallway in a wheelchair. God, the women were beautiful with their starched-white uniforms, white stockings, and shoes. I wasn't lily white; I made crude remarks, winked, and made obscene gestures with my tongue. They smiled or laughed, which encouraged my despicable behavior.

"Let's go have a drink," I said, "the whole lot of you."

I was rolled into a room and a doctor examined me.

"I want you to stay overnight. I want to run some tests," he said.

"Fuck that," I replied. "I'm on R & R from Viet Nam, and I ain't spending it in a goddamn hospital!"

He tried to reason with me, but that didn't work. I got up out of my chair and pretended to wind myself up like I was a toy soldier, and then I penguin-walked behind a particularly good-looking nurse. Several nurses laughed; the doctor and the helicopter pilot did not. Nor did what looked like the head nurse. She was tall, old, and ugly.

"Get him out of here before he wakes up the entire ward," she bellowed. The doctor put his hand on my shoulder. "You had better stay drunk," he said, "because when you sober up, you are going to be in a lot of pain."

We left the hospital. The helicopter pilot wanted to take me back to the base, but I decided I wasn't drunk enough.

"Let's go to a bar," I said. "I'm buying."

I spotted a bar across the street and I began to walk toward it. The helicopter pilot lifted his arms in supplication, and then followed. I stepped inside and up to the bar, and pulled out a wad of bills.

"A round for the house," I yelled.

"You belong in a bloody hospital, mate."

"Yeah, I know. Just get the drinks."

I ordered three straight shots. One I poured over my wounds, to show everyone I was a tough guy. It burned like the flames of hell and so did the one that I drank.

An Aussie stepped forward.

"Let's do some *flaming hooks*, mate," he said.

He said something to the bartender and two more shot glasses appeared. He pulled out his Zippo and ignited the liquid in his shot glass, then he tossed it down his gullet. A flame remained on his lip for an instant. He slammed the empty shot glass on the bar and ignited my drink.

"We call them *afterburners*," I said, as I tossed mine down. I missed my mouth by a smidgen and, despite my alcohol stupor, I could feel the singe on the corner of my bottom lip.

"Want to do it again?" I asked.

I saw the MPs as they walked in the front door, and Joey's promise that we would stay out of jail raced across my brain. The barroom was packed, so I was able to circle behind them and get out the door. In doing so, I lost my helicopter pilot escort. I walked until I found another bar, then another and another. The left side of my face was battered, my shirt was torn, and my shoulder was raw meat. The bartender refused to serve me.

"We're closing," he said. "All bars are closing."

"Can you call me a cab?"

"You're a cab," he said.

I stared at him.

"Yeah, I can do that."

I walked out to a deserted street. A jeep with soldiers wearing white helmets with *MP* stenciled on them rolled past, and I turned my head away from them. They made a U-turn just as my cab arrived, and I got in.

"Take me to the New Odium Club," I said.

"It's closed."

"Take me there!"

I needed to find my woman. She would heal me, hide me, house me. In my stupor, I was sure she would be waiting up for me.

When we arrived, I told the hack to wait as I pounded on the door, once, twice, three times; each time with more force and longer in duration.

"Open up, goddammit!"

I walked around the building trying to find a way to break in. Nothing! "F-U-C-K! Fuck, fuck . . . "

I opened the cab door.

"Take me to the base."

The cabbie woke me up. I paid him and gave him a ridiculous tip. I worked the key in my door with no success. The cabbie watched, then got out of his cab and unlocked the door for me. I entered and fell onto my bed.

I heard the latch turn and the door open. I lay still, assessing the damage and trying to recall the events that led to my present state of nothingness. I opened my eyes just a crack and I saw the bright light that everyone who has died but lives talks about. Shod horses were doing laps inside my head. One of them must have taken a shit in my mouth.

"The maids thought he was dead. He's all yours now," a strange voice said. I heard the door close.

Joey stood before me. He was laughing. "You were the topic of conversation at *breakie* this morning, mate. They said you were chasing all the birds at the hospital." He held out two beers. And he was still laughing.

"A little hair of the dog," he said.

I sat up slowly. The white sheet rose with me. It was attached to my head, shoulder, and hand; bonded with congealed blood. I pried it loose from my hand and reopened the wound. Joey handed me the cold beers and I held them against my temples. He was still laughing while he walked to the bathroom. He returned with several wet washcloths. I opened a beer and downed the contents, then placed a cloth on my bleeding hand. I pulled the sheet slowly off of my shoulder and left side of my face. Joey could not stop laughing. I stood and wobbled to the bathroom. I ripped what was left of my shirt off, removed my shorts and sandals, checked the water temperature, stepped into the shower, and let the water drip over the right side of my body. I dabbed at my wounds with a washcloth and then towel, and when dry I slid into my other set of shorts and a sweatshirt with the sleeves cut off. I pulled the straps on my sandals tight and drank the second beer. I was good to go. Joey took me to the hospital. It looked familiar. The dialogue sounded familiar also.

"I want to check you in, take some X-rays, keep you overnight."

"Sorry. No can do, Doc, we head back to Nam early tomorrow morning."

"Just patch him up, Doc," Joey said.

And they did, with the added warning about staying drunk. I smiled.

"My doc back home tells me to stop drinking, and you're telling me to get shit-faced. I guess I'll settle for shit-faced."

"Good choice, mate," Joey said.

We left the hospital and relocated to the officers club for some chow and a couple more beers. I took a six-pack back to my room and Mr. Big Shot spent his last night on R & R napping, sucking down a six-pack, and watching the *telly*. Somewhere around midnight, I remembered that I missed my Mirage ride, and in my slightly sober state I was able to surmise that doing a header off a motorcycle traveling at 60 knots may have saved my life. Not as spectacular as *pranging* a Mirage, but at least I walked away from it. My bell had been rung and in between dings, I could hear Father William: "How was the Visitation? Jesus Christ, what the hell happened to you, peasant?"

But my last thought before I fell asleep was, I can't wait to get back to Viet Nam where I'm safe.

Chapter 2
Change

They were waiting for us as we disembarked. Earl, my new boss, was sitting in the driver's seat; Father William rode shotgun, and a lieutenant I had never seen before sat in back. He had a charcoal-black mustache, a mustache so bushy that it obscured his philtrum, the concave and normally bare area just above the center of the upper lip, which made his head appear even larger than it was as it sat on his short but compact body. He did not wear a hat. I liked that. He displayed a who-gives-a-fuck demeanor—collar up on his flight suit, slouched perfectly on the seat, twinkle in his eyes—which told me he was battle-tested, and I liked that. Earl started laughing as soon as he saw my wounds.

"How was the Visitation? Jesus Christ, what the hell happened to you?" Father William said.

"I ran into the pavement," I replied.

"He did a header off a motorcycle," Joey said, then added, "But we didn't get thrown in jail."

Earl laughed again.

"Hey, who's this?" Joey asked as we jumped in.

"They call me the Walrus," he said. The fur on his upper lip moved as he spoke. I could not tell whether he was laughing or not. He opened a cooler and handed each of us a cold beer. I liked that also.

"Let's do a 360 and get the fuck out of here," I said.

"How about a 180 instead," Earl replied as he turned the jeep and pointed it in the direction of our hootch. I nursed my beer, but Joey slugged his down and threw the can in the ditch alongside the road.

"Don't litter," Earl ordered.

"Yeah, wouldn't want to fuck up Viet Nam," the Walrus said, and then he added, "and put a cleanup crew of one hundred gomers out of work."

Earl honked, and the mamasans, attired in black pajamas and white conical hats and toting large sacks, looked up and waved as we passed.

"Mamasans picking up litter. Behold: The Beautification of Shit!" Father William said.

"I guess they wear white hats to let us know they are the good guys," Earl replied as he shifted into high gear. The air was hot and steamy. It felt good.

"The Walrus is the new *Smoky* forty-two," Earl, the new *Smoky* forty-one, said as he rolled his head toward the back of the jeep. "He has been flying O-1s up on the Cambodian border."

"Lots of changes," Earl continued. "You, Jefferson, and Carlos now live in a different hootch."

Nothing more was said until Earl stopped the jeep at the opposite end of hootch row.

"This is it."

We all got out. It was an older hootch, maybe the first one built on the row. It had a screen door. The Walrus held it open as we walked in.

"Close the bloody fucking door. You're letting the flies out," Joey said as we entered.

I shook hands with Jefferson and Carlos who also laughed when they saw me.

"Did you have a good time?" Carlos asked with a large grin.

"Put me on the schedule to fly tomorrow," I said as I grabbed my left wrist and rotated my hand.

"You sure?"

"I'm sure!"

"Here's your room," Earl said. "You are all by yourself. We've got a couple more lieutenants back at the FAC hootch that are also going to fly with us."

"Yeah, Frick and Frack," he said. "They are the kind of guys who like to try to light their farts with a Zippo!" I laughed, but he wasn't finished yet. "One of 'em's old man is an Air Force general."

"Which one, Frick or Frack?" I asked.

"Frack."

"Jesus, I trade one who's got a colonel for an old man for one who's the son of a general. Guess I'm moving up in the world. It's got to be some kind of Communist plot!"

"It's a case of two half-wits breeding because they think their kid will turn out to be a whole wit," the Walrus said. We all laughed except Joey.

"I don't get it," he said.

"If you multiply two halves, you get a quarter, not a whole."

"Oh," Joey said. "Like the bloke who stops a Pom and sez: 'If you can guess how many apples I have in this sack here, I will give you both of them.' And the Pom scratches his head and sez, 'Six!'"

Hee, hee! Hee, hee, hee!

The room was larger than the one I shared with Puff. I walked around it, and nodded my approval.

"I'm going to drop Joey off, and then we are all going to head downtown to the TOC. I'll be back to get you in fifteen," Earl said. I nodded.

When Earl and the Walrus returned, I jumped in the jeep for the trip downtown.

"What the hell happened to you?" nearly everyone at the TOC asked. I found a chair off in a corner and sat down. The alcohol was wearing off and my elbow began to throb. I rubbed it tenderly. Actually, it hurt like hell. The Walrus walked over and stood beside me.

"How long have you been up north?" I asked.

"'Bout five months. Working with the S.F.s," he replied.

I nodded.

"A couple of Special Forces types have a villa down the block," he continued. "Phoenix program."

I had heard of the Phoenix program: Special Ops guys who slip into suspected V.C. villages and capture or assassinate enemy agents.

"They got a mamasan who gives blow jobs, if you are interested. She's not much to look at but she is enthusiastic. I give her a high recommendation." I smiled. I was amazed by how acclimated he was for being on board just a short time. I rubbed my elbow.

"Goddamn thing hurts."

"Come with me."

He led me down an alley, then stopped suddenly and rapped on a door. A lad in a green beret opened it.

"My man's got some pain, brother," the Walrus said. "Can you help him?"

The black man in the green beret turned and walked back inside. Several minutes passed before he returned.

"Here, take this," he said as he handed me a small green pill. I took it and swallowed it.

"Thanks brother," the Walrus said and the soldier closed the door.

About halfway down the alley, I doubled over in pain. Only this time the pain was in my stomach. I tried to puke, vomit, ralph, hurl, regurgitate . . . but nothing came up. The Walrus held me and we walked back to the TOC. "Wait here," he said. "I'll be right back." I slumped against the side of the building and slid down the wall. I sat canted to one side. Now, everything hurt. He returned with keys and then he put his head under my good arm and he helped me into the jeep. He started it and we drove off.

"They were watching the movie *The Green Berets*," the Walrus said. "That movie is hysterical. I love the part where John Wayne pulls the pin on the grenade and tosses it inside a bamboo hut. Then he leans against the hut so that he doesn't get hit by the shrapnel." He was laughing out loud now. "As if the bamboo was going to shield him from the blast. It's a fucking classic. You should watch it with a bunch of Green Berets. You will be laughing so hard, you'll get sick."

"I am sick," I said.

"Oh yeah, right, sorry."

He stopped the jeep at the FAC hootch.

"Stay here," he said. "I'm gonna get the doc."

He ran into the FAC hootch and quickly returned with the doc. The doc checked my head, and then he lifted my wounded elbow.

"Motherfucker!" I yelled.

"I've got to get him to Saigon."

"Can do!" the Walrus said. And once again he fired up the jeep and the three of us headed southwest. He drove fast, but he was not reckless, and he dropped the doc and me off at the front of the base hospital.

Despite my pain, I was once again dazzled by the starched-white uniforms, the white walls and ceilings, and the spotless white tile floors. It seemed impossible that something so clean, so pure, so orderly could exist in this shithole called Viet Nam. The doc quizzed me on my recent alcohol intake.

"Incidentally," he said, "your tests came back negative, but it sounds like you gave it a pretty good test of your own in Malaysia. Now what was that pill the Special Forces medic gave to you?"

"It was small and green."

"Could you be more specific?"

"No."

He escorted me to X-ray and took pictures of my shoulder, elbow, and wrist, and I winced in pain as he twisted and turned them into position. Then an angel in white disrobed me and placed me between starched sheets and the doc jammed a needle in my arm.

"The nurse is going to talk to you for the next three hours," he said. "The morphine will relax you. Patients have been known to be so relaxed they stop breathing."

I remember talking to her, impressing her with wild stories that made no sense, even to me. And when I stopped talking, she would ask me to continue.

"Where was I?" I asked.

When I awoke my guardian angel had departed, and outside sunshine had replaced her sunny disposition.

"Good morning, Viet Nam," Doc said as he entered my room.

"We are going to set your elbow," he continued. "There are bone chips everywhere. No flying for seven days."

"Bullshit," I replied. "Set it and get me the hell out of here."

Doc was a funny guy. He was definitely a nerd, but a cool nerd, and he loved pilots, particularly crazy pilots. He had to be around the action, but he was terrified we would get him in trouble, and he would lose his license, or be court-marshaled, or be drummed out of the service, or . . . But those fears didn't stop him; it was like we were his addiction. Crazier still was the fact that his best friend in the Nam was the notorious Doctor Mai Lai. Jefferson told me he once set the doc up for a boondoggle to Japan, using forged leave orders. He was officially covered on the same kind of basket leave I used to go to Malaysia. The doc boarded the airplane, but upon arrival he was so nervous he never deplaned. He just sat in the airplane while it was refueled and reloaded, and he rode it right back to Viet Nam. I thought about these things while he drove me back to my hootch, dropped me off, and drove away.

I wandered around my new abode and it seemed like the air was less toxic here, easier to breathe, and it had nothing to do with the increase in size. I sat in my chair, then got up and walked across the hall to Jefferson's and Carlos's room. No one was home, so I strolled down to the FAC hootch. Halfway there I met up with Joey. He was on his hands and knees, hurling pieces of puke, and when he saw me he started to laugh between upchucks.

"Did you do that?"

"What the fuck are you talking about?" I asked.

"Hit the hootch with C.S. gas—*ba-ruck!*—During bloody daylight hours. Good show, mate—*ba-ruck!*" He rolled over on his back and wiped his face with the sleeves of his flight suit.

"I told you the hootch was going to get hit. You have got to get out of there.

They are going to frag it with a grenade next time . . . Those motherfucking lifers and their Article 15s and fines are going to get someone killed." I knelt beside him. "Move in with me. I've got room."

"Wait till you see this new asshole," he said. "Colonel Fucking PJ. He's the worst of the lot."

Joey rolled back prone, then rose up with one foot and one knee on the ground, and eventually he stood. The whites of his eyes looking back at me through slits and tears were red, and his nose was oozing snot. I held him up, using my good right arm, and we walked to the FAC hootch. Men in fatigues and flight suits were scattered outside the hootch: Some knelt, some stood, some held their stomachs, some rubbed their eyes. One man dressed in striped silk pajamas lay on the ground moaning. Using the door, Carlos fanned the air. A team of investigators arrived. Several wore gas masks. "Is everybody out?" a sergeant asked.

"There's a guy in bed. *Ba-ruck!* Room 6," Captain America said.

The sergeant entered the hootch.

"Why the hell didn't you get him out?" Carlos shouted.

"I tried, but he threw an empty quart of booze at me. Ba-ruck!"

Colonel Fucking PJ overheard him. "I'll see that he's court-martialed," he groaned.

"Give me a gas mask!" Carlos shouted. An airman pulled his off and gave it to him. Carlos held it to his face and ran inside. Two men dragged in a giant fan and inserted it in the door. Air policemen arrived with pistols drawn. Lieutenant colonels arrived with clipboards and cameras. Another group of men wheeled a gas-powered generator to the door and when one of them fired it up, the blades of the fan rotated slowly at first, then picked up speed and the air pulled from inside to outside smelled like sulfur. Another team rolled in two giant spotlights.

"Where's Earl and the Walrus?" I asked.

"They're flying," Joey answered. "*Ba-ruck!* This is shit-hot, mate. I'm proud of you. *Ba-ruck.*"

"Arrest that man!" Colonel Fucking PJ screamed from his position of kneeling with both hands on the ground supporting his upper torso and looking like a bitch awaiting a bone of his own from a rabid Doberman. The colonel lifted one hand and pointed to me, and when he did he rolled on his back and shot puke in the air and all over his satin pajamas. "*Ba-ruck! Ba-ruck!*" The giant fan stopped rotating and two men now moved it aside. Carlos and the sergeant appeared in the doorway; a third man dangled between them. They set him down gently. PAC AF's Junior Officer of the Year slumped to the ground.

"He was sober enough to put his gas mask on, but he was too drunk to get out," Carlos said.

Hee, hee! Hee, hee, hee!

"That's why he is Junior Officer . . . Oh! Oh, *Ba-ruck!*"

While Joey wretched, I visualized the headline in the next *Stars and Stripes*:

Junior Officer of the Year Court-Martialed
Pac AF's Junior Officer of the Year was
court-martialed today for throwing an empty quart bottle
of booze during a drunken stupor at Captain America
who was trying to save him from a suspected fragging incident.
Presiding officer Colonel Fucking PJ . . .

By midnight the hootch was fit for occupancy, and FACs, F.N.G.s, and staff-weenies sat around the bar—everyone but the Kiwi who was paranoid that the spotlights were going to attract enemy rockets.

"Shut the bloody, fucking lights off!" Finally he walked out and choked the generators until they stopped and the big lights dimmed, then died, and he rejoined us at the bar.

The music was cranked way up. Credence Clearwater Revival sang:
Thought I heard a rumblin', callin' to my name
Two hundred million guns are loaded, Satan cries, "Take aim!"

Jefferson worked the volume control, ratcheting it up for the chorus and we all shouted along.
Better run through the jungle!
Better run through the jungle!
Better run through the jungle, Woa, don't look back to see.
Over on the mountain, thunder magic spoke
"Let the people know my wisdom, fill the land with smoke."
Better run through the jungle!
Better run through the jungle!
Better run through the jungle, Woa, don't look back to see.

Woofers rattled, *tweeters* trembled, and notes seemed to bounce off the four walls and collide somewhere in the middle of the barroom. Grown men were back to playing grab-ass and dousing each other with beer. I felt like I was home.

I looked up to see a haggard man dressed in red silk pajamas. Instead of sideburns, he sported *sidewalls*—hair shaved tight from his ears up to the nubs of grey that stuck straight up, about one half of an inch, on the top of his head. He carried a pipe in one hand and a martini glass in the other. His lips were moving but no one could hear what he may have been saying. He walked behind the bar, set his pipe and glass down on it, and again his lips moved. He must have said, "Turn that music down!" because Jefferson cranked it louder. Then Jefferson cupped his ear and shook his head back and forth, indicating that he couldn't hear anything. Colonel Fucking PJ then placed his palms over his ears, closed his eyes, and shook his head. When no response was forthcoming, he turned the knob on the tape deck to "stop." Then he raised his arms as if beseeching a Heavenly Father before being offered up and said, "Please, men. I can't stand it. You got to turn that music down. I want it quiet in here by nine o'clock."

"This ain't no fucking library, colonel!" Joey said.

"You've got to help me. I can't take a year like this. I'll lose my mind."

Joey pushed him aside and turned the knob to "play."

Better run through the jungle!

The man lowered his hands and stumbled out of the barroom, leaving his drink and pipe on the bar.

A *Daredevil* FAC shoved them to the ground and crushed them with his boot.

The next day, out of boredom, I flew with Earl. His movements were precise, mechanical, and learned, unlike Jefferson, a *natural stick* whose movements were instinctive. Jefferson flew by feel or, in pilot lingo, he flew *by the seat of his pants*, whereas Earl relied more on what his instruments displayed. Both pilots handled the airplane with confidence, making smooth corrections. And both pilots respected the machine, knew its limitations, and flew accordingly. I was a composite, I decided. My techniques varied depending on conditions. And then there was attitude; fighter pilots had a presence and so did those who wanted to be fighter pilots. They were the kids who had streamers hanging from the hand grips on their Schwinn Spitfire bicycles, the ones who attached playing cards with clothes pins so the cards would *plink* against spokes, the ones who rode hands off and yelled, "Hey, look at me."

Earl looked like, and was, a lifer; and like Doc, he loved a good time, but he always enjoyed it from the periphery. He might prod but he never initiated deviant behavior. He was itching to mix it up, to fly in combat, but today's mission was strictly reconnaissance. When it was over, the *Smoky* FACs, both old and new, and others gathered at the hootch bar. The Walrus was sitting on my stool, but I didn't mind. Earl sat next to him, then Jefferson, Doc, and several *Daredevil* FACs. Big Al, the Kiddies' Pal, and a raft of F.N.G.s milled around the room. Joey, Miss Sam, and Carlos stood behind the bar. Carlos and Miss Sam were stacking in supplies; the Walrus was talking.

"I hate those fucking C.I.A. types, flying Pilatus Porters, an unbelievable STOL (short takeoff and landing) Swiss aircraft. That motherfucker can launch in 600 feet and land in 400 feet. Not only do the sonsabitches get to fly this gee-whiz aircraft; they make more money in a month than we make in a year. One hundred grand a year! Can you believe that shit? And that's not all. They have a villa in Taipei where their family can stay. They fly three weeks; then they *di-di-mau* to their villa for the last week of the month. Throw me into that briar patch! One day, I jumped one of them, just got in behind him, and I got so angry I fired a Willy Peter rocket right over his head."

The *Daredevil* FACs were not listening to the Walrus. They were building a bazooka—a series of empty beer cans with the tops and bottoms cut out. The cans were then taped together. The end can, or the combustion chamber, had several holes cut in it with a *church key* so that lighter fluid could be poured in. A tennis ball was inserted. Joey loaded the fluid and Carlos ignited it using Jefferson's Zippo lighter.

BAWHAM!

The tennis ball bounced off the far wall, and a host of cheers went up, followed by laughter and pats on the back.

"Let's go for the record," Carlos yelled. "Sixteen cans!" And everyone nodded yes.

"Damn, that means we will have to drink faster," Jefferson hollered. And again everyone cheered. Grown men chugged beers so they could construct a toy gun, and instead of smashing the empty beer cans against their foreheads, which was their norm, they cut the ends out of them. Joey and Carlos taped them together, and soon the bazooka was so long that it had to rest on two F.N.G.s' shoulders. Jefferson dropped in a tennis ball, the front end of the bazooka was tipped up, and the ball rolled down to the combustion chamber. Carlos filled the chamber with lighter fluid.

"Hey, let the doc light it," a FAC yelled.

"Oh, no! Not me," the doc replied. And everyone laughed.

The door on the staff-weenie side of the hootch opened and in came Colonel Fucking PJ attired in his silk pajamas and again holding a martini glass in one hand, but instead of a pipe, he held a book in the other. He looked like a clean-shaven Moses coming down from the mountain. "Gentlemen," he said, "this all-night carousing has got to stop. I told you I want lights out at nine o'clock. Some of us have to be to work at 0700 hours." There was scattered laughter.

"Hey, go fly your fucking desk, colonel!" the Junior Officer of the Year yelled.

"Have a little respect for a senior officer," the colonel pleaded.

"Let's give the colonel a hymn!" another FAC suggested.

"*Him, Him, Fuck Him!*"

"I will take this all the way up to 8th Air Force," Colonel Fucking PJ threatened.

"You are going to get us all killed," another FAC hollered. "Stop issuing Article 15s and fines."

"I'll do nothing of the sort. There will be discipline and order . . ."

I saw the flame from Joey's lighter and I noticed Miss Sam duck down behind the bar before I heard the launch.

BaWHAM!

There was a blur as the ball exited the tube. Colonel Fucking PJ had the best vantage point. From where I was standing, the tennis ball looked like it was heading straight for the bridge of Colonel Fucking PJ's nose, but it missed his head by maybe two inches, punctured the sheetrock on our side of the wall, missed a two-by-four, continued through the second layer of sheetrock on the back wall, and came to rest somewhere in Captain Marvel's room. The colonel dropped his book and martini glass. The goblet shattered when it hit the floor, but the olive bounced once, twice, three times before coming to rest. "Jesus Christ!" someone said, and I was quite sure it wasn't Father William. Miss Sam peeked up over the bar. I stared at Colonel Fucking PJ who was as white and rigid as Michelangelo's *David*. I was actually relieved to see that this prick was still alive, but just barely relieved.

"First time you were ever shot at, colonel?" a *Daredevil* FAC asked.

Doc walked over and talked to the colonel, and then he led him out of the barroom.

"Jesus, you could have killed him, Joey," I said.

"Oh, it's okay for him to get us killed with his goddamn Article 15s," the Junior Officer of the Year said, "but we can't kill him? Fuck that!"

"Let's just put some black pajamas on him, drop him out in the boonies, and let one of our combatants shoot him!" another FAC yelled.

"Where, for fucksakes, do you keep finding these bloody fucksticks?" Joey asked.

"That stupid, fucking doofus walks around in low-quarter shoes, no crease in his cunt cap, and a flight suit full of Strategic Air Command patches, and he harasses guys working their asses off out on the line!" a *Daredevil* FAC growled. "Two days ago, I came back from a flight and an Air Policeman stopped me at the door. 'Where are you going?' the ape asked. 'I'm going to my room.' 'No you're not,' he said. 'You are not going in there until E.O.D. clears it.' He told me a colonel called and reported that a sapper left a bomb in our hootch. 'Who did that?' I asked the ape. He pointed to his clipboard. Sure enough Colonel Fucking PJ, only that's not his real name."

"That's true," Big Al, the Kiddies' Pal, said. "He went running through the hootch yelling, 'Bomb! Bomb!' He's fucking crazy."

"I had to stand outside the hootch for two hours," the FAC continued. The bomb turned out to be a box of fuck books Fast Eddie left for us since he was rotating back to the world."

"Did they confiscate them?" Father William asked. "If not, I'd like to claim them."

"No, they are mine. I earned them," the *Daredevil* FAC said.

"And it's assholes like Colonel Fucking PJ who are causing us to get fucking SAC assignments," the Junior Officer of the Year said.

"That's true," Big Al said. "Air Force did a study and found 50 percent of its pilots had done a tour in Nam, and of the 50 percent who didn't, 90 percent were in SAC. So now they are sending all the SAC pukes over here to fuck up the war, and we get to fill their open slots when we rotate home."

"You can shove that oh-here's-what-I'd-like-for-my-next-assignment-now-that-I've-fought-in-the-war dream sheet up your ass. It is worthless. You are going to get a SAC assignment," another FAC added.

"Yeah, I already got mine," the Junior Officer of the Year announced. "B fucking 52s!"

"Yeah, 'Thanks for fighting the war, lieutenant. Now which base would you like to fly your BUFF, big ugly fat fucker, out of?' Piss on that!" But instead he spit.

"I ain't no fucking bomber pilot," the Junior Officer of the Year said. He stood and threw his beer can against the wall, and then he walked into the head to take a piss.

"Now you know why he was drunk the day you hit the hootch with CS gas?" Joey whispered in my ear.

"I did not dump CS gas into the hootch. Quit saying that I did. You are going to get me in trouble."

"Get *you* in trouble?"

Hee, hee! Hee, hee, hee!

"That's a good one!" Joey said between hees.

The Junior Officer of the Year reappeared. He was trying to free up the zipper on his flight suit—the zipper that allows him to pull out his dong when he had to piss—which struck me as funny: The Junior Officer of the Year and a highly skilled Air Force pilot who can't work a zipper.

"You are on your own," a *Daredevil* FAC said to him. "Ain't nobody gonna help you with that."

I was out in the outback with one of me mates, Joey said. *When I looked over, me mate had his dragon out and was taking a piss.*

Joey held an imaginary schwanz, simulating taking a piss. He even leaned back to give the impression that his member was extra large and extra heavy.

A two-step adder bites me mate right on the end of his dick. "Run to town!" me mate yells. "Find a doctor!" So I ran to town, found a doctor, explained me predicament, and asked him to help me.

"Can't," the doc said. "I'm busy. But it's easy. Just cut a couple of Xs below the bite, and then suck the poison out."

So, I run all the way back to me mate, and he's lying there panting like a dog.
"What'd the doc say?" he asked.
"The doc said you are going to die."

Hee, hee! Hee, hee, hee!

There was a racket at the side door. We could see the knob trying to turn, and then there was someone pounding on it from the outside.

"Open the fucking door!" someone yelled. A staff-weenie walked over to it and tried to open it.

"Unlock the fucker first!" another FAC yelled.

"Jesus Christ! What's he in charge of?" a *Nugget* FAC asked.

"He's our intelligence officer!"

Hee, hee! Hee, hee, hee!

Eventually, with just a little additional help, he managed to open the door, and a tech sergeant entered.

"Hey, get the man a beer," the Junior Officer of the Year said.

"No thanks. I'm on duty. I want to show you something on your airplane. Can you come with me to the flight line?"

"Hell, yeah. I'll be right with you." He tugged at his zipper again. "Fucking zipper! Ah, fuck it! Who's coming along?"

Joey, the Junior Officer of the Year, and I hopped in the sergeant's jeep, and he drove us to the OV revetments and stopped in front of a bird that was backed in. We climbed out of the jeep and up on the airplane, where he showed us a tiny hole in the canopy. Then he pointed to a .50 cal. bullet that was lodged in the ejection seat, just to the right of the spike that ruptures the canopy if it fails to jettison on ejection.

"Must have missed your neck by a half of an inch, lieutenant," the sergeant said.

"Goddamn! I never even knew I took a hit," PAC AF's Junior Officer of the Year, and future B fucking 52 pilot, said. His face turned white, as opposed to red when he was angry and blue when he threw up from drinking too much whiskey; and I wondered if having a patriotic—red, white, and blue—face was factored in during his consideration for Junior Officer of the Year. He said nothing further, nor did we. The sergeant drove us back to our hootch where we switched from beer to whisky, straight whisky, undiluted whisky, forget-to-remember whisky.

Three days later, Joey personally carried Colonel Fucking PJ's belongings out of his room and into another hootch. "Senior officers can't live with junior officers in a war zone," he argued to his new commander, a gentle man who possessed common sense, a commander I didn't mind saying *yes sir* rather than *three bags full* to followed by a sloppy salute. The new commander dropped all charges and fines against the enlisted men and ordered all future harassment of them stopped immediately. And our airplanes loved him. Happy crew chiefs now treated them with tender loving care. Smiles returned to the flight line, and the battle lines between officers and enlisted men vanished.

The next evening, the usual bar stalwarts were flocked around Miss Sam when Doc entered through the staff-weenie door, walked up to the bar, ordered a 7UP, and said: "Colonel Fucking PJ had a nervous breakdown and rotated back Stateside." This was followed by a long period of silence.

"You must be joking," Joey finally said. "He *cracked a fruity* and got sent home?"

"Did I hear you right?" Carlos asked.

"You gotta be shitting me," I said. "Is this a variation of fuck up and move up?"

"Yeah, this is like *Catch 22*, only better. Act like you are fucking nuts and the powers that be will reward you with a trip back home. I don't get it," the Walrus said.

"What the fuck?" Father William said. "This must be the shortest case of combat fatigue ever, only there is no combat, and he wasn't in-country long enough to suffer fatigue."

Upon hearing about Colonel Fucking PJ's free trip back to the world, PACAF's Junior Officer of the Year didn't say a word. He just started throwing things. He threw a beer can at Captain America; then he threw a glass. He tore a book out of Captain Marvel's hands and threw it. He tore a picture of Ho Chi Minh off the wall and threw it. He tore the dartboard off the wall and threw it. He picked up a chair and threw it. He picked up a garbage can and threw it, and a broom, and a barstool, and when he couldn't find anything else to throw, he started tipping things over: a couch, two tables, a bookcase. And when he stormed out of the hootch, he slammed the door so hard it popped back open.

The Junior Officer of the Year wasn't the only one leaving. There was now a great exodus of hootch FACs and staff weenies who had arrived in-country during Nixon's buildup to 600,000 troops. There were lots of going-away parties, lots of trying to get Miss Sam to kiss them good-bye, lots of *"Never happen, GI,"* and lots of F.N.G.s arriving to fill the vacancies. O-1s—a single-engine, super-slow-moving, propeller-driven tail-dragger (a caster at the rear of the airplane for landing, which resulted in many a ground loop)—were being turned over to the Viet Namese. Somehow the Walrus managed to keep his. The vintage airplane looked good on him.

"Where the hell are all the bog rats coming from?" Joey asked.

"Well," Big Al, the Kiddies' Pal, said, "Four months ago, we asked Air Force to send us four FACs. Nothing happened. So the next month we asked for eight. They sent us two. The next month we figured since we asked for eight and they sent us two, we had better ask for twenty hoping to get maybe ten. They just sent us a message saying they were filling our back order and adding a few more so we could expect thirty-six FACs to arrive in the next thirty days. We can't get these guys flying time. We managed to steal a few O-1s back from the VNAF, and we use them to fly spare parts and mail and other small shit out to the F.O.B.s, or forward operating bases. Our F.N.G.s named their new airline: TWATS for Teeny Weenie Air Transport Service."

Two of the new guys became *Smoky* FACs, the ones the Walrus called Frick and Frack. Frick was tall and slender with a wisp of a mustache.

"How do you get away with that bushy mustache?" Frick asked the Walrus. "It must be against regulations."

"Determination," the Walrus answered.

The other guy was plump and short. If he was tall, he could have been labeled an oaf, a galoot, a lummox.

"My father is a general in the Air Force," Frack said.

"Is he on our side?" the Walrus asked.

I could not tell if Frack was warning us or just making conversation, but the words "Big Fucking Deal" flashed across my brain. I did not shake their hands, nor did they offer theirs. Father William entered just as the F.N.Gs were leaving.

"The tall one is alright; the short fat one, the general's kid, is a dork," the Walrus said. "He has already crashed one airplane; landed short. And he brags about it."

Father William sat down and crossed his feet on my new desk.

"How does it feel to be fighting the war again, peasant, now that you have healed? Look at this guy," Father said, pointing to me, "he knows more ways to get out of combat than anybody in the Air Force."

"Why do they call you Father William?" the Walrus asked.

"Why do they call you the Walrus?" Father William answered. And we all just laughed.

"Fucking piss-ant, peasants," Father William said as he walked out of my room with his middle finger held high over his head.

The real *Smoky* forty-two and forty-three, Jefferson and Carlos, were very short now, just days until they would head home, and a huge hole was forming in the center of my gut. They had both flown their fini flights. The fire trucks met their airplanes as they rolled off the active and onto the taxiway and launched a large volume of water from their cannons, drenching both pilot and aircraft. We met them with bottles of champagne, which we shook vigorously and sprayed on each of them, and then we raised the bottles in a salute before handing the bottles on to them. Jefferson shook his bottle and sprayed us back. Carlos drank his. This was followed by lots of smiles and back patting and an adjournment to the FAC hootch bar where Miss Sam refused to kiss either of them. I was positive Carlos would be the first FAC to get a farewell kiss from her since he worked with her behind the bar, bought all the supplies, stacked them in, collected from those of us who imbibed, gave her a ride to the front gate every night she worked, and paid her; but nothing doing. "Never happen, GI" was damned stingy with her kisses.

"Did you know the general's kid *pranged* an airplane?" the Walrus announced at forty-two and forty-three's going-away party. "Landed short... That asshole shouldn't be flying." I just listened.

"Did you know there is a *steam and cream* on the base?" the Walrus continued. *What's a* steam and cream? I wondered. "There is a base within this base, where the Rangers live. You can get a massage and a hand job there for two bucks."

"Sounds like a bargain," I said.

"They use Brylcreem to get you off. *A little dab will do ya.*" He sang the commercial jingo; then he laughed, and I smiled.

"I'm going tomorrow. What to come along?" I cringed at the use of the word "come."

"Nah, ask Joey though," I replied.

"You know Joey's short too," Earl said.

"No!" I was stunned. I could stand to lose Jefferson and Carlos and the others, but I couldn't lose Joey.

"Yes, Aussies have a six-month tour," Earl said.

"Are you sure?" I asked. "I have never heard that."

"Damntooting," the Walrus said.

"Motherfucker!" I looked around the room.

"Where is he?" I asked.

"Over there telling jokes," Earl said. I walked over to the dartboard where he was holding court.

"And she said, mate—" I pulled him aside.

"When are you leaving and why didn't you tell me?"

"I wouldn't leave you. I couldn't leave you. I extended. Me missus decided to change her name to the plaintiff, and I needed the extra money, so I signed up for another six-month stay." I began to laugh. I grabbed him and hugged him. I did not want to let go. "Come on mate, for Christ's sake, let me go. I got a joke to tell." He turned back to the group he was entertaining.

"Hey shut the fuck up! I'm telling a joke . . ."

I had heard the joke. It was a lousy old joke, but fresh and funny when Joey told it. I walked away with a smile on my face and a smile—and I could actually feel it—in my heart. I smiled for the rest of the evening.

The next day I was putting in fighters south of Bien Hoa—it felt good to smash things again, to feel productive, and to feel useful—when I heard a call over guard channel. "Any dust-offs vicinity Bien Hoa, come up three, five, four decimal seven."

There was no mistaking the accent or the panic in Joey's voice. He was calling for a medevac helicopter.

"Any dust-offs vicinity Bien Hoa, come up 354.7."

I tried to concentrate on my airstrike while listening to him at the same time. I heard him make contact with the choppers just as I released a rocket. My rocket sailed past the target. I had to send the fighters through dry and re-mark the target. I wanted to put the war on hold and rush to his assistance but I could not. I had troops below me who were also in big trouble. I could not do both. I punched off guard channel, tried to pretend I had never heard

Joey's call for help, and concentrated on getting the bombs on target. But with each rocket I put in, I wondered what was happening to him. Was he going down? Was he hurt?

I put one set of fighters in and then another. Five-hundred-pound bombs of napalm and C.B.U., or cluster bomb units—miniature grenades—broke the contact. Now it was mop-up time. As my next set of fighters descended, I switched guard channel back on. But all was quiet.

"Lead, you are cleared in hot. Hit my smoke."

"Roger."

Negative transmissions on guard. Had they picked him up? Where were they taking him?

"Two, place it three right. You are cleared in hot."

"Roger, three right."

"*Buster*, *Smoky*. How you doing?"

"Charlie is on the run, *Smoky*. Thanks for the help, man. I have one dead and three wounded."

"Now it was my turn to call for dust-offs."

I continued the bombing until the fighters had expended all of their heavy weapons. They still had their guns, so I held them overhead in case the L.Z. (landing zone) turned hot again for incoming choppers. When dust-off was complete and the dead and wounded were on their way to triage, I sent the fighters home.

"*Dust-off* twelve, *Smoky* forty-four. Have you any information on dust-off activity with an Australian; vicinity, Bien Hoa?"

"That's a negative, *Smoky*."

"Roger, I copy." I needed to head home.

"*Dust-off*, thanks for your help today."

"Anytime, partner."

I turned north and jammed my throttles forward, heading for home plate, getting all of 94 m.p.h. while frantically switching radio channels, asking everyone if had they had heard from Joey. All replies were in the negative. I requested a straight-in approach to expedite my landing. I filled out my forms on final and planted my O-2 on the first brick of the runway, then turned and sped down the taxiway so fast that the airplane actually lifted off at one point.

"*Smoky* forty-four, Bien Hoa tower. Be advised: slow down."

"Yeah, yeah, three bags full," I said to myself while answering them with a double click on the mike switch. I shut my rear engine down but still maintained enough speed so that several crew chiefs scurried out of my way and did not reappear until I jumped on the brakes and shut the rest of the airplane down just outside my revetment. I unstrapped, jumped out, and hollered, "The forms are on the seat." Then I jumped in my jeep and squealed out. I skidded to a stop just outside P.E. and ran inside. There was Joey, face as white as a china doll, eyes empty, vigorously rubbing his hands. I grabbed him by the shoulders. "Are you alright?" He nodded yes. "I heard you on guard channel." I waited for his answer.

"God, it was bloody awful." He shook his head from side to side with such force that it scared me, but I knew the feeling; if he shook hard enough, the vision or thought that was inside his head had to let go and somehow leave his mind forever. But it never lets go, so he had to talk about it.

"He was pulling the pins on my rockets ... and ... and ... he walked right into my prop. I watched him do it, mate. There was nothing I could do. It cut his right arm completely off."

I didn't know what to do or say, so I just held his shoulders and waited for him to continue.

"I heard him scream ... Over the roar of me engines, I heard him scream! ... Fortunately the dust-offs were right there. They picked him and his arm up off the tarmac ... and threw it in the chopper."

He looked through me and straight out the back of my head like he was sitting in his airplane out on the tarmac and looking out his side window. He began to vigorously rub his hands together, first palm to palm, then palm to the back of his hand like he was washing them, only he had no soap so he had to rub faster and with more pressure. And when he finally stopped, his eyes slowly rejoined mine and life returned to his voice.

"They had him on the operating table in Saigon within fifteen minutes ... I just came from there ... He's going to make it. The doctors are going to sew it back on. They are hopeful he will have about 80 percent use of it ... when it heals. ... He was just a young lad, mate. Wars should be fought by men, not kids ..."

"We were all young when we arrived here, you and I and everyone else who fights in this goddamn war. Come on, mate; let's drink it off."

He seemed to think that was a good idea, for that's what we always did, no matter what happened; we just drank it away.

"Yeah," he said, "why not? Let's go over to Long Binh. I hear they have donut dollies there."

"How are we going to do that? I can get off the base. I have a pass. But you don't."

"I reckon I'll find a way," he replied.

We jumped in the jeep and headed for the hootch.

"Grab some civvies," he said. "We'll change on the way." I also grabbed a quart of Jim Beam. "I'll drive," he said, and we hopped in his jeep. The sun was low on the horizon and boring straight into our eyes. I laughed as Joey struggled with it. He was driving like he was already drunk. We were approaching the main gate.

"Do you know how to get there?" I asked.

"I've seen it from the air," he replied.

"Long Binh is damn near as big as Australia. They have like eleven goddamn swimming pools. How are you going to find it?" He didn't answer.

At the gate, an American GI pulled us over.

"You men have a pass?"

"I have one," I said, and I held it up for him to see.

"What about you?"

"No, sir," Joey answered.

"Can't get off base unless you have a pass."

"You wait right here and I'll give you a pass, mate."

Joey turned the jeep around and headed up the road. Five hundred yards back from the gate, he spun the jeep and mashed the gas pedal into the floorboard, releasing it only to move up a gear. The guard spotted us coming and started waving his hands.

"Halt! Wait! Stop!" Perhaps, he was trying to find the Australian word for pull over when he decided instead to dive for cover.

"There's your pass, mate!" Joey yelled and we were on our way.

When we arrived at Long Bien, Joey asked directions to the II Field Force officers club and eventually we found it. Joey parked, and chained and padlocked the jeep. Then we sucked on the jug, passing it back and forth while we slipped into our civvies, worn for anonymity, I assumed, rather than style.

We walked in the main entrance. The bar was quiet, empty quiet. We were the only customers, but we were good customers. We ordered many beers. Then, two donut dollies entered flanked by four bird colonels attired in their dress uniforms, worn to impress the dollies, I assumed. "Look at that asshole! He's got his *gongs* on," Joey said, and he said it a tad too loud since two of the colonels stopped to look us over before they continued on to their table. A couple of birds with four birds, I thought to myself. "What the fuck are *gongs*?" I asked Joey.

"Medals, mate," he replied as our eyes followed the ladies, paying particular attention to their miniskirts as they sat down, exposing raw meat for hungry lions. Their table was off to our left, and we rotated our stools for a better look. We could not take our eyes or minds off these two round-eyed girls. Despite our visual euphoria, we were pissed off. Young chicks flanked by old men, what bullshit. The ladies smiled back at us. I couldn't take it anymore. I rotated back and then hopped off the stool.

"Gotta piss. Behave!" I said as I walked off.

Joey was not on his stool when I returned. I did an eight-point turn looking for him when I spotted his ass inching forward along the floor, surreptitiously moving toward the tableful of full colonels and full-figured women.

"No, Joey," I whispered, but I was too late.

He had made it to one of the dolly's feet and was kissing her ankles and working his way up. The girls were laughing; the colonels were not. One jumped from his chair and started pulling on Joey's legs.

Joey rose to his feet. "You gonna hide behind that skirt, you dickhead? She loves me, so mind your own bloody business before I job you!" The colonel shoved Joey, and Joey countered with a fist sandwich.

I rushed over to help him when the door burst open and several very large military policemen grabbed both of us and manhandled us outside the club.

"Hey man," Joey said, "I haven't finished my beer." And he turned to go back inside. A pair of very large hands clamped down on his neck and spun him into me, sending both of us to the ground. Even though it hurt, I was so drunk that I just started to laugh, as did Joey.

Hee, hee! Hee, hee, hee!

"We've been looking for you two," the MP said. We received a police escort back to Bien Hoa and a warning.

"Don't ever show your face in Long Binh again gentlemen, or you'll sit out the rest of your tour in the Long Binh Jail."

Hmmm ... flying combat missions every day, or read books in a jail cell.

Our squadron commander didn't give us a choice. He just informed us that we were formally banned from the II Field Force officers club for life. And I was thinking: *Who gives a shit?*

One week later, Joey got a letter of reprimand from his Australian commanding officer. In essence, it said:

> *Outstanding job in your quick reaction which saved the use of a young man's limb. Also, we understand that you have put a bunch of fives into an American colonel's face. Please refrain from further encounters with "Yanks" because they do not think the same as we Australians.*
>
> There was a P.S. *We hope you did a good job on the "Yank" colonel, since in dealing with him we found him to be a bit of a prat.*

The letter reminded me of a story told to me by my first boss, a wisp of a mustache chap and bomber pilot named Emory Chessmoreland III, who was a P.O.W. in WWII. Apparently several American GIs wandered into a seedy bar in Singapore toward the end of the war. On a stool sat one lone drunken Limey. "Get the Limey a drink," a GI said to the bartender. "I wouldn't ever take a drink from any bloody, goddamn Yank. You enter the war when she's half over and live high on the hog in my country and steal my wife while I rot in this bloody fucking jungle." The Americans decided to leave him alone. Finally he passed out, dead drunk, and the bartender wanted to call a cab.

"That's all right. We'll take of him," the Americans replied. They took him to a parlor and had *God Bless America* tattooed on his chest in red, white, and blue.

It probably didn't happen but I loved the story.

The Walrus, Earl, and I continued to pound the area just west of *Bearcat* and east of the Dog Bone, and Charlie continued to knock helicopters down, even firing with .50 cal machine guns from the dead section of the jungle we had saturated with Agent Orange. The Walrus suggested that we fly hi/low. One bird down on the deck trolling for enemy guns, the other staying high, and when the bad guys took the bait and started *hosing* away, exposing their position, the high bird rolled in and marked the target; effective but risky.

Jefferson would have vetoed the strategy in a heartbeat, but he and Carlos were gone and by process of elimination only, I was now the mother hen. I did not apply for the job. I did not want the job, but I realized as senior *Smoky*, by time in-country, the call was mine to make. I smiled. I liked the Walrus. He was confident, unafraid, and experienced. And any mammal that could float on his back and crack shells with a rock had to be of superior intellect, as opposed to Frack who could not shit and pee at the same time.

I deliberated for several days, until Buddha lost another of his pilots in a duel with the devil, and I decided what the hell, we would do it, but only if I was the low bird. But today Charlie was smart, or he felt sorry for me, because he did not take the bait. I returned from the mission drenched in sweat, partially because of heat from flying so near to the ground, but mostly because of the heat of the battle, a battle that never materialized.

I returned to the pattern for landing, coming in hot and bleeding airspeed by putting Gs on the airplane, just as Jefferson taught me. I turned left base at the same time as *Dragon* flight, a set of A-1Es driven by experienced Viet Namese pilots who had just placed perfect bombs for me minutes before, turned left base for the parallel runways. I watched as *Dragon* lead came off the perch with a tight, descending turn. "Ah, Bien Hoa tower, *Dragon* lead, final turn."

The pilot had thousands of hours of combat time. His tour of duty was for the duration of the war. He was married to the machine. Today, it was his final turn and I watched as he never rolled back wings level. Perhaps it was the torque of the huge radial engine that sucked him into the earth where his airplane exploded in a ball of fire. Several bullets cooked off to signal the end. The grunts had a phrase they used to sum up the death of a fallen brother: "It don't mean nothing," they would say.

That night I wrote a letter home.

> *There are many changes here, including the weather.*
> *Jefferson and Carlos have gone and*
> *I wonder if I will ever see them again.*
> *Joey and Father William remain and provide lots*
> *of laughs. There is an O-1 driver who looks and*
> *sounds like a walrus. Do walruses, or is it walri,*
> *live in Hawaii? Our trip there is coming up*
> *fast. I can't wait.*
> *Love, Sky King*
> *P.S. I did some fishing today, but I didn't catch anything.*

Chapter 3
WAR STORIES

I am not sure where Joey found her but I do know she was aptly named. Beverly Big Tits was so well endowed that Father William said she should sport rotating beacons on the tips of her breasts, rotating beacons instead of nipples. Very few saw her—it was an in-and-out sort of thing—but many heard her.

"You should be ashamed of yourself," Father William said to Joey.

"Couldn't help *meself*. I had a stiffy," Joey replied.

"Well, go forth and sin no more, my son," Father William suggested.

"Fuck you, Father!" Joey replied.

"Make peace with your maker, not me," Father William commanded.

We—Joey, Father William, Buddha, Earl, the Walrus, and I—sat American Indian style on the floor of my room. We listened to music, drank beer, got lost in our thoughts, and talked intermittently. There were two topics that we would talk about: war and women. We did that most every evening now; no more playing grab-ass or joust, or tearing C-47 kits off of flight suits, or dousing each other with beer. We just sat, listened, and drifted back to the *world*. We turned off the lights, lit candles, and listened to ballads—love songs mostly—mushy stuff, such as "Crystal Blue Persuasion" by Tommy James and the Shondells.

Love, love is the answer, and that's all right.
So don't you give up now, so easy to find.
Just look to your soul and open your mind.

Initially, with extreme concentration, I could travel away from this place to a time and location where I was able to feel love and be loved. But if there was a knock at the door or a candle flickered, any kind of disturbance, the layers of distrust, hatred, and anger—always the anger—smothered the love and wrapped my soul up in layer after layer of chain mail, each layer pulled tighter than the last one until I was nothing more than a steel onion, impervious to emotional pain, unable to love or be loved.

There will be peace and good, brotherhood,
Crystal Blue Persuasion.

I heard the words, but eventually I could no longer feel the message, so I stopped looking.

"Buddha," I said, "I had this dream about Camptown—"

"Oh, shit! I forgot to tell," Buddha interrupted. "You know how he was paralyzed from the waist down?"

I nodded.

"Got word this morning. He tried to swallow a .45. Stuck the barrel in his mouth and pulled the trigger. Did a damn good job, too. They had to have a closed coffin . . . Hey, what was your dream?"

"Three nights ago I dreamt he was dead."

There will be peace and good, brotherhood,
Crystal . . .

The music ended in the middle of song, and the tape broke free from the far wheel and flopped—*whomp . . . whomp . . . whomp*—until the reel stopped spinning. No one said anything. The room was so quiet you could hear a fly fart. Buddha rubbed his belly. The Walrus pulled at his mustache. Joey caressed his beer. Earl grinned. I shook my head back and forth.

"What the fuck?" Father William said. "We are a bunch of combat vets, acting like fucking sorority sisters at a slumber party."

"Only without the chatter," the Walrus added.

Father William stood, walked to the reel-to-reel tape deck, and installed a new tape with songs that changed the mood. The beat was heavier; the words harsher. The subject matter of our conversation was still women but it was lust not love, a topic we all pretended to know a lot about. Father William described the proper art of eating pussy. Joey challenged him. Apparently they did it differently *down under*. Women and war. All other topics were off-limits. No one ever decreed they were taboo, but everyone knew. There would be no probing of feelings or family. Probing usually led to familiarization, but with us it led to alienation. You would be uninvited into our inner sanctum.

In the morning, I walked out into the barroom. Faces had changed. Men seemed to disappear, vanish. They were dispersed, never to be seen or heard from again. Some FACs rotated home while others were reassigned to different A.O.s, as the units they were supporting moved to make room so that the South Viet Namese could take over the fighting; North Dakotans fighting South Dakotans. How could you tell the difference? Staff-weenies were younger now. Cherub-faced pilots replaced Big Al, the Kiddies' Pal, Major Personovitch, PAC AF's Junior Officer of the Year, and others; big shoes to fill. The F.N.G.s were anxious to prove themselves in combat, but there was no combat for them, so they wandered aimlessly, disgruntled and angry, pulling eight-to-five shifts behind desks, shuffling papers, watching the clock, trying to kill one day of 365. Occasionally, they flew a TWAT mission—a mission dreamt up by the brass so the pilots could stay current in their airplane and get their monthly flying pay. Sometimes, if my mission seemed routine, I might let one of them fly with me. My only rule was "Don't speak unless spoken to," which held true both in the air and on the ground.

"Hey you, wanna fly?"

"Hell, yeah!"

"Bien Hoa tower, *Smoky* forty-four, taxi, takeoff."

"Roger *Smoky*. Negative traffic. You are cleared for an immediate takeoff."

We were still pounding the area where the helicopters got shot down. Agent Orange seemed to kill only the foliage, not the little fuckers who were knocking Buddha's boys out of the sky. Earl said that once we got the area softened up, they were going to bring in large plows to scrape the landscape clean.

Boom!

My fighter's 500-pound bomb exploded, followed by a lesser boom and a small fire.

"Got a secondary explosion, *Blade*. Might be a P.O.L. (petroleum, oil, lubricant) dump."

"Roger that, *Smoky*."

And when TAC air was unavailable, we pounded the area with artillery, first one FAC controlling it, then another.

"I'm bingo fuel, Walrus. Take over."

"Got you covered, four-four. Put a couple of beers on ice for me."

"Bien Hoa tower, *Smoky* four-four. Requesting landing instructions."

The sun was setting when the Walrus landed. We reconvened, each sitting in the same place on the floor with two cases of beer in the middle. Tonight, dreaming was out, talk was in.

"And I fucked her good!" Father William said.

It was like we stopped in the middle of a sentence, and when we gathered again someone finished the sentence.

"God . . ." I said.

"Yes," Father William answered. I ignored him and started again.

"I jump out of my skin every time I hear them."

My fellow combat vets looked at me with question marks in their eyes.

"The LERPs," I said. "Long-range reconnaissance patrols of ten men or less, ramming around the jungle looking for trouble and whispering over the radio. It gives me the willies . . . Today, I was flying over an area we hit with Agent Orange when this whispering voice came up my frequency: '*Smoky. Where am I?*' I turned the volume all the way up so that I could hear them better. There was a loud squelch, and I damn near jumped out of my skin. It's so strange, eerie, weird, foreign; almost alien. Everything is dead on the ground below me, yet suddenly this voice whispers in my ear like Marley's ghost from Christmas past, only it's real; it's actually happening. '*Smoky, Smoky . . .*' I never know if I should whisper back. 'This is *Smoky*. Go ahead,' I whispered.

"'*Smoky, I've got boo coo dinks all around me*,' the ghost answered. There was a long period of silence, then suddenly another transmission. '*I don't know where the fuck I am.*'

"'Hold your mike switch down for a direct steer,' I told them. Then, I hear, *Psst, psssstt, pppssstttt*, and the needle on my A.D.F. (automatic direction finder) jittered back and forth. I turned my bird to center the needle; then I rolled wings level. When the needle swung, I looked down, marking my position. They were down there somewhere, in the middle of a decaying jungle, in the middle of a shitload of bad guys, and they trusted me to give them accurate coordinates so they could crawl out, and then we can carpet bomb the fuck out of all the bad little motherfuckers harassing our friends. I checked my maps. There were no prominent features, just rotting jungle all around them. How the hell am I going to give them accurate coordinates?"

"Use the old measure-with-a-micrometer, hit-it-with-an-axe procedure," the Walrus interjected

"Yeah, but guys' lives are depending on an accurate reading from me."

"What did you do?" Buddha asked.

"I encoded my best guess and transmitted the coordinates to them. There was complete radio silence for the longest time. I began to itch, first my face, then my arms. I scratched so violently I drew blood. I stopped scratching and rolled down the sleeves of my flight suit. Finally, I heard, '*Smoky*.'

"'Go ahead,' I said.

"'*Shit, Smoky, I'm on the wrong fucking hill.*'" Everyone in the room broke out in laughter.

"He's on the wrong fucking hill!" Joey repeated.

Hee, hee! Hee, hee, hee!

When the laughter subsided, the Walrus spoke.

"I had one where this LERP was describing how this gook was putting the wood to his girlfriend. Then I heard *BR-rrattt!* '*Oops show's over,*' the LERP said." The Walrus looked to the heavens and raised his arms. "He killed the fucker. One minute this guy is fucking." *BR-rrattt!* "And the next minute he's dead." And we all laughed again, and in between laughs the Walrus added: "No shit. The LERP offed the gook while he was humping his girlfriend. What the fuck?"

"Now that's really shooting your wad," Buddha said. And we all laughed again.

"And what of the fuckee?" Father William asked.

"She's dead too, I guess," the Walrus said.

Now it was a subdued laugh. More like: Okay, we offed the bad guy; he deserved it. But the chick, she's precious and helpless; she deserved to live.

Two days later, there was a problem on the staff-weenie side of the FAC hootch that had all the highers scratching their heads as well as other parts of their bodies. They had no idea what was happening and therefore had no ideas on how to solve it.

"Miss Sam, may I have a beer?" a TWAT pilot asked.

Scratch, scratch, scratch.

"How about a kiss, too?"

Scratch, scratch, scratch.

"I suppose a fuck is out of the question."

Scratch, scratch, scratch.

"Well, then fuck you, the horse you rode in on, and the colonel who sent you!" the TWAT pilot said.

The TWAT pilot looked at us. He looked at us for affirmation, like his profane language now made him one of the boys. I felt only disgust and made a mental note reminding me that this one would never fly with me.

Scratch, scratch, scratch.

Staff-weenies were clawing now at their private parts in public.

Scratch, scratch, scratch.

"You've got the fucking crabs for Christ's sake," Joey yelled.

In the morning, Doc arrived with a fumigation team. The crab trail led to Captain America, who had just returned from R & R in Bangkok. He had finally made a contribution to the war effort. Now, for the first time, scrubbing mamasans had a reason to beat our clothes with rocks. And I couldn't help but wonder if Captain Puff's magic underwear came with a guarantee. "*Now, new and improved, and crab proof too!*" The entire hootch was de-loused, or de-crabbed, or whatever they call stripping beds, burning sheets and blankets, and spraying poison everywhere.

"The shit they're spraying smells like shit," the Kiwi said. "Bloody hell!"

He said it through a gas mask, which he had now added to his ensemble of flak vest and steel pot. No crab or enemy rocket was going to get inside his armor. He wore the ensemble everywhere now that he was very short, just days from departure. He wore it during his going-away party, and he was still wearing it when he boarded the freedom bird. We heard he wore it until he was feet wet: off the coast of Viet Nam and headed back home to New Zealand.

There was a man standing beside my airplane when I approached it with my parachute slung over my back. "I'm a FAC from Me Long," he said by way of introduction. "I've got an in-country R & R to Vung Tau. Folks tell me you might be able to give me a ride down there."

He was dressed in civilian clothes. He looked more like a spook, or C.I.A. type, than a pilot.

"Who is folks?" I asked.

"Actually, the 22nd TASS commander."

"Are you friends with the commander?"

"Oh, hell no! It's just a little *attaboy* I got for a mission I flew last week: one of those we-will-take-the-top-of-the-hill-today-and-give-it-back-to-you-tomorrow missions. I've got a parachute."

I finished my preflight, signed off on the forms, and squirmed in between the copilot's seat and the copilot's yoke; over the throttle, mixture, and R.P.M. levers; and into the left seat. It was another blistering hot day, hellaciously hot my brother might say, stifling hot my mother might say, hotter than hell my father might say; only none of them had ever experienced hot like this, so they would have to find some new adjectives. Motherfucking hot might work I decided, and that would keep with the family theme. Steam rose from the tarmac.

"Get in." I said. "I've got nothing on the agenda, so we can head straight down there unless you prefer the scenic route." He did not answer.

I took off, raised the gear and flaps, and leveled off at 1,500 feet. I set a course for the sandy beaches of Viet Nam and trimmed the airplane so it would fly hands off. Jefferson held the record: forty-three minutes without touching the controls. I was up to eighteen.

"*Smoky* forty-four, forty. State your position."

"I'm over the dead zone," I answered, referring to the cadaver-colored area below me, the area blanketed by dioxin.

"*Buster* has made contact with the enemy. I have ordered up two sets of air."

"Forty-four copies. Give me the specifics."

My side window was soon black with information. I deciphered the coordinates of the contact, but I really didn't need to. I could see the fighting across a ditch running east-west through the kill zone. The enemy was dug in with bunkers tied together by trenches. They could move laterally and perpendicular, to attack or defend. I could see the bad guys moving in tight to our friendlies, a tactic they used to negate our air power. Choppers had less firepower but were more accurate, and right now I needed accuracy.

"*Buddha* contact *Smoky* four-four."

To the east I could see Navy P.B.R.s, which stood for patrol, boat, river, Navy nomenclature, which to me sounded a little bit like *See Spot. Run Jane.* The swift boats were jammed up in a dead-end canal just off the Saigon River and were taking fire on three sides from the banks.

"Any TAC air vicinity Saigon contact *River Rat* on guard." I heard their call for help. The voice was firm but elevated.

"*River Rat, Smoky* four-four. Come up my push 314 decimal 3."

"Roger, *River Rat* copies."

"*Buster, Smoky* four-four."

"*Smoky, Buster.* I'm getting hit bad now, mortars and machine guns. Get me air now!"

"Hang on, *Buster.* Break, break. *River Rat,* how copy?"

"I've got you lima charles."

"*Smoky* four-four, *Buddha* your freq. How copy?"

"*Buddha, Smoky* four-four, state location."

"East of the Dog Bone."

"*Smoky* four-four, *Smoky* four-zero. Fighters airborne. Call signs: *Blade* one-two and *Blade* one-four. Stand by clearance."

"Four-four copies."

"*Smoky* four-four, *River Rat.* Have you got air for me?"

"*Smoky* four-four, *Blade* one-two flight."

"*Blade, Smoky* four-four. Bien Hoa TACAN: 195 degrees at forty-eight miles."

"*Bearcat Arty, Smoky* four-four."

"*Smoky, Bearcat,* go ahead."

"*Bearcat, Smoky.* I've got a fire mission for you."

"Negative *Smoky. Bearcat* tubes are *inop* at this time, over."

"Motherfucker!" I yelled inside the cockpit, and not over the radio. I yelled it to release my anger and to alert my passenger that the shit was really hitting the fan. I pulled my map bag up from between our seats and tossed it on the lap of my civilian-clothed passenger. "Get on the maps," I yelled.

"*Smoky, Buster.* Where's the air?"

"*Buster, Smoky.* It's on the way."

"*Buddha, Smoky.* I've got a tally-ho."

"Roger."

"Have you got a visual on the *River Rats*?"

"Roger."

"Help them, but be careful. I'll be working fast movers to the east of you. Stand by for info."

"Roger that, *Smoky.*"

I turned to my passenger. "*Cack* up the frequencies and call signs, and get them to *Buddha.*" He nodded.

"*Smoky* four-zero, *Smoky* four-four. How's my clearance?"

"We are working it four-four."

"Well, put a fire under their ass, and get me some more air."

"Roger."

"*River Rat, Smoky* four-four. There is a *Hunter/killer* team, call sign: *Mamba* two-eight, over your head." While I worked on our clearance to put in airstrikes, my passenger passed call signs and frequencies on to *River Rat.*

"*Smoky* four-four, *Buster.*"

"*Smoky* four-four, *Blade* one-two. We are two, Foxy 100s, with *snake* and nape."

"*Blade* one-two, *Smoky* four-four. Drop down and set up in left-hand orbit. T.I.C. Bailout to the November Whisky. I'm rocking my wings."

"*Blade* one-two copies and has a tally-ho."

"*Smoky* four-four, *Buster.* I can't hold. We are dropping back. Repeat. I can't hold."

"*Smoky* four-zero, *Smoky* four-four. Where's my goddamn clearance?"

"We are working on it."

"Fuck working. Get it done. Our guys are taking it in the ass!"

"*Buster, Smoky* four-four. I'm rolling in and I have a visual."

Fuck! My fighters were ready; I was ready. The guys on the ground were getting the shit pounded out of them, and we were waiting on some fucking Viet Namese province chief to finish his cigarette or blow job, or to take a piss, or to take a shit: *Who knows what the fuck we are waiting on?* He could do whatever he wanted, and whenever he wanted to do it; I needed permission. I decided to make a low pass, fake marking the target for an airstrike. I pulled the throttles back, rolled the airplane upside down, and started down the chute, bending it right then left, all the way down, hoping to attract the gooks' attention, to draw fire away from the ground troops. I went in low, low enough to see men scurrying back and forth, low enough to see the bad guys looking up and pointing at me with their rifles; then I pulled off the target.

"*Smoky, Buster.* Where's the mark? Where's the air?"

What could I tell him? The only air I could give him was the hot air I was getting. How do you stop the bleeding with a bunch of hot air?

"*Smoky* four-zero. *Smoky* four-four. I need that clearance now!"

"*Smoky* four-four. *We're working it.*"

Fuck it! I was done with bullshit. Fuck the province chief! Fuck command and control! Fuck the rules of engagement! Fuck this war! Fuck the world! Fuck everything! Our guys were getting killed.

"*Blade* one-two, *Smoky* four-four. Set 'em up hot. High drags first. I'm rolling in."

Once again I pulled the power off and banked into the target. I armed my rockets and, pressing the trigger on the right side of my yoke, I let one fly.

"*Blade* one-two, *Smoky* four-four. Two right. You are cleared in hot."

"*Blade* one-two. Understand, two right, and I am cleared in hot."

"Roger that!" I rotated the wafer switch.

"*Buster*, get your head down. Here comes the hard stuff."

I knew I was walking into a shit storm by putting in bombs without a clearance. I knew it, but I did not give a goddamn.

"*Smoky* four-four. *Smoky* four-zero. We have your clearance. You're cleared to drop. How copy?"

Every moving part now seem to proceed in slow motion: The fighters coming down the chute, the bombs falling free from their wing stations, the fireball billowing outward and upward. And in the background, over guard channel, I heard an F-4 jock, flying somewhere in Viet Nam getting ready to bail out. It was like a record running at slow speed in an echo chamber.

"*L-e-a-d, I'm hit and losing hydraulic pressure. I'm turning z-e-r-o, n-i-n-e-r, z-e-r-o.*"

"*L-e-a-d copies.*"

"*It's time to e-j-e-c-t. I'll see you back at the b-a-r.*"

This guy was about to bail out, yet his voice was calm, almost melodic. Grunts tell me they are amazed that FACs' voices are so calm under fire. Well today, mine wasn't. They say it gives them strength to hear our steady and confident instructions, like a babysitter saying, "Don't worry; everything is going to be alright."

The grunts felt we had our shit together, and everything was under control. Under control? Under control, my ass; controlled chaos at best.

I once told the guys on the ground that the fighters were fucked up and didn't know what the hell they were doing, and then I spun the wafer switch and told the fighters the guys on the ground were fucked up and didn't know what they were doing—spread the blame while making damn sure they knew that any fuck-ups did not belong to me. Only I set my radio wafer switch just the opposite of where it should have been, and I ended up telling the fighters they were fucked up and didn't know what they were doing, and then I told the ground troops they were fucked up and didn't know what they were doing. Those are the days I wish I was on the ground instead of up in the air, for it was much easier to stick my boot in my mouth and my head up my ass while sitting on good old terra firma than it was while sitting in the cockpit of a tiny Cessna.

Because U.S. troops did not deploy as a unit—our GIs trickled in and out as individuals—leadership was oftentimes not determined by rank but instead by who was most experienced, who had been in-country the longest. Unlike more disciplined armies, our guys often got more ornery and better organized when the senior ranking officer got hit, because then the natural leader emerged and took charge. Charlie was well-trained. He knew how to effectively wage war against an enemy with superior firepower. He had been at it for decades, against the Japanese, against the French, and now against us. His tour was not for one year but for the duration, unless he happened to die or be killed. He negated our firepower by moving in close, knowing that we feared friendly fire deaths. He would try to kill our R.T.O. (radiotelephone operators), who spent hours trying to figure out ways to hide their whip antennas first. When the radio was neutralized, our troops couldn't call for air or artillery support, reinforcements, or medevacs. Charlie would then try to take out any medics, to demoralize and instill fear in our troops: For if a soldier knew there would be no one to stop their bleeding, they might be less aggressive, less determined to fight. Then they would target officers, who also tried to hide their rank. Charlie preferred wounding as opposed to killing, for it took an addition two men out of action to carry one wounded man.

We countered with *Bouncing Betty*, not a dame or the name of a pole dancer, but an antipersonnel weapon typically used as a booby trap—a buried bomb with two charges: one to raise it waist high off the ground, and the second one to detonate it, instant amputations. It had a kill radius of twenty meters and an injury radius of one hundred meters.

Our grunts told me that breakdowns occured after a firefight, not during, but after danger had passed. Each man reacted differently: some cried while others laughed; some swore while others prayed; some shook while others locked up; some puked while others needed to eat. I just got angry; a fire raged inside my body, and that rage was immediate, and it was intense. Payback violence seemed to be the only act that dissipated it. So I buried it deep inside me, where it was without voice, where it could not surface. Because I had learned payback violence could get me killed.

Then, Buddha got hit.

"*Smoky, Buddha. I'm going down.*"

"I copy, *Buddha.*" And in a millisecond my duties had doubled, or tripled, or quadrupled. Now I was frantically working two contacts, and I was also conflicted. *Should I stop working the contacts and try to save a friend?*

Today's flight was supposed to be a piece of cake, a walk in the park, a little jaunt down to beaches of warm, white sand gently lapped by baby-blue waves. Turned out I was wrong. Turned out that it took four sets of fighters and a slew of choppers to break the contacts and recover my good friend Buddha and his copilot, and then fly cover for the medical evacuation of thirteen wounded soldiers and several dead ones, and the resupply and the reinforcements for the troops still on the ground. Turned out I was wrong about a lot of things. Turned out I was the one who didn't know shit from *Shinola*. Turned out *Sky King* was a fraud; he was just acting, or reacting might be a better word to describe it, and in the big scheme of things, I was about as important as a fart in a typhoon. My son called a noisy fart a "bip," as in, "Mommy, daddy bipped." Then he would giggle uncontrollably, and that's what I did after the fighting was over. I farted and giggled. "Why do farts smell?" I asked my copilot. He shrugged his shoulders. "So deaf people can appreciate them too."

I landed at Vung Tau some four hours after takeoff from Bien Hoa. My passenger got out first, and he waited for me as I inspected the aircraft for hits. I found none. I was rubbing the boom, which connected the tail to the cockpit, and I thought about how small it was. I could just about wrap my hands around it; right thumb to left thumb, right index fingertip to left index fingertip. Inside, with my left shoulder against the side window, I could reach out with my right arm and touch the fuel selector switch located above the right window.

"That was the best piece of FACing I have ever seen," my passenger said before we parted ways. I never saw him again.

I decided to stay overnight. I drank by myself, isolated in a corner of the barroom surrounded by men hooting and hollering, but I was alone. And it hurt.

In the morning, while it was still dark, I kicked the tires and fired up my airplane for another day's work in paradise. While waiting for clearance, a series of random thoughts flashed across my brain.

"Beats drinking beer and fucking women," a *Daredevil* FAC once said.

"It's so much fun we get to do it again . . . and again . . . and again . . ." Father William said.

"Yeah, do it until we do it right," Buddha said.

"I guess we are just lucky to have such a swell job," I said.

"Three bags full!" Father William said.

Sometimes, I could see the image of Captain Puff standing in the doorway of our hootch bar. He was back in the world, yet he still haunted me. I recalled a day when he stood in our room with his arms folded and a scowl on his face . . .

"I want you to hit this bamboo bridge," he said as he pointed to it on a map. "I have been trying to take it out for a month. Now you try."

I tried several times to hit it with a rocket before my bomber, an Australian Canberra with an Aussie crew, arrived on station. The closest I got was about two meters. How would they hit it if I couldn't? I wondered.

The Canberra droned straight on toward the target. "Adjusting for wind," the pilot said, and I got this mental image of an Aussie crew member wetting his finger and sticking it out the window while another wearing a slouch hat stood with his legs crossed in the bomb bay with the bomb doors open and the jungle passing underneath just waiting for word to kick one out. I watched the bomb drop in disbelief as it headed straight for the three- or four-foot-wide bamboo bridge. I watched the explosion and the blast rise up from the creek below with smoke billowing up and out obscuring a perfect hit, or spot on as they would say.

"You got it!" I yelled, and when the Canberra pilot keyed his mike I could hear his crew cheering in the background.

"We will just come around and take a pickie if you don't mind, Smoky?"

"Yeah, yeah!" I said.

Over the radio Smoky forty congratulated me.

I had never before put in a B-66. I was amazed at the accuracy of the bomb drop and it reinforced my admiration, perhaps even hero-worship, for Australian troops. I watched as the lumbering airplane circled and lined up for a camera shot, and when I looked down at the bridge I could see the bomb crater bisected by the still-swinging bamboo bridge. I could not tell them it was still standing.

I could not acknowledge that I had made a mistake in my exuberance. I could not be the one to squash their happiness in this war that only brings misery, disappointment, and death to those who participated in it, even though I knew their embarrassment would be monumental once the photos were developed. I became despondent as I kept up the guise until they departed triumphantly. Two days later Captain Puff said to me: "You reported that you destroyed that bridge but it is still there. Why did you do that?"

I thought about telling him they must have rebuilt it. I thought about how this whole war was a lie and what was one more lie? And then I decided I could no longer justify the deception with yet another lie. I walked away without answering . . .

"*Smoky* forty-four, Vung Tau tower. You are cleared for takeoff. Altimeter: two, niner, niner, five."

I answered with a double click of the mike switch. Better to not say anything. Better to not say anything ever, I thought as I brought the throttles forward.

Another blistering hot day; I had to mop the sweat from my eyes every couple of seconds in order to read my instruments. I had lumbered down the runway, raised the nose of the aircraft and then the gear, made a sweeping, gentle turn to the right, and was heading north to the Thumbtack when I heard the first frantic call for help on guard channel.

"Any TAC air in vicinity of the Parrot's Beak? I'm being attacked by enemy aircraft."

The Parrot's Beak and the Angel Wing were delineated by the Viet Nam/Cambodian border and were notorious as NVA and Viet Cong infiltration routes. The enemy attacked, then withdrew safely to their Cambodian sanctuaries, often in plain view, as if giving us a giant middle finger. I could almost hear Charlie say: "Fuck you, you can't catch me! I'm in Cambodia!" I pushed my throttles forward until they could go no further, and pulled my airplane to the left like a white-hat cowboy turning and then spurring his horse in the direction of gunshots. My reaction was immediate, instinctive, and impulsive; my rage manifested by my death grip on the throttles and yoke, and recognized by the inferno boiling inside me. An American was in trouble! I needed to get there as fast as possible.

For weeks, there had been reports of enemy helicopters operating out of Cambodia; this was the first report of a fixed-wing enemy aircraft. I turned up the volume on my radios.

"This is *Aloft* one-four. I am under attack and need TAC air immediately!"

The voice was firm but fearful. *Aloft* was the call sign of a U.S. Army pilot flying an L-19, similar to the Air Force's O-1, the lightest and slowest aircraft in our inventory, and the aircraft the Walrus flew. An airplane that was absolutely defenseless in any combat situation. The Walrus quipped that there were guns near the border that could put up more lead in a minute than his airplane weighed.

"*Aloft* this is *Blade* zero-three; a pair of F-100s."

"Roger *Blade*, *Aloft* one-four. I am just north of Loc Ninh and taking fire from a propeller-driven airplane."

I immediately firewalled my throttles and turned my airplane north and headed for the Cambodian border. I was driven by adrenaline, anger, and a GI who needed help.

"*Blade* zero-three, this is *Paris Control* on guard. Hold your position."

"Fuck that, *Blade*; go get 'em!" The *wop, wop, wop* in the background identified the caller as a chopper pilot.

"Yeah, kick their ass, Air Force!"

"Fuck 'em up real good, Air Force!" *Wop, wop, wop* . . .

"*Aloft, Blade* zero-three. State position."

Hearing this, my chest swelled. Today, even though I was dressed in faded fatigues, I was proud to wear the blue suit.

"*Blade* zero-three. This is *Paris Control*. Hold your position. I repeat: Hold your position. Do you copy?"

"*Paris*, this is *Aloft* one-four. I'm on the deck and now taking ground fire. I need help!"

"*Paris, Blade* zero-three. This guy is in trouble. We are diverting to his location."

"Negative, *Blade* zero-three. Do not deviate. We are monitoring the situation."

"Come on, Air Force. Grow some balls and help the guy!"

"Yeah, put your wings on the line!"

I bobbed forward and back in my seat. "Come on, come on," I whispered, urging my airplane to fly faster.

"*Paris Control, Blade* zero-three requesting permission to salvo our bombs."

"Negative *Blade* zero-three."

"He's one of us, Air Force. Fuck *Paris Control*!"

"This is *Aloft* one-four on guard. He is making another pass at me! I need help."

"Goddammit, Air Force! Help the man."

"What are you waiting for, flyboys?"

"For Christ's sake, don't be a pussy! Get your ass in there!" *Wop, wop, wop* . . .

And now I was not so proud that I wore the blue suit. The Army pilots were really giving it to us.

"Two, set your switches for salvo. We will drop them in the river."

"Two copies."

And with that transmission, the angry radio calls returned to encouragement and solidarity.

"That's it, Air Force!"

"Get up there and blow that motherfucker out of the sky!"

"That's it, baby! Kick some ass!"

"We got your back, Air Force!"

And then someone keyed their mike, and there was cheering in the background. And again, I felt proud to wear the blue suit. "Come on, *Blade*!" I yelled but my voice sounded hollow in my empty cockpit.

"*Blade* zero-three, *Paris Control*. We are painting negative enemy aircraft in the area. Hold your position and do not salvo your bombs. How copy?"

"Lead is rolling in."

"Lead is off clean."

"Two is rolling in."

"Two is off clean."

"Get after it, Air Force."

"*Aloft, Blade* zero-three. Say type of enemy aircraft."

"I'm not sure. It looks like maybe a T-28. Single-engine prop."

"*Blade* zero-three, *Paris Control*. Return to base. I repeat: Return to base."

I couldn't believe what I was hearing. It made no sense that the North Viet Namese would have a fixed-wing aircraft operating in Cambodia, especially one that we didn't know about it.

"That's a negative, *Paris*. We have salvoed our bombs and are heading north."

"*Blade* zero-three, *Paris Control*. We have identified the aircraft as friendly. R.T.B. Return to base. Do not engage!"

"This is *Talon* one-eight. I have just been attacked by enemy aircraft!" *Wop, wop, wop.* "I am ten klicks north of An Loc and going down."

"*Paris Control, Blade* zero-three. I have a tally-ho on the enemy aircraft, and I'm rolling in. Two, set 'em up *hot*."

"Two copies. Guns are hot."

"*Blade* zero-three, *Paris Control*. Do not engage. Try to get a tail number. I repeat: Do not engage!"

"Bullshit! Air Force, hose the fucker!" *Wop, wop, wop* . . .

"This is a fucking war, man. No pussies allowed. Grease the motherfucker!"

"*Paris Control, Blade* zero-three copies. Two, cover me. I'm rolling in for a look-see."

"Two copies."

Then there was silence, like my radios had stopped working. I banged my fist on the top of the instrument panel. An eerie silence, like the war that lasted forever was suddenly over. The silence seemed to go on forever. I turned up the volume on my radio. Finally, there was a transmission, and when it happened it nearly blew my eardrums.

"*Paris Control, Blade* zero-three."

"Roger *Blade*, this is *Paris Control*, go ahead."

"Looks like a VNAF, A-1E . . . tail number . . . Whisky, Echo, three, niner, eight."

What? One of our guys? The South Viet Namese Air Force drove A-1Es, an old piston-driven U.S. Navy airplane. What the hell was happening? I wondered.

"*Blade* zero-three, *Paris Control*. We have him on radar. Disengage and R.T.B. Break, break *Aloft*. Are you okay?"

"Roger, *Aloft* is okay and heading home."

"*Blade* zero-three flight. Set 'em up safe and let's head home."

"Two copies."

I turned my aircraft south and headed for home also. What the hell just happened? I said this over and over until my grip finally loosened around the throttles and yoke. I felt my lungs expand and contract as I began to breathe deeper and longer. My blood pump slowed and my shoulders drooped, and I sensed pain down my spine from neck to pelvis. I also felt pain in my derriere from a seat of steel designed to protect me from bullets while generating hemorrhoids, or ass-troids as Father William called them, protrusions the size of walnuts. Sweat dripped from my armpits and pooled in my crotch and boots. Little, recently formed, skin-colored stalactites dangled in my armpits and now, just before my R & R to Hawaii, one had appeared on my Johnson.

"*Smoky* four-zero, *Smoky* four-four, Thumbtack and R.T.B."

"Roger. Returning to base. Forty copies."

Earl sat in the jeep fanning himself with his go-to-hell hat and waiting patiently, I assumed, for me to taxi in. I set the brakes, jumped out of the airplane, and hopped into his topless jeep.

"Is it cooler in here?" I asked.

"Hell no!"

"What the fuck happened out there today?" I asked.

"A classic fuck-up. Apparently the Army had decided to put a LERP team across the Cambodia border . . . a super-secret, unauthorized deal. Of course, they didn't tell anyone what they were doing, because the highers would have never approved the mission. The *Aloft* bird was supporting the LERP team. Paris painted the *Aloft* bird on radar as it was re-entering Viet Nam. For political reasons, they scrambled Viet Namese A1-Es to intercept it. "

"What about the chopper that went down?"

"Totally unrelated. Shot down by ground fire." He laughed, shook his head, and started the jeep. I laughed too.

"What a fucked-up war!" I said as we headed back to our hootch.

Joey, Father William, Buddha, and the Walrus were already in attendance.

Hee, hee! Hee, hee, hee!

I immediately started to laugh. I joined the laughter, even though I had no idea what they were laughing about. It just felt good to laugh.

"You are an uncouth, motherfucking heathen," Father William said, as he pointed to the Walrus, "and you are going to hell."

"Who gives a fuck?" the Walrus answered. "I'm already in hell."

Weird thoughts rolled across my brain as I popped a beer and sat down on the floor. Weird thoughts such as: What would happen if we sired a child for every Viet Namese we killed? A weird thought that I did not give voice to. I was getting better at that, better at interrupting the process from brain to mouth because my thoughts were so strange that every now and then I was sure I was going nuts—off my rocker, off the deep end—and I didn't want to let anybody know just how crazy I had become. No, I decided, there would be no downers from me tonight. I just wanted some good old morbid and raunchy GI humor.

The Walrus stood and put a tape on the reel-to-reel. "Listen to this," he said. Rousing military music gushed forth from the speakers. It reminded me of Moondoggie who once proclaimed: "Military music is to music, as military justice is to justice." Then the music faded into a voiceover.

The following statements were recorded when a civilian correspondent interviewed a shy, unassuming Air Force Phantom jet fighter pilot. So the correspondent would not misconstrue the pilot's replies, a Wing Information Officer was on hand to make certain that the real Air Force story would be told.

"Captain, what is your opinion of the F-4?"

"Why, it's so fucking maneuverable you can fly up your own ass with it."

"Ah, what the Captain really means is that the F4C is highly maneuverable at all altitudes and he considers it an excellent aircraft for all missions assigned."

"I assume, Captain, you've flown a certain number of missions in North Viet Nam. What do you think of the SAMs used by the North Viet Namese?"

"Why, those bastards couldn't hit a bull in the ass with a base fiddle. We fake the shit out of them. They're no sweat."

"Ah, what the Captain really means is that the surface-to-air missiles around Hanoi pose a serious threat to our air operations and the pilots have a healthy respect for them."

"Captain, you've flown missions to the South. What kind of ordinance do you use, and what kinds of targets do you hit?"

"Well, I'll tell you, mostly we aim at kicking the shit out of Viet Namese villages. My favorite ordinance is napalm. Man, that stuff just sucks the air out of their friggin lungs and makes a son of a bitchin' fire."

"Ah, what the Captain really means is that airstrikes in South Viet Nam are often against Viet Cong structures and all air operations are under the positive control of forward air controllers, or FACs. The ordinance employed is conventional 500- and 750-pound bombs and 20 mm cannon fire."

"Captain, you've spent an R & R in Hong Kong. What are your impressions of the Oriental girls?"

"Yeah, I went to Hong Kong. As for those Oriental broads—well, I don't care which way the runway runs, east or west, north or south—a piece of ass is a piece of ass."

"Ah, what the Captain really means is that he found the delicately featured Oriental girls fascinating and was very impressed with their fine manners and thinks their naïveté is most charming."

"Tell me, Captain, have you flown any missions other than over North and South Viet Nam?"

"You bet your sweet ass I've flown missions other than in North and South. We get fragged nearly every day for the trails in Laos where those motherfuckers over there throw everything at you but the friggin kitchen sink. Even the goddamned kids got slingshots."

"Ah, what the Captain really means is that he has occasionally been scheduled to fly missions in the *extreme western* D.M.Z. and he has a healthy respect for the flak in that area."

"Captain, I understand that no one in the 12th Tactical Fighter Wing has got a MiG yet. What seems to be the problem?"

"The problem is we got fragged by those peckerheads at 7th Air Force. Those glory hounds sitting on their fat asses in Thailand get the MiG missions while we get stuck with bombing the goddamned cabbage patches."

"Ah, what the Captain really means is that each element of the 7th Air Force is responsible for doing their assigned job in the air war. Some units are assigned the job of neutralizing enemy air strength but hunting out MiGs, and other elements are assigned bombing missions and interdiction of enemy supply routes."

"Captain, of all the targets you've hit in Viet Nam, which one was the most satisfying?"

"Oh, shit, it was getting fragged for that friggin' suspected V.C. vegetable garden. I dropped napalm in the middle of the friggin' pumpkins and cabbage, while my wingman splashed it real good with six of those 750-pound mothers and spread the fire all the way to the friggin' beets and carrots."

"Ah, what the Captain really means is that the great variety of tactical targets available throughout Viet Nam make the F4C the perfect aircraft to provide flexible response."

"Captain, what do you consider the most difficult target you've struck in North Viet Nam?"

"The friggin' bridges. I must have dropped forty tons of bombs on those swaying bamboo mothers and I ain't hit one of the bastards yet."

"Ah, what the Captain really means is that interdicting bridges along enemy supply routes is very important and a quite difficult target. The best way to accomplish this task is to crater the approaches to the bridges."

"Captain, I noticed in touring the base that you have aluminum matting on the taxiways. Would you care to comment on its effectiveness and usefulness in Viet Nam?"

"You're friggin' right I'd like to make a comment. Most of us pilots are well hung, but shit, you don't know what hung is until you get hung up on one of those friggin' bumps on that goddamned stuff."

"Ah, what the Captain really means is that the aluminum matting is quite satisfactory as a temporary expedient but requires some finesse in taxiing and braking the aircraft."

"Captain, did you have an opportunity when you were on leave to meet your wife in Honolulu, and if so, did you enjoy the visit with her?"

"Yeah, I met my wife in Honolulu, but I forgot to check the calendar, and so the whole five days were friggin' well combat-proof; a completely dry run."

"Ah, what the captain really means is that it was wonderful to get together with his wife and learn firsthand about the family and how things were at home."

"Thank you for your time, Captain."

"Screw you, why don't you bastards print the real story instead of all that crap?"

"Ah, what the Captain really means is that he enjoyed the opportunity to discuss his tour with you."

"Oh, Captain, one final question. Could you reduce your impression of the war into a simple phrase or statement?"

"You bet your ass I can. It's a fucked-up war!"

"Ah, what the captain really means is: *it's a fucked-up war!*"

The next afternoon, I flew from south to north over my A.O., circling periodically over suspicious areas, but I could detect nothing that would merit an airstrike or an artillery bombardment. I had no fighters scheduled, and I was bored. The Junior Officer of the Year once told me about a Special Forces camp in War Zone D. I decided to go look for it.

"The N.V.A. (North Viet Namese Army) hit the camp with a regiment of crack soldiers," he said. "The Green Berets were forced to abandon it. But not before they pushed all their nonessential equipment into piles and painted them white."

And there it was. The piles spelled *Fuck the N.V.A.* in letters so big I bet an airline passenger could read it from 30,000 feet. I imagined little Johnny looking out his airplane window. "Look Mommy. What does that spell?"

The mother leans over him and sees the words.

"Oh, Johnny, that spells 'peace.'"

"Yeah, like in 'peace of ass,' huh, Mommy?"

When I related the story to our group that evening, Joey replied, "One day, dirty little Ernie saw his mother naked and asked: 'What's that, Mummy?' And Mummy replied, 'That's where your father hit me with an axe.'

"'Hmmm. Right in the cunt, huh, Mummy!'"

Hee, hee! Hee, hee, hee!

"Girl Scouts wear green berets," Earl declared.

"Don't ever say that to an actual Green Beret. You'll get your fucking head blown off," the Walrus replied.

Now, who would have the balls to say that to a Green Beret? I wondered. And then it hit me. Joey might. And he would probably get away with it. Instead of busting him up, they would probably buy him a beer.

"The Berets on the Cambode border are animals," the Walrus said. "Many are on their second and third tours. Once a week they have gross-out night. They grease the bar, then hire a Cambode broad to strip and lay on it, with pussy and tits pointed skyward. If you are hungry, they just slide her down to you. Gobble, gobble." We all laughed.

The Walrus continued. "On another gross night, they scrounged up a bunch of ping-pong balls. They lined the girls up, put a ping-pong ball in their pussy, and then bet on which broad could shoot their ball the farthest." Again, we all laughed.

Father William handed out another round of beer. When the cans were all popped open, the Walrus spoke again. "Our TOC was in a old run-down French villa a couple of miles from our hootch and runway. Around three in the morning, we got a call to *scramble*. Our radio operator jumped in our jeep and raced to the TOC to order up some air. I ran to my airplane. After a couple sets of air, we broke the contact. A couple of days later, the province chief paid us a visit. He said our radio operator hit a Viet Namese when he was driving through the village on his way to the TOC the night of the scramble, and the victim was suing the U.S. government for a million piastres or some bodacious amount of money like that. Our airman was in big trouble. That night, I was in the S.F. club and I told the story to a Beret. 'What's the guy's name?' the Beret asked. 'Kittridge,' I said. 'No, not his name; the gook's name?' 'Why?' I asked. 'I'll get a couple of Cambodes, and we'll go slit the guy's throat.' I told him the gook's name. The next day, charges were dropped. Seems the gook had disappeared."

"He was probably a V.C. anyway," Buddha said. "Got what he deserved!"

"Yeah, don't fuck with the United States Government," Father William replied. He said it with contempt, but it felt a little bit like his contempt was for us and not the government or the gook.

"Do you know the difference between the Boy Scouts and the Air Force?"

Earl asked. Those who knew began to chuckle. Earl and I studied faces. Buddha didn't know, and to my astonishment, neither did Joey.

"The Boy Scouts have adult leaders," Earl said. And as we laughed, Father William policed the room by gathering up the empty beer cans.

"I heard the Army had a tube," Father William said, "that was getting ready to fire its one millionth round, and they want to do a photo op. You know, like it was the one millionth shopper in a supermarket or some stupid fucking thing like that."

"Who's counting?" the Walrus inquired.

"How the fuck should I know?" Father William replied as he gave the Walrus his hate stare. "Anyway, before I was so rudely interrupted by the heathen over there, they flew in a four-star general to pull the lanyard. Everyone was lined up, the cameraman was ready, the general had the lanyard in one hand and probably his dick in the other, and while flashing a big smile, he pulled the cord and the cameraman shot the photo. Of course, the Army failed to clear the airspace above, and the shell blew a C-7 caribou right out of the goddamn sky: and a bunch of unsuspecting GIs were killed . . . They gave their lives so this fucking general could get his picture in the *Stars and Stripes*."

"I hope he framed that photo and put it on the mantel over his fireplace, so he could look at it every day . . . remind himself that his vanity took the lives of good men," Earl said.

"When something like that happens, it's just not your day, huh?" Buddha added.

"Guess not," I answered. "I heard another one about a guy who had finished his tour and was waiting to board the freedom bird when the base got hit with rockets and mortars. He ran to a bunker and hunkered down and a 122 rocket went right through the roof of the bunker but it didn't explode."

"Wow! He was a lucky bastard," Joey said.

"The rocket impaled him. Killed him right there in the bunker on his last day in-country."

"Motherfucker!" Father William summarized. He got up and walked over to the tape deck.

"Yeah, put some hard rock on. Janis Joplin, Steppenwolf . . . anybody." And he did. And nothing further was said. We tried to muster up some energy by singing along, attempting to reignite some good vibes, but the good vibes seemed to be gone. We were just hanging on, counting the days and hoping we were going to make it to 365.

The next night we assumed our positions. "I heard," the Walrus said, "there is a $10,000 bounty on our heads. Kill a FAC, and collect the reward."

"That's a bargain!" Father William said. "I've read where we spend $333,000 to kill one gook."

"No shit?"

"No shit!"

"Yeah, I heard that B-52 pilots have a $10,000 bounty on their heads also," Buddha said.

"Now, that's some pretty shitty company," Father William interjected. And we all laughed. Everyone but Father William.

"Earl, you were in B-52s, weren't you?"

"Yeah, I was a copilot. I volunteered for Nam to get out of SAC."

"Does that mean if the dinks kill your ass now, they could collect $20,000?" Father William asked.

The Walrus tilted his head, like a dog trying to understand a human.

"$10,000 for being a B-52 driver and $10,000 for being a FAC, for fucksakes, Walrus," Father William explained. The Walrus nodded.

"Fucking peasants!"

"I can see some zip gunner yelling, 'Hallelujah, I hit the daily double! Two for one. Now pay me my goddamn money and send me back to those swinging slope heads in Hanoi!'" the Walrus exclaimed. And again we all laughed.

"I was flying D models out of Thailand," Earl said, "bombing mostly the Ho Chi Minh trail and along the Cambodian border. Occasionally, we would get a target in Laos."

"Oh, you mean that country we are not supposed to be in?" Father William asked.

"Yeah," Earl answered. "Country X!" We laughed and he continued. "Once, we hit Vinh, their southernmost MiG base. We hit it with six cells: eighteen B-52s, each one carrying one hundred and eight 500-pound bombs. All but one B-52 hit the runway. Eleven days later, using their wheelbarrows, hoes, and rakes, they were flying out of there again."

"Why those little motherfuckers!" Father William said. He said it with admiration in his voice instead of his usual causticity. Then, as if catching himself, he added: "How about I kill the Walrus here, and we all split the ten grand?"

"Fuck you, Father William," the Walrus said, and he punctuated it with a middle-finger salute. And we all laughed.

"I wish someone would!" Father William said.

"Would what?" the Walrus asked.

"Fuck me!" Father William said.

"Well, bend over," Buddha said. And everyone laughed again, everyone but Father William.

Then Buddha spoke. "A Special Forces sergeant told me he was sent in after a B-52 strike to assess the damage. You know what he said?"

"How the fuck would we know," Father William answered.

"He said, and these are his exact words, 'There were bodies *festooned* all over the trees.'"

"*Festooned*?"

Hee, hee! Hee hee, hee!

"I like that word," Joey said. And we all nodded in agreement. We clanged beer cans. Then Joey asked, "What the hell does festooned mean?"

Hee, hee! Hee, hee, hee!

Earl took a long swig of beer, wiped his chin on the back of his hand, and began again. "Colonels came from everywhere to strap on a flight, get their combat pay and tax deduction, buy stereo gear, fuck a *tealot*—a live-in whore—then buy jewelry to appease the wife back home. The navigator and bombardier sit under the pilots and there is a *relief tube* behind the navigator. It's very dark down there and when we had a strap-hanging colonel, we would put Saran wrap over the tube and the colonel would piss all over himself."

Hee, hee! Hee, hee, hee!

"B-52 strike! Scared the piss right out of him," Joey said. "Suits the slimy bastard!"

"What if someone had to take a shit?" Buddha asked.

"There's a honey bucket behind the copilot's seat. Anybody who dares to use it has to buy a case of beer for each crew member."

"Hey," the Walrus said, "that's like the fighter pilot who joined on a cargo plane's wing. 'Watch this,' the fighter pilot said, and he did a barrel roll around the airplane. The cargo pilot said, 'That's nothing. Watch this.' Nothing happened. Five minutes go by. Finally, the cargo pilot asked, "Well, what did you think of that?' And the fighter pilot said, 'What? What did you do?' And the cargo pilot replied, 'I went in back and took a shit.'"

And we all laughed, everyone except Father William.

Then it was Joey's turn. He stood.

A young lad found a shirt with pilot wings on it. He tore the wings off the shirt and pinned them on his. Joey paused, made a ripping motion with his hand, pinned the imaginary wings to his shirt, sucked his gut in, pushed his chest out, and patted his left breast. *Just then a bus rolled up. An old hag—two hundred stones, maybe more—waddled down onto the street. Both her arms had casts on them. Her fingernails were full of dirt. Her hair all tangled. And she had a gigantic canker hanging from her nose. Just here . . .* Joey pointed to the tip of his nose, then moved his index finger some six inches away from his nose, indicating that the length of the growth was approximately six inches.

"*Can you help me, little man?*" *the hag asked.* "*Can you carry me groceries?*" *The lad just stood there. The bus driver handed the lad two bags of groceries.* "*Follow me,*" *the hag ordered. And the lad followed her.* Joey teetered with his arms cradled as he walked, portraying the lad trying to balance a heavy load.

They reached the hag's house and the lad set the groceries on the counter. "*I have to go to the bathroom. Will you help me?*" *the hag asked.* Joey hunched over and held his arms out.

"*I guess so,*" *the lad said. So they walked into the bathroom.*

"*Lift up me dress and pull me knickers down,*" *the hag ordered.*

The lad did as she asked. Joey lifted up an imaginary dress and pulled imaginary panties down. Then he fanned the air in front of his nose. *The lad just stood there staring at her matted fur.*

"*Would you like to kiss it?*" *the hag asked.*

And the lad said, "*Hey look lady, I'm not a real fighter pilot. I just found these wings.*"

Hee, hee! Hee, hee, hee!

And of course we all laughed with him, including Father William.

"You are going to hell, all of you," Father William said as he extended his hands, palms up, and I expected to hear him say the words "Dominus vobiscum"—the Lord be with you—but he didn't. Instead he said, "Fuck you all!"

"Father William," Earl said. "You'll like this one . . . When these asshole colonels strap along on their B-52 ride, the EWO (electric warfare officer) has to fill out a form . . . a DD (Department of Defense) 680 or some number like that. After we were briefed on the target, the chaplain stood up to give his spiel. And he ended it with, 'May Michael the Archangel fly with you.' And my EWO hollers, 'Question! Question right here.'" Earl waved his arm frantically.

"'What is it?' the chaplain asked. 'Do I have to fill out a goddamn DD form 680 for this Michael guy too?'" And we all laughed.

"Behold, peasants!" Father William stated. "We are fighting in a war where the tactical bombers are doing the strategic bombing, and the strategic bombers are doing the tactical bombing." Heads nodded in agreement.

"God, I hate those B-52 arc light strikes when I'm out there flying around," I said. "'This is Portcall on guard with a heavy artillery warning to 38,000 feet from 1300 to 1315.' Let's see. Three B-52s in a cell; 108 500-pound bombs to an airplane. That's 324, 500-pound bombs that are going to rain down on my ass any second now. I check my watch. Do I have time? I check my position. Oh, shit! Which is the fastest way out of the box? I push my throttles to the firewall and wish I had afterburners. I check my watch again. And then I see the bombs falling. BOOM! BOOM! BOOM! Three hundred and twenty-four BOOMS! I can feel the ground shaking even in my airplane. I see a long cloud of dust rising with red-orange mini-explosions at the base of it. It's goddamn terrifying."

"There are a lot of ways to die over here, my son," Father William said. "When you get killed from the heavens, it means the Almighty has taken a personal interest in making sure your ass is grass. What did you do to piss him off, heathen?"

I did not answer.

"I heard about a LOACH driver," Buddha said, "who was flying with an intel type who wanted to check out an area. 'Get down on the deck, where I can see,' he said to the pilot. 'No way,' the pilot said, 'that area is loaded with .50 cals.' The intelligence officer insisted; the pilot complied and they were immediately shot down. The pilot grabbed his M-16, some extra clips of ammo, and split. He was hauling ass through the jungle when he came to a clearing. And there were the gooks patting each other on the backs, cackling, and pointing to the sky, congratulating themselves for knocking the LOACH out of the sky. The pilot was so pissed off he fired off a clip, taking several gooks out. He went to reload and discovered he had lost his extra ammo, and the footrace was on. He swears he ran for four and a half straight hours before he got away from the gooks. One of my boys picked him up. He was damn near dead from heat exhaustion. Never found the stupid fucking intelligence guy."

"I heard about a Navy jock in Da Nang," Joey said. "He took off at night in an A-6 with a full bomb load. He had an electrical problem and lost all radio contact, so he decided to come around and do a front-end barrier engagement. He dropped his tail hook, but he missed the cable. His hook missed the cable!"

Hee, hee! Hee, hee, hee!

"He didn't think he could get airborne, so BOOM! he banged out. The airplane roared down the runway and made a perfect rear-end engagement."

Hee, hee! Hee, hee, hee!

"His hook grabbed the cable at the end of the runway and the plane just sat there running at full military power with no canopy and no pilot. The firemen stood around scratching their heads." Joey scratched his head using only his index finger. "Suddenly, the firemen saw a man in a flight suit. He ran up to him. 'Excuse me,' the fireman said. 'Do you know how to shut this aircraft down?' And the pilot said: 'I fucking well ought to; I just banged out of it.'"

Hee, hee! Hee, hee, hee!

"I had a bogus target once," I said. "Out in the swamps where a 500-pounder just goes blub. I asked the VNAF A1-E pilot if he ever tried to drop all his bombs on a single pass. 'Never, *Smoky*' he said.

"'Do you want to?' I asked. 'Can do, can do,' he said excitedly. 'Let's do it,' I said. So he set up to pickle all twelve bombs on one pass. Down the chute he came, releasing the first two just as he started his dive. Then three and four came off, five and six, and when he got to ten he was so low that I was sure he was going to fly through his own frag. Shoot himself down. I figured he would stop, but no, he started his pull and here comes eleven and twelve, two 250-pound napes. And all I can think about is when I put a rocket off the range back in Florida. These two bombs are tumbling end of end and they jump the river and are heading for a rice paddy where I can see gomers working. And I'm thinking, 'Oh, shit. He is going to cook them.'" I swallowed some beer. "But the bombs just kept going, and they are on a direct line with a farmer's hut, right up the front sidewalk, if they had one, and about two to three clicks long, just tumbling along for what seemed like forever, but I know they are low because I can see their shadow on the ground. And suddenly there is this big fireball, the flames only a few meters from the hootch, and I got the hell out of there before someone spotted me. Scared the shit out of me. I'll never try that again."

"Jesus Christ!" Father William said. But the rest of the men just laughed.

"Reminds me of a time when we were putting in strikes near the Parrot's Beak when this VNAF A-1 driver got shot down," the Walrus said. "We tried all day to get him out, but the ground fire was too intense. The next day we picked him up and brought him to our hootch for a party. 'How was that?' a Beret asked the rescued pilot. 'What?' 'Spending the night on the ground?' 'Oh,' he said. 'It was very dark. I was very scared. I could hear them looking for me . . . I jumped at every noise . . . V.C. catch you, they treat you not so bad. Not what you used to, but not so bad. Oh . . . V.C. catch me, they treat me very bad . . . and for very short time too.'" And we all roared with laughter. The Walrus continued: "Later on, he puked; but he did it in a pail. 'I very neat Viet Namese,' he said. And one of the Berets yelled, 'Save the big pieces!'"

And when we were all laughed out, I told this story.

"I read a snippet . . ."

"Wait a minute. What the fuck is a snippet?" the Walrus asked.

"It's like zip it, only it's a snippet, you cretin," Father William said.

"I read an anecdote..."

"Wait a minute. What's an anecdote?" the Walrus stopped to look at each of us and when no words of wisdom were forthcoming, he shrugged his shoulders.

"It's a short personal account," I said. "Anyhow I read it in *Reader's Digest* several years ago. Apparently it happened in 1937 or so. There was a history teacher who was certain that a World War was about to break out and he wanted no part of it. He gathered all the books and maps he could find that might help him find a place where he could peacefully sit out the war. And after much careful study and deliberation, he finally settled on the small, insignificant island of Guadalcanal."

Two days later, Earl and I were flying together, he in the right seat, I in the pilot-in-command or left seat. It was a quiet day, and out of boredom we decided to see how high this overloaded aircraft might fly. I pointed the nose toward the stratosphere.

"I put you in for an instructor pilot," Earl said. "I told them you were the best pilot I have ever flown with."

"And?"

"And the DASC colonel doesn't like you. In fact, he hates you. He said there was no way in hell he would let you be an instructor pilot. What's the deal with that?"

I told him about our showdown in the officers club and how the diminutive Ranger poked him in his belly and said if he ever fucked with me, no one would ever find any of his body parts. Earl laughed as I nudged the aircraft higher. We were through 18,000 feet, or flight level one eight zero or angels 18,000 as the Navy would say, and we were barely ascending. We had been at it for over forty-five minutes and when we hit 18,600 feet, the airplane would not climb an inch higher.

"Might be a record, Earl."

"*Smoky* forty-four, *Smoky* forty."

"Forty, forty-four. Go ahead."

"Got ground troops taking fire. Ready to copy info?"

"Roger, shoot it to me."

"Want to spin down?" Earl asked. And when I heard the word "spin," all I could think about was the time in pilot training when the tweety bird flipped upside down and into an inverted spin. I felt the fear ripple through my body.

"You gotta be shitting me?" I said.

"No," Earl replied. "We can do it."

I ignored him and began a steep descent with clearing turns, left then right, as I copied forty's info on my side window. I decoded the coordinates and checked my map. Our guys were just west of the road running south from Long Binh to Vung Tau. The east side of the road belonged to the detachment from Thailand, the ones I had supported but the highers said I didn't so they could deny me a medal on my first solo combat mission. I noticed an O-2 in a lazy, left-hand turn.

"Who's that?" Earl asked.

"Not sure. I am assuming it is a Thai FAC, call sign: *Snake*. I've got a bad feeling about this."

"*Buster*, *Smoky* four-four. What happening?"

"We are taking mortars from the east and we are returning fire."

I looked up the call sign for *Snake*.

"*Snake*, operating just north of *Bearcat*, rock your wings." We watched as the O-2 rolled back and forth.

"*Snake*, *Smoky* four-four. I am in your four o'clock rocking my wings."

"*Smoky* four-four. *Snake* one-two has a tally-ho."

"*Snake*, *Smoky*. I think our allies are firing on each other. Have your guys cease fire and I will do the same, and let's see what happens."

"Roger that, *Smoky*."

"*Buster*, cease fire. I repeat cease fire."

"No can do, *Smoky*. We are under heavy fire."

"You are firing on friendlies."

"My counterpart says the Thais initiated the contact."

"I don't give a damn who started it. Cease fire!"

"*Smoky* four-four, *Snake* one-two. I am having trouble getting my troops to cease fire."

"Myself, *Snake*. Fuck 'em. Let them kill each other. I'm going home."

"Roger, *Snake* copies."

"*Buster*, *Smoky* four-four. You are on your own. I am going home."

"Everybody hates everybody here, Earl," I said. "The Viet Namese hate the Cambodes, the Thais, the Montagnards, the Chinese, and the Laotians; and everybody hates us. What the hell are we doing here?"

I parked the airplane, and we dropped our equipment off at P.E.

"Let's stop at the mail room on the ride home," Earl suggested.

"Roger that." I jammed the gas pedal to the floor for a couple of counts, shut the engine off, and coasted into the parking area. I didn't quite make it. The jeep stalled out in the middle of the road, where I got out and walked to my mailbox. Earl followed. He did not ask why I left the jeep in the middle of the road; I liked that, and I did not offer an explanation. Colonel Buzz Cut spotted me and began to run at me like he had to take a major shit.

"Why did you leave that jeep in the middle of the road where it is blocking traffic, lieutenant?" he roared. And then he recognized me. "Oh, it's you," he said.

"Yeah, it's me," I answered.

"Where's your hat? I told you to wear a hat. And why didn't you salute me?"

"You ask too many questions, Buzz," I replied. I opened my box and pulled out a couple of letters; then I unzipped my pocket and pulled out my hat. It was by now the ugliest officer's hat in Viet Nam, sweat and beer stains everywhere and a frayed silver braid on the top edges. I was proud of it. I placed the cunt-cap on the back half of my head.

"Take that hat off," he ordered. I obeyed.

"Put it on, take it off. Can't please anybody around here," I said. Earl laughed and we jumped back in the jeep and drove off. "The boys on the tape got it right, Earl," I said.

"What's that?"

"It's a fucked-up war!"

Chapter 4
SOMETHING IS MISSING

Father William rode shotgun while I ran the jeep up to maximum speed and then cut the engine. We began to coast.

"You're pulling a Jefferson," he declared.

I nodded.

"Have you heard from him?" he asked.

"No." I said.

"Do you miss him?"

"Every day."

The jeep slowed. Other jeeps lined up behind us. The drivers were making ungentlemanly statements.

"Moron fucks. Get off the road!"

The vulgarities seemed to increase in direct proportion to our decreasing speed.

"Give them your blessing, Father William," I ordered. He turned and flashed the middle fingers of both his hands at them, pumping them up and down like an engineer blowing the whistle on a freight train. I turned off the perimeter road. We were moving so slow now, a rock stopped our forward momentum. We were ten feet short of my parking space.

"Dammit!"

I restarted the jeep and pulled into our assigned space. Then I walked back and searched for that rock. When I found it, I picked it up and threw it. It bounced along the tin roof of the *Buzzard*'s hootch.

Pling, pling, pling.

Father watched without comment. I waited for some sort of snide remark. None was forthcoming. We entered our hootch and took our places on the floor. Joey and Buddha were already there, and the beer was stacked up in the center of the room. But something else was brewing. I could feel the tension stirring inside me, and it was looking for a way out. I did not know the cause. Joey, Father William, and Buddha were edgy also, and that night there were lots of *fuck yous*—not the usual jovial ones, but fuck yous voiced with anger; confrontational *fuck yous*, which nearly led to fisticuffs on several occasions. Finally Joey said, "This is bullshit! Let's get into the turps! Do a pub crawl."

The tension immediately left my body and was whisked out of the room. We began to plan on how we were going to get shitfaced, the four of us; a drink to the death, an intoxicating marathon to excise all our demons and quite possibly create some new ones. We didn't do much of it anymore, rowdy drinking that is. Had we matured? I doubted it. Had we mellowed? Perhaps. For me, it felt more like I was worn out. We had done everything; there was nothing new.

> *An Indian child was talking to his father,* the Walrus said. *"Daddy, how did I get my name?" the child asked. His father pointed to his son's sister. "She was born as the sun rose. Therefore, we named her Morning Dawn. And when your brother was born, the wolves were howling as if to announce his birth. So we named him Howling Wolf. Why is it that you ask, Two Dogs Fucking?"*

Hee, hee! Hee, hee, hee!

When Joey started his laugh, it was impossible not to laugh along. We laughed till our sides hurt, and when we could laugh no more, Joey said:

> *Me father got into the grog most every night. And when he staggered home, he would wake me mom and ask her to cook him some breakie. She heated up some dog food and put in on a plate, to teach him a lesson. But me dad loved it. So every week me mom would send me to the store to buy more dog food. One day I walked in the store and said, "I'll take some bread, and some soup, oh and a hunk of cheese . . . Hmm . . . that's it I guess." And the grocer said: "Have you forgot the dog food, Joey?" "No," I replied. "Doesn't you father like it?" he asked. "Well," I said, "I guess he still likes it, but last week he was lying out in the middle of the street licking his balls when he got run over by a truck."*

Hee, hee! Hee, hee, hee!

Kiddies were everywhere and more seemed to be arriving daily. We had abandoned the hootch bar as our party headquarters. The bar was now manned and occupied by TWAT pilots along with other frustrated desk-flying lieutenants, staff-weenies, and F.N.G.s. Captain America and Captain Marvel were the reigning dignitaries simply because they had been in-country the longest. We needed to reclaim it for a big blowout. One where we would get *mongrelled*, as Joey so aptly referred to it. One where we could release the pressure generated by pent-up internal anger. Personally, I sensed that it needed to occur soon, before something bad happened. Our group was agitated and surly. Caustic remarks were no longer funny. They were cutting and cruel. We all sensed it. We made our first rule. Weapons would be banned from our nightly sessions. Tonight, Joey had somehow requisitioned several large cans of tomato juice, which we would mix with gin and ice. It was genius; a hangover cure before we got drunk.

Father William blew first. Two *Nighthawk* FACs waited for me as I taxied in after a four-hour flight. "Have you seen Father William?" one asked.

"He's not in my airplane if that's what you are asking."

"No shit!"

"Why do you ask?"

"He is on a bad drunk."

"Have you checked the O club?"

"No."

I ran to my jeep, jumped in, cranked the engine, and, with tires spinning and a rear end swerving and spitting dust, I sped out of the parking lot and onto the perimeter road. I found him at the O club. He was sitting at the bar, with a shot glass of whiskey in front of him. He was slumped over with pen in hand and was writing on a napkin.

"Letter to the Thessalonians?" I asked

"Just a minute," he replied and continued writing. I ordered a drink for both of us and waited. When it arrived he sat upright, dropped his pen, and shoved the napkin to the center of the bar.

"More booze," he said as he downed the shot. "My boss just chewed my ass for saying *fuck* all the time . . . me, a Father." He laughed. "But he has no problem with *crispy critters, step-ons, dead gooks, body count* . . ." I said nothing. He looked up at me and continued, "Jesus, I think I'm going nuts."

"Know the feeling," I said. He reached for the next shot and I reached for the napkin. "Can I have this?" I asked.

"Yeah," he said. "It's about you." I glanced at the napkin and saw verse.

"Hey, I didn't know you wrote poetry."

"Only when I'm drunk," he replied. "I've got drawers full of it. Now, get the fuck out of here!"

I studied him. He stared at his hands, wrapped around another shot glass. I moved to a booth. I could watch him from here. I sat down, opened the napkin, and read:

> *Twas '69, discovered a friend.*
> *Aggressive, insecure, no certain allure.*
> *Slow to show beyond façade,*
> *The true person within the bod'.*
>
> *Keen and sensitive, a hustler's grace,*
> *Emanated from that youthful face.*
> *Rounded to the nth degree,*
> *Stalks a man of integrity.*
>
> *Proud to be within his grace,*
> *Known his impact in thy fate.*
> *Pray his life not turn to waste,*
> *But share tomorrow's tribulates.*
>
> *Life can be that fickle friend*
> *And loving souls; sour goals.*
> *Ne'er accept that second best*
> *After passing all tests.*

I stared at Father William. He was slugging down another straight shot. I folded the napkin and placed it in my upper-left pocket, right next to my heart.

When his head bounced off the bar, I walked over, and with the help of another man I loaded him in my jeep and headed for his hootch. His upper body lurched sideways with each corner. I had to reach out and steady him on at least three occasions. I pulled into the parking lot and wrapped the chain around the steering wheel. I hooked the padlock and then closed it. I got out of the jeep and walked behind it to Father William. I put his arm around my neck and dragged him into his hootch.

"You found him," the man who had met my airplane said.

"No shit!" I replied.

The pilot grabbed Father William's other arm.

"Where did you find him?"

I wanted to say, *No, this isn't really him. It is just an exact replica!* But I welcomed his help, so I held my tongue. We pushed and pulled Father William down the hall, into his room, and onto his bed. I stooped to take off his boots and then unbuckled his fatigue pants, and that was as far as I was going to go.

"Have I told you God takes care of little kids and drunks?" Father William mumbled just before his eyes closed.

"Keep an eye on him," I said. The pilot nodded, and I walked out of his room, out of his hootch, and into mine.

"He has been sleeping for nearly twenty-one hours," Father William's roommate said when I walked over to check on him. I grabbed his big toe and shook it, and then rotated it in ever-increasing circles until he stirred. He squeezed his lips together, then opened them. "Water," he moaned. His roommate handed him a canteen. Eventually, he sat upright. He accomplished this incrementally: first he pulled his head out of his ass; then he let his feet fall off the side of the bed; then he propped himself up on one elbow, pausing, I assumed until the room stopped spinning; and then sat up, with the bulk of his weight now resting where it should have been, on his ass. "Come on," I said, "I'm heading to the mail room."

"Who the fuck would write to you?" he mumbled.

He dressed with deliberation, yet he mis-buttoned his fatigue shirt three times in a row. I laughed.

"Fuck you, peasant!" he said.

We walked outside, and when the sun hit him, he dropped to the ground as if shot by a sniper. "Goddammit!" he yelled as he shielded his eyes. Again I laughed. He rose carefully, checking to see if his body was still intact, and when he was convinced it was, he got into the jeep. We drove to the mail room and stopped. I looked around for Colonel Buzz Cut, but he was nowhere in sight. Two other lieutenant colonels were on the prowl.

"He must have been a terrific haircut colonel," I said to Father William.

"Who?"

"Colonel Buzz Cut."

"Why?"

"Because it took two lieutenant colonels to replace him."

"Who gives a fuck?"

I sauntered over to my box, spun the combination, opened it, pulled out a letter, and returned to my jeep while avoiding both of the haircut colonels.

"Fucking assholes," Father William said.

"Want me to check your box?" I asked.

"I don't have a box. I have a cock!" he replied.

We drove back to the FAC hootch. Earl, Buddha, the Walrus, Joey, and several other *Daredevil* FACs were sipping beers at the bar. I sat down and opened the envelope. A newspaper clipping and a letter fell out. I picked up the letter and started to read it.

"Miss Sam, get us all a couple of beers. And chalk it up to dipshit here," Father William said as he pointed to me.

"What day is it?" I asked after reading the letter.

"I don't know," a *Daredevil* FAC answered.

"Maybe Tuesday?" another FAC said.

"No fucking idea, mate," Joey said.

"Don't look at me," the Walrus said.

"Who gives a fuck?" Father William said.

"I do!"

"Why?"

"Because I think I have the *worst letter of the week*. In fact, it might be the worst letter of the year."

"Who gives a fuck?" Father William said.

The door opened and a slew of staff-weenies walked in.

"What day is it?" I asked.

"Wednesday," four staff-weenies responded in unison.

"Can anybody tell me why the hell we are over here?" I said. "The goddamn Viet Namese don't appreciate us and neither do the people back home."

"Did you just figure that out?" a *Daredevil* FAC asked.

"I didn't expect it from my brother," I replied. "Listen to this shit."

> *I went to a peace rally last night where I witnessed the most powerful speech I have ever heard. An American Indian dressed in full Indian regalia: buckskins, eagle feathered headdress, and beaded moccasins stood before the audience and waited for complete silence. And when the murmur stopped, he said: "Our government says the reason we are in Viet Nam is because we have to honor our treaties." And then he sat down. He never said another word. I was deeply moved and I thought about you. I don't know how you can go on killing innocent people. This war is wrong . . .*

"Okay, that's enough," another *Daredevil* FAC said. "You've won *the worst letter* for the entire year."

"Fucking-a!" another FAC agreed.

Then the staff-weenies opened up.

"Is your brother some kind of long-haired, hippie bastard?"

"Yeah, some kind of draft-dodging, radical son of a bitch?"

"Yeah, some kind of commie, pacifist wuss!"

"Hey, maybe he's fucking Jane Fonda!"

"I doubt it," I answered.

"I was just trying to give him an out," the FAC replied sheepishly.

"I can't believe your brother is a fucking pinko, hair-bag Communist!" Another FAC shook his head. "Why can't they just shut their yap?" he shouted.

"Yeah, what do they know?"

"Not one goddamn thing! That's for sure!"

"They don't know diddly-squat!"

"I hate those protesting motherfuckers!"

"Yeah, we should put a big fucking airstrike right in the middle of one of their protests!"

"Napalm baby."

"Put them all in jail or let them go to Canada or Russia or wherever the fuck they want to go!"

"Yeah, why the fuck are they complaining? They're not over here! They should cork it shut, sit back, and enjoy the good life."

"Let us do the fighting, and stay the fuck out of it!"

"I'd trade places with them anytime and anyplace," Buddha said.

"Well, I tell you what," the Walrus added, "we'd better finish it soon or our kids will be over here fighting."

"You don't have any kids, do you Walrus?" Earl asked.

"Not that I know of."

And everybody laughed.

"No way! It's going to end for us. Nixon's going to turn the fighting over to the Viet Namese, and we are all going to go home early," Earl said. And again everybody laughed.

"The Viet Namese? Shit, they couldn't last ten days!"

"Who gives a fuck??" Father William shouted, and the room went silent.

"Let's go to the O club," someone suggested, and we all ran to our jeeps.

I sat in the driver's seat, and we waited for Father William. Joey was in the front seat. He leaned over to honk the horn, only there was no horn. So he placed his foot on mine and pushed the throttle to the floorboard. With my other foot I jammed on the brakes, and the battle between throttle and brake caused the jeep to shake. If I released the brakes, we would plow straight into the hootch. Joey didn't seem to mind.

Hee, hee! Hee, hee, hee!

"Come on, come on. Let's go!" he shouted. Finally, Father William emerged from his hootch and joined the Walrus and Earl in the backseat.

"Move over, goddammit!" Father William yelled, followed by, "What's your fucking hurry?"

"Times a wasting," the Walrus replied. "We only got about 120 days of fun left in Viet Nam."

"Only 120 days. Ain't that a pisser?" Father William replied.

The next night I sat alone in my room. There was a hollow in my gut now. Jefferson, Carlos, and Captain Puff had rotated back to the world. Perhaps it was because I now had a room of my own; perhaps it was because I had moved past the halfway point in my tour; perhaps I was just burned out; perhaps it was because I would be seeing my wife in Hawaii soon and I was nervous about it; perhaps it was none of these things. The door opened; Joey, Father William, and Buddha entered. Joey and Buddha immediately sat on the floor and opened four beers from the case they carried in. Father William removed my hard rock tape from my reel-to-reel and replaced it with ballads. No one complained. Then he placed candles on the floor and lit them. I turned out the lights and joined them on the floor. We all sat American Indian style; men acting like women, but without the constant yakking. We followed this ritual for more than one month, flying, and then coming together to reflect and dream of home.

One night, Joey stood up and yelled "I can't stand it anymore! I need another pub crawl!" And with his words, I could feel my ticker's boost pump kick in. A devilish grin appeared on Father William's face, and the right corner of the Walrus's mustache quivered. Our sunken eyes seemed to open wider. Color had returned to burned-out pupils. The blood in our eye sockets seemed to rejoice at the opportunity to get loaded up once again. We planned it out like a combat mission. We had our names scratched from the flying schedule. The day of and the day after. The day after would be devoted entirely to recovery.

I had been moved back to my original room in the house of Puff, the room of a highly decorated combat coward, or maybe a man smarter than I; I was not sure anymore. We started at noon. We stood in a circle in the center of the room while Father William walked over to the tape recorder and switched on Iron Butterfly's "In-A-Gadda-Da-Vida."

"They are trying to say, 'In the Garden of Eden,'" the Walrus yelled over the recording.

"No shit, Sherlock!" Father William answered.

"You eat with that mouth, Father William?"

"Only pussy. How about you?"

"No I just shove my food up my ass. Saves a few steps processing it, if you know what I mean."

We clanged beer cans high over our heads, chugged the contents down, then smashed the empty cans on our foreheads, and threw them on the floor where Joey and the Walrus squashed them further, stomping on them with their combat boots, now all a part of a pagan ritual dance they were improvising. They stomped down extra hard every time the Butterflies sang. Father William continued to hand me beers, which I opened with an extra-large church key, and then I handed them off to the dancing heathens as they circled past me. And when the song and our beers were finished, we headed to our hootch bar where a crowd was forming as word must have gotten out that the lunatics had been let out of their cage and were about to get mongrelled. I ordered an F.N.G. off of my stool, and Joey sent Captain American and Captain Marvel to their rooms. I spotted Doc. I walked over to him and yelled in his ear that I wanted to talk to him.

"Absolutely," he replied as he rubbed his ear with his thumb and index finger. I leaned in close and I thought I detected a look of fear behind his triple-paned glasses.

"It's kind of private," I whispered.

"Come in to my office," he said

He motioned for me to join him in the john.

"What's the problem?" he asked.

I looked around to make sure no one could listen in.

"I've got these things growing on my dick."

"Show me," he said.

"Are you sure?"

"Of course I'm sure. I'm a doctor."

I looked around the room, and then I looked under the stalls. I saw no one.

"I hope no one walks in," I said as I pulled out my Johnson.

He grabbed it and turned it over. He called the growths by a medical term as opposed to referring to them as little Johnsons. I liked that.

"I'm going on R & R, Doc."

"No problem. We can cut them right off." I didn't like that.

"When you say we, you don't mean you and Doctor Mai Lai, do ya?"

"No, no, I'll do it. It will only take a second." I liked that.

"It sounds painful."

"Don't worry," Doc said. "I'll stick a needle in it and numb it." I didn't like that.

I cringed, grabbed my Johnson back, and stuffed him inside my flight suit. Then I zipped it shut.

"What the hell are you two doing?" Joey asked.

"What the hell are you doing?" I fired back.

"I have to drain me dragon," he said.

"Well, me dragon is growing horns. Doc here is going to cut them off."

The Walrus walked in.

"Hey, you know why turds are tapered?" he asked.

"No," we all answered.

"So your asshole won't slam shut!"

Hee, hee! Hee, hee, hee!

"I like him," Joey said.

I walked back to the bar.

"Did you heathens have a little prayer meeting in there?" Father William asked.

I did not answer.

We each grabbed a six-pack of beer and began our pub crawl down hootch row. Father William led the procession. Secretly, I wished I had made up a six-foot cross for him to use as a giant swagger stick, to give nonverbal commands as to where and when we should stop and congregate so that he could enlighten the multitudes, and when he had finished he could pick up his cross and we would follow: Joey, the Walrus, several TWATS and F.N.G.s, weenies, chicks, and a few staff pricks.

We stopped at the *Nighthawk* hootch where Father William introduced us to an O-1 driver who was in his pilot training class and just happened to be in Bien Hoa for the night on a spare parts run and would be flying a mission from here in the morning. His mustache was half the size of the Walrus's—in length, depth, and density— and it was blond instead of bushy black. Father baptized him Walrus the Lesser. We christened him with beer, drank several ourselves, picked up two more processioners, and it was off to the next hootch, which was occupied by A-37 drivers. Before entering, Father William issued a warning that this hootch featured the *word of the day* and if it was uttered, the utterer would have to buy a round. The word today was "shack": a perfectly placed bomb.

A FAC in giving B.D.A. (bomb damage assessment) at the end of a strike might say to fighter lead: "Two shacks, and all bombs within three meters." The word apparently referred to a shack located on a Texas bombing range during

World War II. The bombardier would place his crosshairs on this shack. This word was seldom used in the vernacular, and it obviously would not challenge first or second place on the all-time list of most beers bought. The number-two word was *napalm*. The number-one word, and recently retired forever, was *fuck*. Therefore, despite the large amount of Father William followers, chances for a free beer because someone uttered the word "shack" were slim. Fortunately, there was always a weenie ready to impress. When Father William asked a TWAT pilot—whose mouth switch always seemed to be stuck in transit—"What's the word for a perfectly placed bomb?" The weenie promptly yelled out: "Shack."

"Ah yes," Father William said. "It is written, the first shall be last and the last shall be first. Set 'em up barkeep!"

Hee, hee! Hee, hee, hee!

We walked out the side door of this hootch and into the next one. It was the hootch where I played cards with Lucky Larry before he was killed. I stood in the doorway. My body buzzed with nervous feelings. I could not enter. I stepped aside and stayed there until the procession continued its march.

"You alright, mate?" Joey asked.

"Yeah," I answered. I forced a smile.

At the next hootch, I sat at the bar feeling more secure now with a layer of men surrounding me. I sipped my beer. An enlisted man, a crew chief on an F-100, sat next to me; the lines in his hands grey with grease, and his fingernails, although clipped painfully short, had tips outlined in black. And when I heard someone say "Altoona" and the crew chief answered, my head lifted and I studied this boy-man.

"Are you from Altoona?" I asked.

"Yes sir."

"Do you by any chance know a guy by the name of Elwood Smirk?"

He slapped his hand on the bar and his cheeks rippled like the waves on a lake, only this was the result of a massive grin that also lit his eyes.

"Woody. Goddammit, sir, Woody is my best friend back in the world. How do you know him?"

"I don't really," I replied.

He told me about the good times they had growing up together, chasing girls, dragging main street, getting into fights . . .

"Do you know the movie *The Birds*?" he asked.

"Yes," I answered.

"There was this old theater in downtown Altoona," he said, "and it had a balcony. Woody called me up and asked if I could get a package into the theater. I said I could. I knew the usher. But he wouldn't tell me why. When he picked me up—he drove a chopped '49 Merc—he handed me a gunnysack. My usher friend had propped open the back door. We entered and snuck up to the balcony. The movie was *The Birds*. You've seen that movie where the damn birds attack humans?"

I nodded yes.

"Well," he continued. "The gunnysack was full of fucking pigeons! And when the birds in the movie were going nuts attacking everything and everybody, Woody emptied that gunnysack and people went rip-shit, jumping over seats, fighting to get out. I heard later that someone even had a heart attack. It was goddamn crazy. We still laugh about it. Woody, he's a character, sir . . ."

Altoona finished up with how Woody got married, and he was the best man, and how each of them now had a kid.

"Woody was smarter than I was. He knocked up his old lady and got that draft deferment. I fucked up and waited . . . and ended up over here . . ."

I was the last one to leave the hootch. I asked him if he would like to join us. He said he couldn't, but he jumped off his stool and pumped my hand up and down about a half-dozen times, all the time still sporting that massive grin. I hated to leave him and this eerie connection we had back in the world. I hated to leave his memories of childhood innocence, peace, love, and raising hell in a hick-town called Altoona.

"But wait," he said. "How do you know Woody?"

"Woody is my brother-in-law," I said, "but I have never met him. His old lady is my wife's sister."

"No shit?" he said.

"No shit," I replied.

I told Father William about meeting the guy from Altoona. I told him what a strange experience it was hearing about a man who was related to me but I had never met. I must have mentioned something about peace and love, because he cut me off.

"You're not turning into some kind of goddamn commie, hippie-freak, are you, heathen?"

"No, Father," I replied.

At the end of hootch row, the Messiah decided we should move our procession to the Army helicopter driver's officers club. He dispatched several TWAT pilots to commandeer jeeps for the short ride to their club. We loaded seven jeeps—six with men, one with a driver and the beer—and we descended en masse. All jeeps stopping with brakes jammed flush up against the floorboard. The jeep with the beer actually crashed into the corner of their club. The driver was summarily dressed down and replaced for putting the beer at risk. And when we entered, Joey immediately went to the front of the club and sat down in a seat reserved for their battalion commander, a man we had never met. Joey refused to move, despite repeated requests and threats from the Army. "I'll move when he gets here!" he hollered back.

Walrus the Lesser, perhaps insulted by his diminutive moniker, decided he would make a statement. He began tossing down straight shots, then chasing with beer. It was an impressive show. At the bar stood two Special Forces officers attired in tiger-striped *cammies*, a captain and a lieutenant, both quiet, maybe sullen, and both with don't-fuck-with-me looks on their faces. I slid in beside the lieutenant and listened.

"I'm the only captain battalion commander in Viet fucking Nam," the captain said. He stared straight into my eyes. "I'm the Mike force commander. I've got 500 *Cambode* mercenaries under my thumb." He squashed his thumb into the bar until it turned white. On payday, I order up a couple of fully loaded Cobra helicopters to hover a few feet over their heads. Any slackers got half-pay. If they had an argument, I'd tell them to talk to the Cobra." The captain laughed; the lieutenant did not. He leaned with the palms of his hands resting on the bar. The captain continued talking. "We cross the border and fuck up Charlie real good." He smiled as if remembering a time when he fucked up Charlie real good. "Hey bartender, get everybody at the bar a green gasser, on me."

"Let me get it!" I protested.

Neither the captain nor the lieutenant said anything. Both men glared at me. The lieutenant's eyes were shiny and bloodshot. The captain's eyes were dull, maybe even dead. The bartender lined up a dozen or so empty glasses. Starting with whisky, he poured a shot of every different kind of hard liquor he had into each glass: rum, gin, vodka, scotch . . . When finished, he opened a bottle of cream de menthe and topped off each drink. He handed a glass to the captain, who held the finished product up and into the light. Using his index finger and thumb, he slowly rotated the glass, inspecting to make certain the green color of the drink was consistent and worthy of consumption by Green Berets and friends. He nodded to the bartender, who then distributed the remaining glasses. When everyone at the bar had a glass raised, the captain chugged the drink and we followed.

"That's a *green gasser*, gentlemen!" he shouted and we all cheered.

"Your lieutenant is kind of quiet," I said to the Special Forces captain.

"Show him!" the captain ordered.

The lieutenant lifted up his shirt, then ripped a bandage loose exposing a ten-inch scar, scarlet in color, where recent stitches were pulled tight. His stomach was sunken. It looked like he was missing internal parts.

"Damn, he belongs in a hospital," I said.

"That's why we are here!" the captain roared. "The fucking REMFs (rear-echelon motherfuckers) wanted to ship him Stateside, but he wanted to be with his troops."

The lieutenant patted the bandage back in place. He released his shirt.

"Gotta see a man about a horse," he said. He turned and walked away.

The captain moved into the vacated space. He placed an arm over my shoulders.

"I call him Lieutenant Gut Check," he said, giggling. I nodded and smiled. "He's a hell of a soldier," the captain continued. "We've got a little camp up against the Cambode border, right beside a rubber plantation. Every night we get hit with mortars. They are lobbed in from that fucking French-owned plantation. Gut Check puts on his dress uniform. He managed to get some flowers from somewhere. He knocked on the front door of the villa. 'Excuse me, sir,' Gut Check said as he handed the Frenchman the flowers.

"'Oh, how nice. For *moi*?' the Frenchman said.

"'Yes. You see, I'm from that Special Forces camp just down the road . . .' Gut Check stopped talking. The silence is freaking out the Frog. Gut Check lifted him off the floor and pulled him in real tight, making sure Froggy is paying attention.

"'If we take one more mortar from your plantation, I will grow bamboo shoots up your asshole! *Comprenz-voux*, motherfucker?' Gut Check threw the Frog to the floor, turned, and walked out. We never took another mortar from that plantation. In fact, I heard Frenchy booked a flight—di-di moi'd—the fuck out of here the very next day."

There were cheers in the background. I turned toward them just in time to see Walrus the Lessor chug another green gasser. On the other side of the room a rowdy crowd pawed and roared at Joey, trying to get him to move from the chair belonging to the helicopter battalion commander. The Walrus grabbed me by my elbow.

"Gotta go!" he said.

Buddha and a couple of his pilots rescued Joey, and we all formed up behind Father William who departed with some warm words for one of the Army pilots.

"Go fuck a duck!" he shouted as we withdrew to our jeeps.

We headed back to do the opposite side of hootch row. I jumped in the lead jeep with Father William, Joey, the Walrus, and a few other reprobates, peasants, heathens, heretics, and limp dicks, as Father William had labeled us. No one passed Joey on our way back home. Joey jammed on the brakes. Some of us disembarked; others were launched due to the sudden stop; while others were simply pushed to the dirt. We were all laughing. It felt so good. I smiled as I picked gravel from my palms. It was dark out now, darker than I have ever seen it back in the world. The Walrus tripped. He ripped his flight suit and some flesh out of his thigh. "It's so motherfucking dark here," he said, "I feel like I'm crawling through a tunnel of sphincter muscles."

"Do you pray with that mouth, heathen?" Father William asked. The Walrus gave him the finger.

"Age or I.Q.?" Father William asked.

"It's the number of times I'm gonna take any more shit from you!" the Walrus answered.

"Oooh! Fear that!" Father William responded.

We began to work our way back down the other side of hootch row. The procession was now so long that when the lead element exited, the rear element entered. When we got to the *Buzzard*'s hootch, the place where I spent my first terror-filled night in Viet Nam, my feet would not cross the threshold. All the alcohol that I had consumed in the last ten or so hours, and the nearly eight months I lived in-country, had not dulled the foreboding feeling of dread that consumed me as soon as the door to the hootch was opened. I felt like I would be struck dead if I set one foot inside. So, I sat outside, with my ass in the mud and my back up against the outside wall of the *Buzzard*'s hootch, and I relived that night: hearing the sounds of outgoing artillery, hearing the voice of an American pilot threatening to kill me. But most of all, I felt the humiliation of being a scared little boy, alone and scared shitless in a violent foreign land. I felt like I didn't deserve to be called a combat vet.

The Walrus joined me. "You know," he said, "the guys I worked with on the border went out in the boonies for three weeks; then the brass brought them back in. They roped off a big area, took anything that might be used as a weapon away from them, fed them, and let them drink booze until they never wanted to drink again. Then, they hosed them down, paid them, sent them to the PX, and sent their young asses back out into the bush. What a miserable fucking way to live, huh?"

"Yeah," I said. "We got it made in the shade."

"Fucking A!" he said.

We sat in silence, listening to a chorus of drunken pilots singing rock music backed up by the occasional roar of jet engines and outgoing artillery.

In honor of Big Al, the Kiddies' Pal, Father William led a gaggle of troops to the top of the hootch's roof and was positioning them for a mortar stomp that ended with more men sliding down the sloped metal roof and falling on the ground than stomping.

The Walrus spoke. "I was at a fire support base once. They did a thing called a *mad minute*. At a specified time, every gun on the base was fired for one full minute. Jesus it was terrifying . . . and fun too. I got to fire a *fifty*. Rat-a-tat-tat-tat! Only for one minute. Can you imagine? You're Charlie sitting outside the perimeter waiting to launch a *sapper* attack and suddenly, without any warning, every fucking rifle, mortar, tube—anything with a barrel—starts pouring lead at you?"

"Yeah, kind of like shopping the day after Thanksgiving."

"One day," the Walrus said, "I was flying around bored. So I called up the TOC and said: 'Ready to copy a *Papa Romeo*?'

"'Roger,' they replied.

"'I've got 500 *Papas* moving to the *Sierra Whisky*,' I said.

"'Roger, we copy; 500 Papas moving to the *Sierra Whisky*.'

"'That's affirmative,' I said.

"About ten minutes later I called them back and asked: 'Do you know what a *Papa Romeo* is?'

"'No,' they answered.

"'It's a parrot report!' There was a long pause, then: 'Geez, I just sent someone to wake up the old man and tell him we had 500 *Papas* moving to the *Sierra Whisky*.'"

I laughed.

"What a fucked-up war, huh?" I said.

We ended up back at our hootch where Walrus the Lesser tossed back another shot, and he just kept going until he was flat on his back upon the hootch floor. He was out cold and completely rigid. We stood over him, staring at him as if waiting for Father William to say a few words over him. He did.

"For Christ's sake, move him before rigor mortis sets in!" Nobody moved. He was Father William's friend. No one else knew him.

"Toss the Loser, I mean Lesser, in a bunk," Father William ordered. "He is fucking up our drinking." Two TWAT pilots—one grabbed his ankles; the other held him by the back of his neck—lifted his laid-out body out of the barroom and onto a spare bunk. The blowout continued. There were several toasts to Walrus the Lessor. After all, he more than held his own against the Green Berets.

"To the Lessor. He represented us well!"

"Hear! Hear!"

About five minutes later, Captain America showed up and said, "I think your friend is dead."

We walked to his room where the Lesser was splattered facedown on the floor.

"He did a half-roll off the top bunk. Excellent!" Father William said.

Joey stooped, rolled him over, and listened for a sign of life. "Well, he ain't dead," Joey said.

"Press-to-test his eyeballs," Father William suggested, a procedure we used in our airplanes to check malfunctioning lights on our instrument panels. "I can give him last rites," Father William continued. "Throw him back up there. And this time tie him in," Father William ordered. "He's interrupting our drinking."

Having secured the body, the entourage moved back to the barroom but I kept going. It had been a classic pub crawl but, as Joey would say, "I had the claw." I collapsed on top of my bunk and fell asleep.

I stirred when the door opened and the light was switched on.

"Anyone here know a guy called Father William?" a voice said.

I sat up on the edge of my bed. "Yeah, I do," I answered. "Why do you ask?"

"Some guys in the *Buzzard*'s hootch are getting ready to kill him!"

"Show me," I said. I followed him out of my room, through the barroom, out the side door, down hootch row to the *Buzzard*'s hootch, and into their barroom.

"Oh, fuck you, peasant!" I heard Father William say. He was surrounded by a group of angry pilots.

"And you, and you, and you," he continued, while pointing to several of his tormentors. "You don't know dick shit, any of you. You bunch of troglodytes! You cretins! You walking dildos!"

"Pleasant fellow, your friend," the man who woke me said as I moved into the huddle.

"Come on, Father; let's go home," I said as I put my arm around him.

"You a friend of this asshole?" a big man asked me.

"Yes!" And again I felt the fear, not because of the man's size but rather a re-living of the terror that consumed me in this hootch on my first night in-country.

"You better get his ass out of here before I knock him on his ass!"

"Come on, he is a priest," I joked, but no one laughed.

"Yeah, fuckers!" Father yelled. "And I won't be giving you last rites after I kick the shit out of you!"

"Some priest," the big man answered. "Get him the fuck out of here!"

I pushed Father William toward the door. He growled at one man and made a half-hearted attempt to reach over me and get to him. The man growled back. I pushed him through the crowd. He pumped his middle finger on each hand high in the air as we staggered toward the door.

"Fucking heathens!"

"Yeah, yeah. Just keep going!" they shouted. He went limp as we exited the barroom. I could not hold him up. He slumped to the ground. And then he started to sob.

"How come everyone loves you and they all hate me?" he mumbled. I held him with one of my hands around his bicep as my other hand clasped his shoulder. I held him like that for a long time, until he grew weary from crying, and then I walked him home and put him to bed. I stopped in our barroom and tossed down a shot of whiskey. I drank it because I felt fear. I drank it because I felt sadness for my friend. I drank it because I was angry that this shithole of a country could reduce a proud man to a sniveling crybaby. I drank it because I still had many months left in-country. And I drank it so maybe I could get back to sleep.

The next morning, Doc entered my room and shook me awake. I was lying on my bunk in a beer- and mud-soaked flight suit, boots unzipped but still on, and my dick hanging out from when I most likely took a piss sometime during the night and forgot to put it away.

"I see you are all ready for our little operation," the doc said as he opened his black bag and pulled out a syringe about the size of a toilet plunger. I sat up. My temples felt like the chained Sampson had pulled the pillars down on me, but I was happy that I was hung over and could scarcely give a shit what anyone would do to my body, for whatever it was it would be an improvement over how I felt now.

"Stand up and take it like a man," Doc said.

"It looks like it is going to hurt," I replied.

"A little pinprick," he replied. "No pun intended."

I turned my head to my right and looked down at the floor.

"Yeah, a little prick, for the prick with the little prick," I mumbled with complete surrender.

He stuck the needle in and pushed the plunger—like he was chambering a bullet—allowing a deadening agent to flow into my Johnson. Then he removed the needle, dropped the syringe in his bag, and pulled out a scalpel.

"To shave the little growths," he said, "free up your Johnson for future business."

And as he shaved I could hear Joey in my head saying, "Circumcise the lad! Give him a clear head for business."

"You know," the doc said, "that friend of Father William's who fell out of his top bunk last night?"

"Yeah."

"He broke his nose."

"Uh, huh."

"He wouldn't let me set it until after he flew his mission this morning. I don't know how you guys do it."

"We stay drunk, Doc."

Day after day, I flew up and down and across our A.O.; north to the Thumbtack, then east along a river flowing out of the Thumbtack to an abandoned village. Occasionally, I dropped down on the deck, soaring low over the huts, and I wondered what had happened here. My instincts told me that the V.C. visited it one night and intimidated, indoctrinated, or killed the elders; scrounged for food; and recruited at gunpoint all its young men. The peasants were defenseless. They just wanted to live out their lives peacefully. Then some American general who lived in a villa in Saigon or maybe a townhouse in Washington, D.C., concocted the Strategic Hamlet program, and the villagers were forced, again most likely at gunpoint, to move to an area that would be better for them. That's what the generals said. The villagers moved. They were crammed into a place of squalor, filth, and sickness; a place where we could keep a watchful eye on them; and a place that was easier for us to defend.

Hadn't we tried this before? The only difference once again was the choice of words used to describe it. The strategic hamlet was nothing more than a small reservation. If all this had transpired, then why wasn't this village destroyed, wiped off the map, erased from the earth? This village was an enigma, the only one I had ever seen with hootches still standing. The encroaching jungle and the elements had reclaimed several of the structures, but others looked worn but intact. I never asked anyone if they knew what had happened here. I'm not sure I wanted to know. I continued to fly over it, studying it, analyzing it: hoping I would discover its secret. If I was a Viet Namese peasant, I would go to this village and hide in it with my family and live out the war peacefully.

There was a large structure, perhaps built to accommodate village meetings, maybe weddings and funerals. On one side, the thatched roof had collapsed. I would live in the other half. I would partition and reinforce the good side, and leave the other side in disrepair and looking like no one lived there. A slight waterfall in the river—just enough for audible enjoyment—would provide purified water and excellent fishing. I could throw a line with a bucket attached to one end and dip for water from that hootch there. I pointed the left wing of my airplane at a hovel nearest the river. Under the structures held up by stilts, I would plant several small, covert vegetable gardens. I would restore laughter in the rooms, laughter at simple things like listening to my eldest son say, "Dad, I swallowed up." There would be no alcohol, no swearing, no orders—given or taken—no *nightdreams*, no deaths, no war. It would be paradise. I would have Father William over to bless it and Joey over to remind me that this peace was international.

And then, suddenly, I realized that this was exactly what I was doing now; I was flying over it to ride out the war peacefully. It was my sanctuary, and that was the reason I never asked what happened here. If I did, they would tell me to destroy it. Destroy this haven, this abandoned village sitting on the edge of a river.

I would bet that when the inhabitants, who had lived here for generations, were forced to vacate it, they were disconsolate. They watched as families were broken apart, as guns replaced gaiety, as bomb craters replaced rice paddies, as fear replaced solemnity, as violence replaced love, as foreign occupation forces replaced village elders, as hovels in a refugee camp replaced their bucolic homes on the banks of this river. Of course, as Americans, we had done this before, with the forced relocation of the Cherokee Indians and their "Trail of Tears."

"*Smoky* forty-four, *Smoky* forty."

"Forty-four, forty go."

"I haven't heard from you for a while. State location."

"I'm near the Thumbtack."

"Roger, forty copies. Time to kill some Cong. I have a fire mission for you. Are you ready to copy?"

"*Smoky* forty-four is ready."

That night, when we congregated, Father William asked a question.

"Know why they call it *the Viet Nam conflict*?"

"No, why?" Buddha answered.

"They call it a conflict because it is unwinnable. A war you win or lose, but a conflict denotes a draw, stalemate, tie, everybody back to square one."

"It sure is *stale*, alright," Buddha said. And we all laughed. Joey handed out the beers.

"Enjoy it, mates. We are running low," he said.

"Here, use my ration card," the Walrus said as he tossed it to Joey.

"Anything that is worth a shit is rationed over here," Father William snarled.

"Ain't that the truth!" Buddha answered.

"And anything you need, you can't get!" the Walrus said.

"Ain't that the truth!" Buddha answered.

"Saw a couple of TWAT pilots sitting at the bar this afternoon. They had gas masks on and were doing shots. They would unhook their masks, toss a shot down, and then hook it back up again. It was kind of funny," I said. The group chuckled. We admired creative drinking.

"The U.S. gets this order from Russia," Buddha said. "Twelve grosses of rubbers, twelve inches long by six inches in diameter."

"Huh?" the Walrus said. "It takes a big fucking prick to fill a rubber that size." He held his hands up, making a circle with his thumbs and index fingers.

Buddha continued, "The State Department figures this is a propaganda stunt, but they don't know what to do with it. All our big mucky mucks are sitting around a conference table discussing it."

The Walrus scratched his head to imitate the mucky mucks, and we did the same.

"Finally, the guy who was hired to pour the coffee said: 'That's easy. Package them up, stamp them *medium*, and send 'em off.'"

Hee, hee! Hee, hee, hee!

At 3:35 the next day, I spotted the Walrus flying slow and low, below 1,500 feet A.G.L. or above ground level, and therefore vulnerable to small arms fire. His focus was on the ground, so he did not see me coming. I rolled in, picking up speed as I did. My objective was to make a high-speed—high-speed being a relative term when driving an Oscar Deuce—pass alongside of him, maybe scare him a bit, to discourage him from flying so low without a high bird monitoring his position. When I flew by him, I was still in a steep dive, and as I passed I instinctively rolled my aircraft, an aircraft not stressed for acrobatics, an aircraft that should never be rolled at such a low altitude, but I did it without thinking; it just felt like it was the natural thing to do.

"God, that was beautiful," the Walrus said over the radio.

"Get off the deck! And stay off it!" I yelled back into my radio. I said the words with such force, I thought I heard them echo across the airwaves.

"Don't do that!" I told him again when we were both on the ground. And I repeated Jefferson's mantra: "Your job is to stay alive. This war is unwinnable and not worth your life."

His mustache quivered slightly, but he said nothing. He stared at me for a while, and then he walked away; and I realized he heard but would not heed.

The next day, I flew low, just above the trees, looking for signs of enemy activity. Jefferson would have chewed my ass for doing it, but he was gone. Not gone, but home—back in *the world* I assumed, for I had not heard from him. The Walrus watched from his perch above, on the lookout for enemy gunners who might want to take a potshot at me. We had reached an agreement: if we were going to troll for enemy guns, then I would be the low bird. I did not tell him that I could not stand the pain if he was the low bird and something happened to him; I'd much rather sacrifice my life than live with his death.

"Get off the deck," he said over our radio frequency. "I'm bingo fuel and need to head back to base."

"Yeah, yeah," I replied. I had spotted a few trails, and I was following them, hoping they would lead me to a base camp.

"I mean it," he said. "Get off the deck."

"Okay," I replied. I banked my aircraft to the left, heading back to pick up the trail again. I was now *jinking*, making rapid turns to the left and right, making my airplane a difficult target in case the bad guys wanted to take a potshot at me.

"Ah, there's the trail," I said to myself, as I was able to again see it through the trees. I was starting my turn to the left when I heard an explosion under my right wing. The concussion forced my airplane upside down, with my nose pointed at a large tree trunk. I was inverted, and I was so close to the tree that the trunk filled my windscreen. I knew that recovery was impossible in the time I had left before I crashed into it. My mind began to whirl. I wondered if this was how Billy bought it. Then, I visualized an officer knocking on my wife's door. She opened it while cradling my youngest son, my oldest son standing at her side. "We regret to inform you . . ." the officer said as I awaited impact. Then, an eerie, strange, perhaps miraculous thing happened. Somehow, I was flying straight and level; my altimeter read 1,500 feet. "What happened? Had I died?" I wasn't sure. I checked my instruments again, and I noticed my hands shaking. Something must have happened. It was like there was a time warp; one second I was upside down and awaiting impact, and the next second I was safe. Did it happen? How could it have happened? Was I dead? Was I crazy?

"*Smoky* four-four, *Smoky* four-two. Are you off the deck yet?"

"*Smoky* four-four, *Smoky* four-zero. State your position." What happened? Obviously, I was flying on the deck. *Smoky* four-two's radio call confirmed that.

"*Smoky* four-four, *Smoky* four-zero. Do you read me?" But how had I missed that tree? In my mind, I could still see it filling my windscreen.

"*Smoky* four-four, *Smoky* four-zero on guard. If you read me, come up *Smoky* frequency."

"*Smoky* four-zero, *Smoky* four-four. I read you loud and clear. I'm heading home plate."

"Roger four-four. You had me scared there for a minute."

"Sorry about that, four-zero."

What could have caused that explosion? Maybe an R.P.G. (rocket-propelled grenade)?

But no one had ever talked about having an R.P.G. fired at them. And then I remembered I had rotated the yoke full left, so far left that my fist holding the yoke was up against my lap, and my left foot mashed the rudder pedal to the floor. I actually recalled slouching down in my seat to make sure the rudder peddle was tight to the floor and could go no further. But why would I put in left aileron instead of right aileron, which would have rolled the airplane back to where it was before the explosion? Nothing made any sense. I landed the aircraft. The Walrus was waiting for me.

"Have you ever heard of anyone having an R.P.G. shot at them?"

"No," he said. "Why do you ask?"

"Just wondering."

"Did something happen up there? You look pale."

"Nah, just wondering," I replied.

When we got to the hootch, I told Frick to take me off the flying schedule for the next two days, for on the third day, I would be departing for Hawaii, and I wanted to be alive for it.

Earl drove me to Saigon where I would be boarding an airplane for my trip to Hawaii.

"Thank you," I said as I removed my small bag from the back of the jeep. "It seems strange to be wearing a khaki uniform and shoes instead of combat boots."

"You look good. Have a great time," he said as we shook hands. I listened to the jeep as Earl shifted gears. I felt a smile forming on my face. Like Jefferson, he drove the jeep like he flew: mechanical, robotic, devoid of feeling. I walked into a building, stood in line, and when I reached the front I traded in my MPCs for U.S. greenbacks. I stacked the money, mentally thanked those who gave it to me in poker and dice games, folded it, and stashed most of it in my pocket. When I was sure no one was looking, I jammed the rest in my right sock.

"Step over here," an airman said. And I found myself in yet another line. This one led to the men's room and when I got to the front, another airman handed me a bottle and said: "Piss in it." He gave the order like he outranked me, which he didn't, and it pissed me off. But he did have power over me. He could stop me from getting on that bird and out of this shithole and on to Hawaii to see my wife. He ordered me to piss while he watched me; I wanted to aim it at his leg. I was so angry, I was surprised the piss was not crimson in color.

"Drug test," he said as he held the cup up to the light.

"Three bags full," I replied as I walked away.

I was still fuming when I climbed the stairs to the freedom bird, entered, nodded to a smiling stewardess, and dragged my bag down the aisle looking for my assigned seat. I passed rows of Army enlisted men with cherub faces; men who, like me, got caught up in a vortex that taught them how to kill and then deposited them in a strange stretch of land, a land fraught with death traps and old men who used men as bait.

"Would you like a pillow, lieutenant?" a made-up, young lady with round eyes and dressed in a blue uniform asked.

"Yes."

I tucked the pillow under my head, for I planned to sleep the entire flight so that I could somehow reverse the twelve-hour difference between Viet Nam time and my wife's Central Standard Time. But when I closed my eyes, all I saw was a massive tree before me and I was a millisecond away from being crushed. The inside of the airliner was dark when I snapped awake. I sat upright in my seat, restricted only by my lap belt. My left arm whipped through the air and my left foot pressed against the seat in front of me.

"Hey, what the hell?" said the young troop in the seat in front of me—the seat I had kicked—as he turned to glare at me.

"Are you alright?" the trooper beside me asked.

I did not answer. Instead I excused myself and walked back to the galley. Two stewardesses stood beside the metal containers.

"Could I have a cup of coffee," I asked the prettiest one.

"Absolutely. Cream and sugar?"

I smiled. She looked like sugar tasted. "Black, please," I said.

I cradled the cup in my hands, waiting for it to cool.

"Will you be meeting your wife in Hawaii?" she asked.

I nodded yes.

"And the best man at our wedding," I said, "my roommate from college. We both took advanced R.O.T.C. And we partied a lot. Too much maybe

. . . It was going to take us five years or more to graduate. We were in no hurry." I took a sip. Both stews waited for me to continue. "Winter quarter the R.O.T.C. department contacted us. They said if we didn't graduate at the end of our fifth year, we would be drafted as enlisted men. That built a fire under us. We found out the only way we could graduate was to take and pass a correspondence course in Spanish from the University of Indiana. Did you ever have a nightmare where you were taking a test and you were not prepared?" They both nodded and smiled. "I managed a D and graduated. My roommate flunked. I got Viet Nam. He got Hawaii."

There was a long silence.

"So I will be seeing him there," I said.

"And your wife too," the pretty stewardess said.

"And my wife too," I said. I drank my coffee and returned to my seat.

My God, I got excited when I heard the pilot announce: "We have begun our descent into Honolulu."

My first thought was of Jefferson and all the time he spent perfecting his announcements from the cockpit. But that didn't last long, nor did that thought excite me. It was the idea of seeing my wife, the mother of my two sons, and the thought of clean white sheets and sweet-smelling air and food I hadn't tasted in more than six months. My stomach felt like it was experiencing just the right amount of tickling and my head felt like it had been emptied and was waiting for something very special to enter. I could feel a smile on my face, and it did not leave but only became bigger and brighter when touchdown, taxiing, stopping, and disembarking occurred.

I thanked the crew as I exited the airplane. I walked down the stairs and across the tarmac, and when I looked up I saw my roommate. We hugged. It felt strange to hug another man. We talked and laughed and drank a few beers for the next three hours while waiting for my wife to land. The tickle in my stomach increased during the wait; it increased so much I could hardly stand it. When it was time, we walked to the railing and studied the faces of the passengers now deplaning, looking for her—no, that's not her—thinking each time the next face would be hers. We waited and watched until all passengers had entered the building.

"Could we have missed her?" I asked my friend.

"Did you see her?" I asked my friend.

"Is it possible that she wasn't on that airplane?" I asked my friend.

"I don't know," he answered. "I studied every face that got off that airplane and I didn't see her."

And then someone tapped me on my shoulder. I turned. I did not recognize her—my wife—who had dyed her hair or was wearing a wig or something, and I felt lousy when I took her in my arms because I didn't recognize her.

"I dyed my hair," she said when I released her. "I thought I would surprise you."

I could not answer. I took her hand and we walked to luggage where we again waited, this time for her bag to appear. She dropped my hand and opened her purse and pulled out my wedding ring. I put it on. It felt strange to have it on, for a man in combat traveled sterile, never carrying or wearing anything that might give the enemy an edge in case of capture. We gathered her bag and my friend drove us in his car to our hotel. We checked in, drank some beers, and talked on the hotel room's balcony overlooking the ocean. After a couple hours, our friend left.

"I'll pick you up tomorrow about ten and show you the island," he said just before he walked out of the room. I had my arm around my wife as we said good-bye, and when the door closed we kissed and made love.

"I'm hungry," she said as we showered. She stepped out and wrapped a towel around herself; I stood and let the water pound against my body. It was the first time I felt clean in a long, long time. We dressed, rode the elevator downstairs, and ate supper outside in the veranda: hot food, warm breezes, cool jazz music, clean skin, linen napkins, and a beautiful woman. I felt that tickle in my stomach once again. We finished eating, ambled along the beach, kissed in the moonlight, and rode the elevator back to our room where we made love once again.

"I'm sleepy," she said. And she fell asleep in my arms. It was nine o'clock in the evening her time, 2:00 a.m. Hawaiian time, and 9:00 in the morning my time. I stared at the ceiling, checked the clock periodically. When it read 3:00 a.m., I rose up, walked out on the balcony, and smoked a cigarette, then another, then another. I stepped back in the room to study her. She radiated peacefulness, and I wondered if I would ever again be able to rest and sleep at the same time. At 5:30 Hawaiian time, I pulled the sheet back and crawled in with her, and at 7:00 I sat straight up, frightened by a massive tree glued to the insides of my eyelids.

"Are you alright?" she asked.

I laughed.

"I had a *nightdream*," I replied. Exhausted, I fell back on the pillow and at 9:00 a.m. Hawaiian time, she woke me with a kiss, coffee, and a cinnamon roll. I stared at the roll for a long time, trying to remember its taste, and when it would not come to me I ate it in small bites, savoring both the taste and the moment. We made love again, and when I got out of the shower, my roommate arrived. We traveled the island, stopping occasionally for a swim and food, and more often for beer. We laughed and talked of old distant times when we were young, somewhat innocent, and brimming with life. And when the sun set, our best man got up to leave. We said long good-byes to him, as my wife and I would depart for Maui in the early a.m. Hawaiian time.

Maui was spectacular. We rented a car and drove the island, from the developed end to the pristine end, and in the middle we drove to the top of the dormant volcano Haleakala. We walked up to the edge and then we walked down inside the cone where I kicked some rubble. Grey dust rose, touched, and merged with the swirling grey clouds. It looked like a large bomb crater dusted with Agent Orange. A tour group arrived. I studied the faces and movements of the American tourists and decided they didn't know there was a war being waged, and suddenly I felt nervous, closed in, cornered, and threatened. I had to get away from them. We climbed back over the edge where I noticed a guest book. I walked over to it and read several of the glowing comments beside names and hometowns. I took the pen in hand, wrote our names, and in the comment section I wrote: "Sure beats the hell out of Viet Nam." We got back into our rent-a-car and started our descent, heading downhill for the first time since I landed. "What are you thinking about?" I asked. "Oh, nothing," she replied. We ate supper and returned to our room. We skipped the lovemaking and tried to talk. I wanted to hear all about the kids; she wanted to forget the burdens of motherhood. I was tense, spring-loaded. She was relaxed, sleepy. She wanted to talk about the war; I did not. There was a long stretch of silence, and when I could endure it no longer, I stood and walked out to the balcony where I brooded with beers and cigarettes while she slept.

The next day we embraced the sun and sand and watched whales blowing fountains of water while they frolicked in the ocean before us.

"I want to do something different tonight," I said to her.

"What would that be?" she answered.

"I want you to sit at the bar with a drink, and I will come in and try to pick you up."

"Sounds interesting," she replied.

She wore a red dress that evening and looked stunning sitting at the bar all alone. I watched her from the doorway and when a man approached her, I rushed in front of him and sat on the empty stool next to her. We talked and drank. She ordered some kind of lady drink, a strawberry daiquiri with an umbrella or something like that, and I drank beer. We talked and laughed and imbibed.

"Would you like to come to my room?" I asked when I felt the time was right.

"Maybe," she replied.

"Okay," I said. Then I beckoned the barkeep.

"Can I help you?" he asked.

"Check please," I said, taking her answer as a yes.

There was a line of clothes, both men's and women's, from the door to the bed; only we never made it to the bed but instead lay on the floor where again we made love, with the ocean breezes from the open sliding glass doors gently flowing over my back and cooling my overheated body. We slept together, there on the floor, for the entire night, and when I felt a chill I pulled the bedspread down and wrapped our bodies in it. We were both now on Hawaii time.

When I awoke the next morning, instead of the bliss I felt the night before, I felt angry; angry because I realized that soon I would have to get back on that airplane and return to Viet Nam. I desperately tried to push this thought from my mind, or put it in some rarely used niche, but I could not. It was more than a thought; it was a fact.

"What's the matter?" my wife asked several times over our remaining days. I could not answer. How could I explain to her the things I was experiencing in Viet Nam? I couldn't. How could I tell her that when I looked at her, I saw her answering the door when the officers came to inform her of my death? Why ruin her day? Why cause her needless worry? She had her hands full with the children and running a household.

I could feel the distance between us growing, and even though we were inches apart, the gulf seemed to be greater than the miles between my hootch and our home back in the world. I hurt knowing I was the cause of her pain. I physically tried to close the distance between us, but the emotional distance loomed large. The magic had disappeared, vanished, dissipated. And now I could not wait to get back to Viet Nam, where I had no feelings of love. The jungle and the war had encircled me and my *steel onion* was the cause of her tears.

I tried to comfort her, but all I could think of to say was what the grunts said when one of theirs had been killed: "It don't mean nothing." So that is what I said, nothing. And while I held her, I realized I felt more comfortable in the jungle. I felt exhilaration there. I felt respected there. I felt like I belonged there, and my soul remained there even though I was thousands of miles away from there. I felt unworthy here. I felt like I would taint her if I touched her, but I never told her these things.

I remember kissing her and returning my wedding ring before I left to board the airplane back to Viet Nam. It was an unemotional kiss, and again I was unable to speak. I watched as the cherubs kissed their ladies good-bye. And then we walked—the cherubs and I, a gristly old man of twenty-six years—like cattle in groups of one across the tarmac. I could feel her eyes upon me, but I could not look back. If I did, I would never have gotten on that airplane.

The flight back was solemn; no one spoke, only the dull roar of the jet engines playing back up to my thoughts. How did I miss hitting that tree? Why did I put in left aileron and left rudder? What happened between impending impact and recovery at 1,500 feet? *Rrrmmmm* . . .

"How was your R & R?" Earl asked as I jumped in the jeep. "Did you get plenty of rest and relaxation?"

"More like repair and re-evaluation," I replied as I looked around at the guns, and bunkers, and barbed wire; and a sense of calm rushed through my body. "And I can't wait to get these khakis and low-quarter shoes off, and my cammies and combat boots back on."

Chapter 5
BACK TO NORMAL

When I was flying and I had no airstrikes scheduled, I had time to think. Inevitably, the tree I should have crashed into worked its way back to the front of my brain. I still didn't understand why I put in left aileron and rudder, when right aileron and rudder would have been the normal response. I reenacted my actions, snap rolling my airplane until I was nearly upside down with my nose below the horizon, and every time I tried it, I instinctively rolled it back using right aileron and right rudder because that was the shortest distance back to wings level. But that day, my memory was that I used full left aileron and full left rudder, and then I blacked out. I tried it again, and again, and again. And when I sat on my stool at the hootch bar, I performed the maneuvers again—only this time inside my head—with the exception of my left arm, which rolled and pulled the airplane, and my left leg, which shot straight out. Sometimes, my reaction was so violent, I slid off my stool as I tried to get more extension on my rudder pedal. In my dreams, I always crashed into the tree.

"What you do?" Miss Sam asked.

"Oh, nothing," I replied.

"You have good time with your wife in Hawaii?"

I nodded yes. It was easier to lie with my head than my mouth. I turned my head as Joey walked in.

"Yeah, he *boom-boom* real good," Joey said.

"*Numbah* ten! You speak *numbah* ten!" Miss Sam said.

"What were you doing," Joey asked, "with the hands?" He mimicked my action.

"Oh, I was just wondering why I put in left aileron and left rudder."

"You were doing a roll. Hey, Miss Sam, give me six to go," Joey said. Then he looked at me.

"I have to fly out to division and spend the night." He stuffed the six beers under his arms. "Something big is up. Hey, why are chickens so ugly?"

I shrugged my shoulders. "Damned if I know."

"You'd be ugly too if your pecker was on your face."

Hee, hee! Hee, hee, hee!

And he walked out.

His words rolled around my brain. Not the "ugly" words but the "You were doing a roll." Is it possible that I would roll the airplane so close to the ground? And if so, why? Let's say I did roll the airplane. So instinctively, I rolled the airplane through 360 degrees. I was now flying with my right hand as my airplane.

"You *dinky-dao*," Miss Sam said as she wrinkled her nose, nearly closing her slanted eyes.

So I rolled it through 360 degrees since I knew I would crash . . . there wasn't enough time to roll back wings level after the explosion . . . so I rolled left, in an airplane that wasn't designed to roll, because it was the fastest way to wings level . . . "Then what happened?" I said this out loud as I maneuvered my hands. "My nose was below the horizon line . . ." I returned my hand to straight and level, palms down. "There was the explosion under my right wing, which flopped me upside down, with the nose of the airplane below the horizon." Again I moved my hand through a left roll. I stopped to think. Then I performed the maneuver again, again, and again, trying to visualize what had happened. "If I rolled left . . . . then I could start my pull early . . ." I tilted my hand down halfway through the turn. "But then what happened? And why didn't I hit the tree?" My head was starting to hurt; the pain was just behind my eyeball. It felt like someone had my head in their hands and was trying to compress it. "It doesn't make any sense!" I said out loud. I drained the beer from my can and hoisted the empty to the garbage can. I missed. Miss Sam stooped to pick it up.

"You bad shot!" she said. Two TWAT pilots walked in.

"Yeah, fuck you," I whispered, and I walked out.

Earl called a meeting in my room. The Walrus and I sat on my bed; Earl sat in the chair; Frick and Frack stood.

"We've got this new directive," Earl said. "There's an airstrip called Kotum, just this side of the Cambodian border, and every time a re-supply bird lands, they get shelled. So TASS wants us to give it as much cover as we can, which means we orbit over the fucking airstrip for as many daylight hours as we can. You two will take that." He pointed to Frick and Frack.

"Yes sir," Frack said. The Walrus and I chuckled.

"They have also decided to bring in some plows to level that area to the south where we've lost so many helicopters. The rest of us will be working that mission. Any questions?"

"Yeah," the Walrus asked. "When are the Viet Namese going to take things over? They can have my piece-of-shit airplane anytime."

"Don't know, haven't heard," Earl answered.

"I'll take the noon flight," I said.

"I'll relieve him," the Walrus said.

"When I am done, there won't be any war left," I replied. "You'll be able to float on your back and crack shells on your tummy, Walrus."

"Fucking sea otters do that!" he said.

"Okay, let's go drink," Earl ordered.

The time was 1530. I had just landed after flying around, under, and through thunderstorms all the way back to Bien Hoa. The weather was so bad that even the Rome plows had shut down. I radioed back and told the Walrus to abort his mission. No sense challenging Mother Nature; she usually won. Now I sat on my corner barroom stool, stinking of sweat and enjoying a cold beer. I was all alone, since the staff-weenies were still flying their desks. Miss Sam entered, walked behind the bar, opened another beer, and set it in front of me.

"How did you know I wanted one?" I asked.

"You always drink and talk *numbah* ten, every time."

"You're like an old schoolmarm for Christ's sake."

"What that?" she asked. I did not answer. Instead the phone rang. I had never heard that phone ring before. In fact, I didn't even know it was there. She lifted it up with the receiver still in the cradle and placed it beside my beer. I stared at it. It was still ringing. I did not want to answer it. It was like I was still playing that game with Jefferson. Whoever answered the phone first would have to answer all further calls. I placed my hands over my ears.

"Stop ringing goddammit!"

"See *numbah* ten. You speak *numbah* ten all the time."

"How about Buddhadamn then, for Christ's sake?"

Ten, eleven, twelve rings. I finally lifted the handset and spoke.

"Hello, is Joe there?" I said.

"What?" the voice at the other end of the line replied.

"Is Joe there?" I repeated.

"No."

"Okay, I'll call back later." And I hung up. It wasn't but a second and it started to ring again. At eight rings I picked up and said: "This is Joe, any calls for me?"

"What? No!"

"Okay. Thank you." And I hung up. It was an old telephone game we played as kids, when we were bored. We would also call any *Wolf* or *Wolves* listed in the phone book late at night, and when they answered we would howl into the telephone until they hung up. The phone rang again. I picked it up, and before I could say anything, I heard: "I'm looking for *Smoky* forty-four."

"By God, you got him. What do you want?" I finished my third beer, pushed the empty toward Miss Sam, and started on my fourth.

"This is Master Sergeant Birmingham. I am the N.C.O.I.C. of maintenance for the 22nd TASS," the voice on the other end said. Hmm, my brain, although foggy, translated non-commissioned officer in charge of maintenance but I did not recognize the voice or the name. He continued talking. "Chief Master Sergeant Zane's father is dying in San Francisco. We have got him manifested on a C-141 scheduled to take off from Tan Son Nhat at 1930, flying direct to San Fran, and we need to get him over there. We got an O-2 gassed up and ready to go."

"Hey, Sarge, I'd like to help you out but I just landed from a mission, the weather is shitty, and I've been drinking. There's a shitload of pilots sitting at desks over at TASS headquarters; why not give a call over there?"

"I'll try." Click. I put the phone back in its cradle and pushed it toward Miss Sam. "Get the fucking thing out of my sight, will you please?" She grabbed it and stowed it under the bar. "*Numbah* ten! *Numbah* ten, all the time *numbah* ten!" she quacked. If she wasn't so pretty, I would have told her to shut the fuck up, like I did to the mamasans every morning until they were trained, and now there was a hush just as soon as I strode into the crapper. But she was, so I didn't.

Two *Daredevil* FACs entered, followed by the Walrus, Earl, and Frick and Frack. Suddenly, I had four beers in me and two more stacked up in front of me. And when the staff-weenies and TWAT pilots showed up, I figured it was time to adjourn to our room. *Ring! Ring! Ring!* I ignored it and Earl picked it up.

"*Smoky* FACs," he said, and then he handed the phone to me.

"Can't get anybody to fly him over there, lieutenant. We are running out of time. You are our last hope," the voice said. I tried to remember how many beers I now had in me; was it six? I started to beg off.

"The man's father is dying."

I was pissed off that none of the weenies would take the flight, and the anger seemed to sober me up. "Okay," I said, "I will be right there."

"Thanks, lieutenant. Just come to the airplane. Everything will be there for you."

"Roger that." I hung up the phone. "Got to go fly," I announced.

"Jesus, the weather is horseshit," Earl said.

"Just going to Saigon, I'll be back in a jiff."

I stepped outside. Stateside summer rain is like a gentle caress from Mother Nature; Southeast Asia monsoon rain is like a snarling slap from Father Time. I pulled my collar up around my neck and waited as the rain swirled past me, then dashed to the jeep, unchained it, started it, and headed for the runway. The rain was so dense at times I could hardly see through it. I was scared to inch forward in my jeep; how the hell was I going to fly in it, I wondered, knowing that fear could turn to terror in a second when flying in extreme weather. But I rationalized. Once airborne, I decided, I would be safe while climbing and turning. It was the descent and landing that might be a heart-starter. I wiped my eyes and wondered how I always managed to get myself into these pickles. I hydroplaned and skidded off the pavement. When the tires grabbed dirt, the jeep lunged forward. I had hydroplaned on the road. What, I wondered again, was it going to be like when I was rolling down the runway? Flashes of lightning illuminated the bottom of churning clouds, the color and consistency of a cauldron of boiling tar. The rumbling thunder sounded like a B-52 strike: continuous explosions of more than one hundred 500-pound bombs. Streak lightning zigzagged its way from ground to clouds. I decided only a fool or a drunk would fly in such weather, and I was both. I would try to fly below the clouds, maybe 200 feet A.G.L. (above ground level). I stopped beside an O-2. There were a slew of top-level sergeants standing beside it. Some stomped their feet; all were soaked. When they saw me, they snapped to and saluted. I felt unworthy. These men had sacrificed twenty to thirty years of their lives, working twelve to fourteen hours a day, seven days a week. I had not yet finished three years. I flew for four hours and drank beer for eight. I returned their salute.

A man with five stripes under and one over stepped forward. "I'm Master Sergeant Birmingham. This is your passenger Chief Master Sergeant Zane." Chief Master Sergeant: the highest rank an enlisted man could achieve. A man twenty-five years my senior, yet three ranks junior to me in grade, stuck out his hand waiting for *me* to shake it. I shook it vigorously. I considered it my honor to shake his hand: his five stripes under with three over meant more to me than any stars on a general's collar. One man earned his pay with his hands; the other with his mouth. One man wore fatigues; the other a suit. One man was more concerned about how he performed; the other was more concerned about how he looked. Jefferson had a saying for it: "How's your picture and sound today?" he might ask.

I identified with the one who worked with his hands. I felt like I worked with my hands. His tool was maybe a wrench, a voltmeter, a can of oil; mine was an airplane; while the general's tool was an order. One man carried a lunch pail to work; the other was a lunch bucket, and most of the time he was out to lunch. I had respect for one, and contempt for the other.

"She's ready to go, lieutenant," the lowest-ranking sergeant, sporting only five stripes, said. I did not doubt him. Where had they been hiding this airplane? I wondered. It looked *cherry*, like it had never been flown. The insides and outsides were both freshly painted and spotless. The pins were pulled. I jumped in, and as I got ready to crank the front engine, I watched as those assembled shook hands and slapped the back of my passenger. He took the seat beside me, and I shook his hand again. Neither of us spoke. I cranked my front and then my rear engine, checking the gauges as I taxied out. Tower advised me the runway was closed due to inclement weather. I ignored them, took the active, and pushed my throttles forward. Streak lightning chased us down the runway, thunder cracked like a sonic boom, and the wind tried to tip us over. Otherwise, the takeoff was uneventful. I struggled to control the airplane. With my brain clouded by alcohol, I was late on all my inputs. Sweat gushed from my pores; the airplane was flying me. I was just hanging on. The aircraft bounced, rolled, and yawed. I leaned forward, as if moving my eyes eight inches closer to the windshield would let me see better. I lowered the nose and followed a road to Saigon. The weather improved as I approached the city; the runway strobes flashed and disappeared into the base of the clouds. I switched to tower frequency.

"Tan Son Nhat tower, *Smoky* four-four. I am an *Oscar Deuce* on short final, requesting landing instructions."

"*Smoky* four-four, Tan Son Nhat tower. Go around. I have an airplane ready to take the active. Break, break. *Guppy* one-four-eight you are cleared for takeoff. O-2 on short final will go around." The C-141 heading for San Francisco, the very airplane my passenger needed to catch, was then cleared for takeoff and I watched as it began to inch forward.

"Roger, Tan Son Nhat tower, *Guppy* one-four-eight is taking the active."

"*Guppy* one-four-eight, *Smoky* four-four. Hold your position. I have a passenger for you."

"Negative, *Smoky*. We have been on a weather hold and we are way behind schedule."

I reached up and armed a rocket.

"*Guppy*, *Smoky* four-four. If you take the active, I will put a Willie Peter right up your ass." I was not kidding. I was drunk enough to put a rocket right beside him if he continued to roll. I would kick right rudder and cook one off. All was quiet. I imagined the conversation inside their cockpit.

"Copilot, do you think he means it?"

"Sure sounds like it to me!"

And the plane abruptly stopped. I flared and nearly shoved my gear into the underbelly of my airplane as we collided with the runway.

"Sorry about that," I said over intercom. I swung my airplane around and taxied up to the giant C-141, which opened a door and gobbled up my passenger.

"Would you have actually fired that Willy Peter, *Smoky*?" *Guppy* asked.

"I would have put one close enough to start your heart, *Guppy*."

"I thought so."

"Thanks for waiting."

"Roger that. Maybe I will see you in a stag bar sometime. I'll buy you a beer."

"I've had too many."

"This is Tan Son Nhat tower. Maybe you two ladies could knock it off so we can get some work done."

I was feeling feisty and proud that I got my man safely on his way home. I keyed my mike.

"Three bags full, buddy." I lit a cigarette and watched *Guppy* one-four-eight disappear into the clouds, and when I was sure his wake turbulence had dissipated, I headed back to Bien Hoa. Once again, I pranged the landing. And while taxiing back to my revetment, I added *never fly while drinking* to my list of things not to do ever again.

Bien Hoa, Da Nang, and Tan Son Nhat were now three of the longest and busiest runways in the world. The air transport business, both people and product, was booming. Our government had already formed an airline, called Flying Tiger Air, to handle GI traffic in and out of Viet Nam. Supplies were stacked up on docks and flight lines. I had heard there were eleven support personnel behind every one combat troop, and each one of them needed supplies. The black market was also booming. Anything or *any body* could be bought, sold, or traded for.

The headquarters of the 19th and 22nd TASS, which controlled all the FACs flying in III and IV Corps, were located in Bien Hoa. From there most FACs were assigned to F.O.B.s (forward operating bases) where they lived with the grunts for the duration of their tours. Near the end of their tour, they received DEROS (date estimated to return from overseas) and Stateside assignment orders. They usually spent their remaining days in-country back at Bien Hoa: out-processing, getting drunk, purchasing souvenirs, and touching up on their suntans before boarding a freedom bird that would take them back home. After spending months living in sandbagged bunkers, surviving rocket and mortar attacks and occasional ground probes, while trying to stop enemy infiltration from sanctuaries in Cambodia, it was a well-deserved respite.

The *Nugget* FACs had moved out of our hootch and north in order to be closer to their assigned division of Army troops. This move shortened lines of communication and response time. Intelligence was garnered from *Kit Carson* scouts—V.C. prisoners who had surrendered under a PSYOPS (psychological operations) enticement program called *Chu Hoi*, which roughly translated to *open arms*, or *welcome back*, or now we are going to let you lead us back to your old buddies' haunts so they can shoot at you instead of us.

Two short-timer FACs moved into the room across from Joey. Since we had access to jeeps, Joey and I would drive them over to Buddha's officers club for a late breakfast. Joey and I would then go fly, and they would read books, write letters, and lounge in the tropical sun in between monsoon rainstorms. They had survived. I loved to watch them eat, wolfing down actual bacon and eggs instead of the C-rats, or C rations, of canned ham and eggs that they were used to.

"You got kids?" Joey asked them one morning. The muscular one had two, and the skinny one had four. From the little bit I knew about fucking, it seemed to make sense that the skinny one would have more kids. But mostly they talked about their time spent in the boonies living like jungle rats and how the troops they were supporting looked like children yet were extremely brave when it came to fighting a wily enemy, which they respectfully referred to as *Mister Charles*, as opposed to *dink, gook, slope, gomer*. I was a wee bit jealous of them. They would be home soon. Once, while we were eating along with a club full of Army helicopter pilots, a round-eyed woman walked in. She was not particularly good-looking, or even stacked. There were a great many prettier Asian women walking about, bartending, waiting on tables, busing dishes. But the round-eye walked with her head up; she commanded attention as she scanned the room. She smiled with her eyes. Her walk was the kind of strut that would illicit wolf whistles and overt sexist remarks from construction workers, or any man who might let his urges take control of his mouth. But here in this foreign land—this land filled with horny, virile, and violent men—she was treated to a standing ovation: no cheering, no catty remarks; just a rousing, respectful applause that started with one clap from one man standing in the back corner of the room and then spontaneously spread to each table until all were standing. She grinned, and as I sat down I realized it was a moment like this that brightened my day. But it also caused me great sadness, knowing that I was so far from home, so far from the arms of my wife and children, and had so long to go before I would see or hold them again. When we finished eating, the four of us stood—as we did each morning—and we shook hands before heading back to our hootch. How it started or why we did it, I did not know. I only knew that it seemed natural, and it felt damn good.

Two days later, the outside air was just the way Father William liked his broads: hot and heavy. The sun sizzled as I pounded the area east of Saigon and south of Bien Hoa. I had been flying in-country now for more than eight months, and I still had a difficult time realizing that in my A.O. the closest way to the ocean was flying due south. Viet Nam was shaped like the profile of a pregnant woman, and I was now flying and pounding the underside of her belly. The plan was to level the area, turn the jungle into a moonscape. To do the job, three giant Rome plows—named for Rome, Georgia, the city where the plows were made—were brought in, accompanied by several A.P.C.s (armored personnel carriers) to provide protection. The plows were Cats with a sharpened two-ton blade attached to the front. The blade cut down 200-foot trees, which had stood unmolested for more than 200 years, with little more than a blast of smoke as the operator gunned the throttle. The plows worked in tandem in ever-decreasing circles, with the A.P.C.s on the perimeter and us above. In the late afternoon, the plows pushed the brush and trees into a pile that was then burned.

In the morning, we would again *prep the area*, which meant we would pummel the inside of the circle with bombs, shells, and bullets before the plows began their ever-decreasing concentric circle of destruction. The only thing that stopped them after they got rolling was a planted explosive device strategically placed to blow a track off of the Cat. If they missed the track, the giant plows would just keep grinding away with only the sound of the explosion interrupting the operation.

I landed, and two jeeps full of sergeants were waiting for me. A master sergeant saluted and handed me a beer.

"What kind of food do you like?" he asked.

I shrugged my shoulders.

"Chief Master Sergeant Zane called us. He said he was able to spend a day with his father before he died. He ordered us to thank you and to take care of you. Jump in. We have a case of beer, and we can cook whatever kind of meal you like. Chinese, Italian, Soul food, Mexican, Hungarian, you name it."

"Italian," I said.

"Chiapponne, you're up!" the sergeant yelled over his shoulder to another sergeant.

"Can do, sarge," the other sergeant said. "Would you like wine with it?"

"Beer is fine," I replied while lifting my can.

They met my airplane every afternoon after each of my missions for eight straight days; each time with a different cook, a different meal, and lots of laughs. I felt like a king, a sky king.

"You know those candy bars called Zeros?" Sergeant Washington asked.

"Yes."

"I used to call them *officers*. I walk up to a machine and say, 'I guess I'll have an officer today.' And I would pull the handle marked Zeros. I've been in the Air Force twenty-six years, and you are the first officer I've ever liked."

One evening, the sergeants took me to their *top three club*, a bar for the top three enlisted ranks, *only*!

"No officer has ever set foot inside of here," Sergeant Rogers said as he opened the door.

"Attention!" he roared as we entered. "No one fucks with my man, the lieutenant here! He's the pilot who flew Chief Master Sergeant Zane to Saigon."

Several of the men at the bar were not happy. One of the sergeants walked over and said: "If he is gonna drink with us, we had better strap him in so he doesn't get hurt. And they pulled up a stool and motioned for me to sit on it. Then he took off his belt—he was a huge man—and he wrapped it around me and the back of the stool and cinched it tight. Then he pushed the stool up to the bar and ordered me a beer. It reminded me of a story Joey once told. The Kiwi was present in the audience so Joey inserted him into the story:

A Kiwi and his girlfriend were out drinking and got surrounded by a gang of bikers. One of the bikers—a man called Gash, because he had a scar on his face beginning just below his hairline and running through an eye that wandered about so much it was difficult to tell what he was looking at, and then it sliced down to his lips so that he could talk only out the good side of his mouth and finally ended up across his throat, where stitches made the scar look like a zipper— traced a small circle with the heel of his boot. He picked the Kiwi up by his ears and deposited him inside the circle. "Stay inside this fucking circle!" he said to the Kiwi. The biker then walked up to the Kiwi's girlfriend, slapped her hard across her face, and began groping her. Gash snapped his head around to make sure the Kiwi hadn't moved.

The Kiwi was still in the circle, but he was smiling. Gash then tore off the girl's shirt and bra and, grabbing her by the hair, he began to suck on her tits. Gash again snapped his head around. The Kiwi was still standing in the circle and still smiling. Gash then forced the girl to her knees and began to unbutton his trousers. Once again he snapped his head around to look at the Kiwi. The Kiwi was still standing in the circle and still smiling.

Gash ran over to the Kiwi and inserted his fingers inside the Kiwi's nostrils. "What's so goddamn funny?" the biker asked out of the good side of his mouth.

And the Kiwi said, "When you weren't looking, I stepped outside the circle."

On the eighth straight day of flying and fine cuisine, I returned to our hootch. Our new *Smoky* ALO, the major from Vung Tau and the man who was always after me to join his *Smoky* FAC contingent on the beach, stood at the bar.

"Can I talk to you?" he asked.

"Of course."

"How would you like to kick ass and take names?" I rolled those words over in my head and then laughed.

"You've got me confused with someone who gives a shit, major."

"It's big. It's going to be dangerous. And I don't want to send any green kids in there to get killed."

"I'm getting *short*, major."

"It won't last long, a month maybe two."

We knew something big was up. Convoys were moving north every day. *Vietnamization* stopped. Supplies were being stockpiled. Airstrips were being improved, but nobody knew exactly what was going to happen.

"What is it?" I asked.

"Can't tell you," he answered.

"Green kids." The words bounced around in my brain. *Green kids*, like Frick and Frack, and the TWAT pilots; fuck-ups who needed to be sheltered so they wouldn't kill themselves or, worse yet, someone else. I thought about the fact that he had asked instead of ordered.

"One month?"

"Give or take." Dangerous words. I'd been victimized by them before. "So that's the whole nine yards, huh?" I asked.

"That's the whole kit and caboodle!"

"You are not even going to try and baffle me with bullshit?"

"No baffling bullshit."

"And when it's done, I have an R & R to Hong Kong, and then I will be really short."

He remained quiet.

"You promise me no one will fuck with me after it's over?"

"I promise."

I shook his hand. It was all that was needed between two men who respected each other. He pulled a piece of paper out of his pocket.

"Here are the coordinates of your targets and several call signs. You will launch at 0400 tomorrow. We are going into Cambodia. Your maps will be at P.E. Be ready. That's all I have for now. Good luck." And with these words, my dinner dates with the sergeants had come to an end.

That night, the eve of May 1, Father William rousted me from an early sleep. He pulled me out into the hallway where there was light. He pulled out a map and knelt on one knee.

"Look at this shit," he said, pointing to the map. "Gun sites everywhere. And big stuff too: 37 mm, Z.P.U.s, and quad fifties." He raised his head. "I am supposed to launch right away. I'm not going unless you go with me."

"I can't go. I've got dawn targets. I've got to get some sleep."

"I'm not going unless you are in the right seat running the starlight scope. They can court-martial my ass." I hated to fly at night, especially in hostile country. Somehow I was in another pickle. I looked at him. He was dead serious.

"Let me sleep to the border and on the way back home."

"Done!" He folded the map and jammed it in his pocket.

"Let's go!"

"Wait! I've got to get my boots on, for Christ's sake."

"Well hurry up, goddammit!" Father William, the blasphemer, said to the infidel.

When we showed up at P.E., we checked out every available weapon we could carry: knives, pistols, rifles. We found a place on our body for all of them. I asked them to pull my SAR (search and rescue) file, and I reviewed all the data: personal information including codes and answers to questions such as "What is your dog's name?" Questions that needed to be answered before the SAR boys could pick you up. And I recalled a story I had heard in survival school about a pilot who was shot down over the North and was so exhausted and frightened that he could not answer any of the questions confirming his identity. The Jolly Green rescue chopper, sensing a trap, was reluctant to go in when the downed pilot yelled: "Goddammit! Fuck all that bullshit! Get your ass in here and get me the fuck out of here."

"Sounds like a GI to me," he said, and they went in and successfully rescued the downed pilot.

I smiled, and Father William spotted it. "What the fuck is the matter with you, peasant? Are you crazy or something?" he said.

"Oh, I just thought of something. Nothing important," I lied. When I was certain I had all the pertinent information filed away in my head, I closed the file, rubbed my dog tags with my index finger and thumb, and renewed my commitment: death before capture. I donned my flak vest, and as I snugged it tight I could feel adrenaline being pumped throughout my body. But a strange thing happened when we got to the airplane and I strapped in. I pulled my tinted sun visor down, blacking out nearly all light, and fell asleep before takeoff. I did not stir until Father William again shook me awake.

"Wake up Rip Van Winkle. We're here."

"Terrific," I replied as I raised my visor.

For the next couple of hours we flew over Cambodia, quietly covering covert special ops insertions to secure landing zones and generally looking for any enemy activity. But all was quiet. I again slept on the way back. We landed, and I returned to my bunk but could not get back to sleep. At 0400 hours I launched, and the sun and I arrived at the border at the same moment. I rotated radio frequencies. There was chatter on all channels.

"This is *Paris control* on guard with a heavy artillery warning up to 37,000 feet from 0500 to 0530 . . ." B-52 strikes, tons of falling 500-pound bombs. Obviously, I couldn't climb over them so I had to go around them. I grabbed my map just as the ground below me shook. And then the concussion hit my airplane, bouncing me up and down while the bombs detonated. Whoever came up with the term *rolling thunder* got it right. Today, B-52 Arch Light strikes seemed to happen every fifteen minutes. I was continuously banking left and right trying to avoid them. Then, I heard two mighty explosions. In dawn's early light, I watched as mushroom clouds rose over the explosions.

"Jesus Christ, Nixon is using nukes and sending me out in a Cessna. You gotta be shitting me. What a fucked-up war." It was the start of a long day.

It began as the Gulf of Tonkin *Incident*, which turned into the Viet Nam *Conflict*, and now it was the Cambodian *Incursion*; but for me it felt like a war. It had all the ingredients: death, destruction, despair. My flights were longer in duration now. Driving to and from Cambodia gave me time to think. I wished Jefferson was here to give me advice, but I was the mother hen now. I was the one who was supposed to know everything. I began to burn my aux fuel tanks first to get my flying time. Captain Puff would have been proud. It was different for me now; I felt alone. Joey had moved north, flying from a F.O.B., as his troops would be leading the charge into Cambodia. I continued to launch at noon, so our ritual of a late breakfast with the short-timers remained, only without my missing Aussie mate.

"They're putting us back into action," the muscular short-timer said.

"You gotta be shitting me?"

"Yeah, they say they need us."

"What a bunch of bullshit. Did you try to fight it? I mean . . . what have you got left? A week, ten days?"

"Actually twelve days." The skinny one said, "But the good news is that we get to fly together . . . What's it like over there?"

"It's a cluster fuck as usual. Gaggles of airplanes and choppers, confusion on the ground, horseshit command and control, not enough artillery support; the weather is always shitty, the dinks are dug in with eight to ten feet of overhead cover while our guys are exposed . . . it takes about three direct hits to even put a hurting on the gook bunkers . . . a lot of folks are going to get killed."

After that, we ate in silence. When finished, we stood and shook hands—first with the father of two, then the father of four; eight kids between us. I kidded them once, "Six kids. I bet you came here for a break."

"Some break," the muscular one answered.

I dropped them off at headquarters to be briefed on their mission, and I continued on to the flight line where I started my engines and launched for a flight into the Cambodian morass. I had a set of fighters scheduled for every half hour, banging away at those bunkers that seemed to be everywhere. I returned fatigued and in need of a beer, and when I switched to Bien Hoa tower frequency I heard a familiar voice.

"Bien Hoa tower, *Nighthawk* two niner requesting an emergency landing." I could hear him twisting and turning between deep breaths. He had a stuck mike and he probably didn't know it. Every noise in his airplane would be transmitted out over tower frequency. And when he said: "Goddammit, motherfucking piece-of-shit mutant of an airplane," I knew for certain it was Father William. I landed and taxied in behind him, and when he finally got out of his airplane I was waiting for him.

"So, what's wrong with the motherfucking mutant airplane?" I asked.

"Everything!"

"And why are you flying during the daytime?"

"They are sending me north, II Corps . . . flying into Cambodia."

"Join the crowd."

He scribbled all the things that were wrong with the airplane on the forms, signed his name, and slammed the book shut.

"Get me another bird!" he shouted to a passing crew chief. "Preferably one that can fly!"

"So, you were going to just sneak off before you could give me your blessing, huh?"

"They didn't give me any notice, peasant. They just woke me up and said: 'You are going to *didi-mau* up to Plieku.' No invitation, no going-away party—nothing . . . What they forgot to add is: 'and you get to do it in a broken-down fucking airplane!' The fucking dildos!"

"Got one ready, lieutenant," the crew chief said. We shook hands, like we always did, and then we hugged, which we never did.

"Ora pro nobis," he said.

"Yeah, cunnilingus," I answered.

"Fucking infidel."

I smiled, turned, and walked away—just a few steps though—and then I looked back. When he saw me, he turned his back and walked away, but not before he stuck both of his middle fingers up in the air.

I checked my weapons, maps, and parachute at P.E., then debriefed and headed back to our hootch. When I opened the door, I saw two footlockers in the hallway across from Joey's room, and then I noticed a hasp and padlock on the muscular one and skinny one's door. "Motherfucker, this can't be!" I yelled to no one but myself. I walked to the bar and slammed the heel of my hand on the bar. Earl and the Walrus were there; Miss Sam was behind the bar. No one said anything. I recalled the laughter with Joey talking at breakfast on the days leading up to today. The skinny one had a hearty laugh; the muscular one preferred a big grin. I couldn't help but smile. I scratched my head, shook it, and looked at Earl and the Walrus.

"How did it happen?" I asked.

"Midair with a chopper," Earl answered.

"Cut them right in half," the Walrus added.

"One of them shinnied up the risers with no legs to escape the napalm. He was still alive when they got him in the chopper but died on the way in." Again I shook my head.

"That's one tough son of a bitch," I mumbled.

"No shit," the Walrus said. "I just got done breaking bread with them... What a lousy fucking war!" I was too exhausted to feel the pain; I was too tarnished to feel the love; I was a steel onion. I visualized the knock on their doors. There were large "welcome home" signs, grieving wives and kids, but I felt nothing. My thoughts were personal. I no longer cared what happened to someone else; I didn't even care what happened to me. I was now one with my machine: efficient, united in purpose, soulless. I only wanted to get out of this shithole and sit by myself, perhaps on some deserted island with a dog as my only companion, or maybe a jug of whisky. Physically, I hoped to make it home in one piece so I could care for myself and not have to depend on someone else. I would not have to carry out another order, not have to make concessions. I smiled... "cut them right in half..." I wanted to say, "So there was twice as much to go around," but I didn't.

I had screwed up. I had let them in. I guess I figured it would be alright since their tour was over. They would survive, go home, and live happily ever after. But it didn't happen that way and now their deaths hurt, like a kick in the nuts, only the pain never goes away.

Two days later, the lockers that sat on the floor across from Joey's old room disappeared. I assumed they were shipped back to their families along with their remains. *Remains*, what a strange word I thought as I walked by the space where there once was something and now there was nothing. *Remains*: a wartime euphemism connoting a peaceful passing. *Carcasses* would better describe the condition of their corpses. They died a violent death. Only this time, *remains* might work since their hearts and heads were sent home, but their legs would remain in Viet Nam forever. I walked into the bar area where a major stood sipping a beer. It was easy to see that he was barrel-chested and battle-tested.

"Grab a beer and your gear and come with me," he said. "You are now a *Red Marker* FAC, flying for the Arvin airborne." I did not answer. I grabbed the beer Miss Sam had placed before me, went to my room, and tossed some items in my duffle. The major stood in my doorway and watched. When I zipped my duffle shut, he stepped aside so that I could pass him by and take the lead. But I did not know where we were going, so when I reached the hallway, I stopped and let him pass; then I fell in behind him.

We drove to the flight line, where he got into the left seat of an O-2 and I strapped into the right. We took off and headed north and west, dodging thundering, monsoon rainstorms and getting bounced around like a Mexican jumping bean whose diet consisted of tequila and hot peppers. He let the airplane yaw and roll and gain and lose altitude, not fighting it but just going with it. Eventually, we came to a short airstrip with a wooden control tower. He began his straight-in approach several miles out. As he came down final, the winds were so strong that at times it felt as though we were hovering with no forward motion. I could see he was battling a wicked crosswind using full left aileron and cross-controlling with full right rudder. He was fighting it now, trying to hold the bird straight so he could touch down. I admired his tenacity and flying expertise but questioned his judgment. I would have backed off and tried again under more favorable conditions. He chopped power and we touched down. I decided he landed with willpower; he was not going to let the machine or weather deter him. He had willed the airplane onto the ground. And the entire ordeal had occurred with no words spoken between us since he said: "Grab a beer and your gear and come with me."

He led me to a sandbagged bunker with a metal roof and three layers of sandbags on top of that. Tanned men were sitting shirtless on other sandbags. One of them strummed a guitar. He played like me: clumsy and slow. Jefferson would have cringed and probably walked away. He was just another GI trying to kill some time. Another pilot was practicing his Viet Namese, serious stuff. Not just the usual: *didi mau, gook*. Several stood and greeted me. One of them led inside the bunker and pointed to a cot enshrouded with mosquito netting, and I wondered if it might be a good idea to start taking malaria pills: pills the size of marbles, pills that liked to lodge in your throat, pills that tasted like shit, pills that made me feel sick. I threw my duffle on the cot and walked back outside to join the band of merry men. On the way, off the entrance, I spotted another bunker that was dug deeper and reinforced better. I sat next to the man strumming the guitar and listened. They were pilots who operated out of Saigon. Most were younger than me, and all had less time in-country. One pointed to a centerline fuel tank. It was removed from an F-100 and was now suspended by timbers.

"We've got the only shower on the base," he bragged. "You can sell your time under there for twenty bucks." I nodded. Then I spotted a ragtag band of U.S. grunts. They looked like they had walked to and from Cambodia, rolled in red clay there, and brought back all they could carry. Red clay was in their hair and formed the outer layer of their skin. It covered their unbuttoned and untucked fatigue shirts. Their belts were cinched tight, like they had lost twenty pounds or more, and their boots had the color and look of cardboard. Their leader—I assumed he was the leader since he was walking point, the man at the front of the pack—stopped. His rifle was riding on the nape of his neck. Both arms dangled over it.

"Gonna frag a sergeant in the next hootch tonight," he said, then added:

"Don't take it personally." They walked on by. Not one pilot said a word. There was a noise behind me and I jumped up and turned to face a Viet Namese soldier.

"Little jumpy there, aren't you?" the Strummer said. "It's only Sergeant Trung. He takes care of us: shines our boots, sends our laundry to the cleaners..."

"Yeah, right," a pilot said, and they all laughed. Sergeant Trung limped toward me. He was wearing a red beret and camouflaged fatigues with airborne insignia; part of his jaw was missing. He stuck out his hand and I shook it.

Then another pilot, the one who was studying Viet Namese, whispered in my ear, "He has been shot up something like seven times. They only assigned him to us so that he can maybe live out the war." I nodded. That night, we were listening to Hanoi Hannah on the radio when we heard the explosion in the hootch next door. Several of us flinched, but no one said or did anything. It wasn't our problem. This was followed by a round of mortars getting walked in, a sound I have never forgotten. I scurried along the ground and into the reinforced bunker.

"Hey, where the hell are you going?" I heard someone say as I wrapped my knees with my arms. The sounds got louder. The bunker filled up.

"How the hell did you know that?" the Strummer asked.

"You've been living in Saigon too long," I answered.

"Yeah, we've got a sweet deal. The Arvin airborne is the palace guard. We live in a villa just off Tudor Street. Word is we will spend three weeks here and then rotate back for a week in sin city."

"Yeah, we get T.D.Y., temporary duty pay. It isn't much, something like a buck and a half a day, but we are the only ones who get it."

"Yeah, sweet deal," I mumbled.

"Hey, how'd you get this assignment?" he asked.

"Just my lucky day, I guess." He nodded.

"What do you do for booze here?" I asked.

"Army's got a hard-ass commander. He closes the club at eight o'clock."

I shook my head from side to side, got up, and walked over to my bunk. I parted the mosquito netting, crawled in, pulled my poncho liner over my head, and tried unsuccessfully to empty it of all thoughts. Sometime during the night, I awoke lying in a pool of sweat. Everything was black; only the explosions inside my head lit the room...

My plane was heading for that tree: the tree I was going to crash into, the tree that was impossible to avoid. I jammed left aileron and rudder and pulled. Why left aileron? Why left rudder? It should have been just the opposite. How had I missed that tree? Was it a miracle? I saw the faces of Billy, Moondoggie, Mike in the Jungle, Lucky Larry, the muscular one, the skinny one. All were looking at me, all were smiling . . .

The next morning I rose with the sun. I couldn't remember the last time I saw the sun rise. Most of my fellow pilots were sitting outside our bunker eating C-rats: ham and eggs in cans inside a cardboard box; one of the better meals.

"What kind of cigarettes did you get today?" a FAC asked. The Strummer opened his box and pulled out a package of four. "Chesterfields," he said.

"Trade you for a pound cake," the other FAC said.

"Fuck that! It takes two canteens of water to get a pound cake down. They should call it a ton cake. Here, you can have my cigarettes." The Strummer tossed them to the sitting FAC. Then the Strummer rose and stripped naked, and walked over to the F-100 centerline tank and pulled the cord for a quick shower.

"They're fucking with him," the smoking FAC said. I nodded, indicating I needed more information.

"He was working a contact. An Army helicopter was expending on friendly troops. He tried to raise the chopper pilot on guard channel, but apparently the chopper pilot had his guard channel punched off. The chopper was killing friendlies. So every time the chopper made a hot pass, the Strummer would fly his airplane between the chopper and the ground troops . . . you know . . . so the chopper couldn't fire without hitting him. Motherfucker! That took some balls." I nodded.

"Anyhow, the chopper pilot finally turned his radio to guard channel and hollered at our guy to get the fuck out of the way. 'You're killing friendlies, you dumbshit!' he yelled back." He flicked the ashes from the end of his cigarette and exhaled a long stream of blue smoke. "Now the Air Force is fucking with him. They've started an investigation, giving him shit about needlessly putting his life at risk or some kind of military horseshit that can only be drummed up by some rear-echelon motherfucker in Saigon. What the fuck, it's his life! He ought to be able to do whatever he wants to do with it. And they ought to be giving him a medal." He paused and then he ground out the cigarette with the heel of his combat boot. He didn't stop until it was shredded and indistinguishable from the red clay. "I hate the fucking place!" he said as he stood and walked back into the bunker.

Chapter 6
A BEER AND A BROAD

We continued to pound Cambodia until it looked like the pock-faced Viet Nam. I didn't seem to give much of a shit about my life either, as I flew recklessly—too low and too often—while putting in airstrike after airstrike. When I was finished, I headed for home plate. I aimed my airplane at the wooden tower at the middle of our runway, building speed, actually wanting to crash into it, and then just before impact, something inside compelled me to bank hard right, away from it. Each day, after every mission, I experienced the same powerful draw to destroy it and me simultaneously, each time getting closer and closer to colliding with it. At first, the men in the tower thought it funny, and then they thought it was a little bit intimidating, and then they threatened to shoot me down if I continued, and then I thought it was funny. I landed, taxied in, shut her down, and got out. My crew chief approached.

"Take a look at this," he said. He showed me where I had taken a hit in my rear engine. Hell, I wasn't even aware the bad guys were shooting at me. I signed the forms, and when I looked up my new ALO (air liaison officer) was waiting for me.

"You've got to go down to Bien Hoa this afternoon and fly a check ride," he said.

"You gotta be shitting me?"

"No, I am not. Just go down there and fly the goddamn thing and get back here."

"And what if I flunk it? Will they ground me?"

"You had better not! I need you."

"For fucksakes, I fly a check ride every day. If I live, I've passed. Besides, who is going to check me out, some goddamn nobody who has never flown a day of combat in his life?"

"Just do it!" he said. And then he read my mind. "And you better not try to flunk it."

"Three bags full, boss." I said it reverently and with a smile. He returned my smile.

I jumped back into my airplane and flew to Bien Hoa. There was an official letter waiting for me. I opened it. It was my assignment back to the States. I had filled out my dream sheet—an official document where I rated my preference of aircraft assignment and location—first, second, and third. Plane assignment was specific; location was generic, such as Southeast or Northwest. I had filled it out early since I figured I may get it in before I got locked into a SAC assignment. Just to make sure, I wrote in the comments section that I would take any aircraft anywhere in the world, but please don't give me a SAC assignment. I was positive that the clipboard colonel reading this, and realizing that I had just lived through a FAC tour, would be able to find something to accommodate me. He did. The motherfucker gave me B-52s, a SAC assignment to Rome, New York. I crushed the paper, then shredded it into as many pieces as was physically possible. I was still rip-roaring, red-faced mad when my check pilot—a doofus with about five months in-country and a handful of combat missions—appeared. An ass-kisser, I assumed, who got this dandy assignment by performing above and beyond the call of duty by shoving his head and shoulders so far up some colonel's ass that you could only see the soles of his boots. In fact, that's what the Aussie's called a guy like him: *boots*.

"I guess we can waive the airstrikes," he said. I stared at him. "We will just go out and shoot some touch-and-go landings." I continued staring. He rose, and we walked to our airplane. I cranked engines, taxied, and took off. He ordered me to fly to a strip I had never heard of. I was so angry that I was being evaluated by this ex-SAC weenie—an ass-kisser of extraordinary proportions—who finally got his ass over here and brought all his bullshit rules and regulations with him to fuck up our war; and worse yet, he left a slot open back home that ensured all of us rotating back would get a SAC assignment. I discovered, once again, it was hard for me to fly while angry with someone in my cockpit, my space, my face. It was a night ride with Captain Puff: Déjà fuck vu! Only this time, it was fuck me. I couldn't concentrate. I was way too low on final approach; dragging it in, carrying full power, the stall horn wailing, the controls mushy, the airplane wanting to fall out of the sky, and my check pilot so nervous that I caught him reaching for the controls on several occasions. I pranged the airplane on the runway and then lifted off for another go at it. "I guess that's enough," he said. It was the shittiest approach and landing I have ever flown. Had I been him, I would have flunked me on the spot, taken control of the airplane, and refused to let me touch the yoke and throttles until we were taxiing back at home plate. But he did not. He gave me a passing grade.

I entered the landing pattern back at Bien Hoa and pulled a *Jefferson*, flying in with my airspeed approaching redline and then bleeding it down with a wicked 90-degree turn. I rolled it back wing level and landed on the first brick. I had not said a word the entire time I was with this asshole. A dipshit who may not have actually been an asshole. He may have just been interested in getting promoted, which I guess would put him on the asshole-in-training list. I envied the fact that he would get a chance to wear the blue suit for many years, when I knew I would not.

"Just a few questions," he said as he shuffled some papers. "What's the definition of an uncontrolled airstrip?"

"I guess that would be one the bad guys own," I said.

"No, the actual definition is an airstrip without a radar-controlled approach." And I was thinking about the fucking strip I had been landing on lately: a strip where I sometimes had to fly a low approach to get the fucking water buffaloes, goats, chickens, and peasants off the runway so I could land.

"What are the minimums for putting in an airstrike?" he asked.

"Well, if our guys need our help and the fighters are willing to work, I guess I'm not too concerned about minimums. But I guess the book answer might be, ceiling: 250 feet; visibility: 1 mile."

He raised his head, turned a page, and peered at me.

"Well, you got it half right," he said.

"Where the hell are you getting these questions and answers?" I asked.

"Oh, we have sent them out in distribution."

"Distribution? What the fuck are you talking about? We don't even get mail!"

He asked several more stupid questions, several of which I probably didn't even try to answer with words. I was thinking more like answering them with a fist to his mouth and a couple to his kidneys and a knee in the nuts.

"I am afraid you failed," he finally said.

I stood, smiled, and offered my hand, which he took. "Thank you," I said. "I guess I won't have to fly anymore." Since I was now *grounded*, I had to call my ALO to tell him the good news. He would have to fly down and pick me up. He screamed at me, first on the phone and then shortly thereafter in person.

"I told you not to flunk that check ride!"

"Just a minute," I answered calmly. "Let me ask you a few questions." And when he could not answer them, I said, "Sorry, I guess you are grounded too."

He spun on his heels and headed for the squadron commander's office. He didn't wait for anybody to open the door, nor to shut it. He did that himself, with the force of a typhoon, and then he started screaming in a voice that could be heard halfway to Hanoi. I noticed that he left no opening for a response. Suddenly the door opened.

"You are *un*grounded," he said. "Now get your ass back up there and start flying!"

The next afternoon I was back in the saddle, all set to take off, when tower informed me that there was an inbound Cobra, call sign: *Mamba* twenty-eight, and the pilot wanted to talk to me. "*Buddha*," I whispered.

"Tower, *Red Marker* two-seven. Requesting clearance to take the active, turn off at midfield, and taxi to the helio-pad."

"That's a Charlie, *Red Marker*." I taxied my airplane to the helio-pad and parked it nose-to-nose with Buddha's chopper, so his Cobra could get reacquainted with my Skymaster. They had met several times before, in the sky where a dog fight broke out between the *snake* and the Skymaster. The Cobra could stop, hover, and swivel, an absolutely unfair advantage. But one time I rolled inverted and pulled it through. A *split-S*, another maneuver my airplane was not designed to perform. I pulled out—with the wings still attached—decidedly lower and headed in the opposite direction from Buddha. I never gave it a thought that I might tear the wings off; it just seemed like the natural thing to do.

"Wow," Buddha said. "What the hell was that?" I smiled at the memory.

Now I watched as this huge man lumbered over to my bird. I opened the door. He leaned in and placed his elbows on the right seat, this man twice my weight: two hundred and sixty pounds, most of it located in his belly.

"Just stopped by to say good-bye," he said. I looked away. "My tour's up," he continued. I shook my head from side to side. I felt sadness and anger at the same time.

"Well then get the fuck in and let's go fly." He hesitated, and then with a great deal of effort, he squeezed in.

"Kick the seat back, for Christ's sake," I ordered with a smile. "I can't even turn the yoke." He did, and when situated, he gave me a thumbs-up. I called the tower and got clearance to taxi back to the front end of the runway. The sodden air seemed to stop all breezes. Low clouds hung like un-milked udders on a lactating cow. Heat vapors wrinkled up from the runway. Sweat poured forth from our bodies as I brought both throttles forward and we rumbled down the crude runway. I glanced at the airspeed indicator looking for rotation speed, and it became clear that we were going to run out of runway before we attained it. I pulled back on the yoke, but the plane did not separate from the ground. I pushed the yoke forward with one hand, and with the other I pushed on the throttles to make sure they were supplying all the power available. There was no overrun. The end of the runway was marked by a small barbed wire fence that restricted some animals—both the four-legged ones and the two-legged ones—from entering the base and overweight airplanes from leaving the base. I had not planned for Buddha's additional weight or the dense, stagnant air that impeded both thrust and lift. I knew I could no longer stop the airplane without crashing through the fence and into the minefield that waited for us on the other side. When I ran out of runway, I popped the nose up, and with the stall horn wailing, I immediately raised the gear, which gave me extra inches to clear the barbed wire. The plane staggered over a few trees and then began to claw its way into the ether.

I had six pre-planned airstrikes scheduled in half-hour increments in and around the Angel Wing. We had time before the first strike, and with the clouds now broken and the storms isolated, I decided on some leisurely sightseeing. We flew around the white and black virgin mountains: Nui Ba Ra and Nui Ba Den. The latter rose out of a flat landscape and reached a height of 2,232 feet; the former, 1,000 feet higher. I wondered if my airplane could make it to the top with Buddha in the right seat. It did. And when my fighters checked in, I descended to 1,500 feet and we went to work. Three hours and twenty-nine minutes later, we landed. Buddha crawled out several pounds lighter, and I followed. It was a flight I never wanted to end. He wrapped his huge arms around me and then he rocked back, which lifted my feet off the ground. Suddenly, he released me, and without words we shook hands. He stepped back smartly and saluted, and I returned it. And when I did, he turned and walked back to his aircraft, cranked the engine, and lifted off. He flew low over the field before raising his nose and climbing out. I stood and watched. I watched until this giant of a man turned into a distant speck; and then it, too, disappeared.

"The weather is horseshit up along the border," the Strummer said the next day. I nodded and slid into my airplane. "I wouldn't go if I was you," he warned. I started my front engine. He shrugged his shoulders and walked away. Once airborne, I could see the line of thunderstorms and a wall of rain running parallel to the border. My target was on the other side. It was the kind of weather the enemy loved. I dropped down to 500 feet, just below the clouds, and looked down for landmarks to confirm my location, and up for a hole to punch through. Our Viet Namese airborne troops were fighting with valor but were getting hammered by crack North Viet Namese units. They needed my help. I droned on. The pounding rain drowned out the hum of my engines. Eventually, I found an opening. I could see blue sky above and ground below. I ran my finger along my map and then peered out my side window looking for landmarks. I repeated this procedure, while flying in a tight circle, until I was sure of my position. It was my lucky day. The fighting was taking place just below me. When my fighters checked in, I rose up to meet them, climbing above the clouds. When they spotted me, I led them down through the hole I had found. I put in two sets of fighters and sent them on their merry way before I noticed my circle of blue sky was closing fast. It was time to go home.

Then, almost instantaneously, blue sky turned into black clouds. I turned on my instrument lights and rotated the rheostat all the way right as I tried to climb up through the dark, dense clouds, hoping to break out on top. But the tops were too high. I could not get above the storms. My aircraft bounced up and down, right to left, and then up and down and right to left simultaneously, depending on which pocket of turbulent air I happened upon. I inadvertently lost 100 feet of altitude in the time it took a bolt of lightning to flash. My aircraft dropped violently, so violently I thought it may break apart. I decided to try to get under the clouds. I watched as my altimeter unwound: 500, 400, 300 feet. Outside, I saw nothing but heavy rain. A blast of thunder terrorized me.

I knew there were mountains in the area, specifically the black and white virgin mountains. Every muscle in my body was knotted tight. With each forward motion, I felt like my airplane might crash into the side of a mountain and fold up like a cheap accordion. Artillery shells were most likely ripping through the clouds. My TACAN needle was spinning, and because I could not see the ground, I had no way of knowing where I was. My only defense against an artillery shell disintegrating my airplane was luck. I checked my fuel and did a quick calculation: thirty to forty minutes. I was in trouble. I *squawked* emergency on my transponder and began a climb, knowing that the higher I got the better chance I had of getting painted on a radar screen in Saigon. I checked my map. I needed to get above Nui Ba Den at 3,200 and some feet. I climbed to 5,000 feet, still in the soup and still getting bounced around. I turned to a heading of 090 on my whiskey compass and hoped for the best. I dialed in different channels on my TACAN, Saigon, Bien Hoa, and waited for a spell. Looking for a lock-on, but the needle kept spinning. I repeated the process, switching channels back and forth, studying my instruments. The needle appeared to stop. I had a lock-on. Then the needle rocked back and forth from ten o'clock to two o'clock. It did this several times before it resumed spinning. I droned on, watching my wings, checking to see if they were still attached. I checked my gauges. I was running low on fuel.

"This is *Paris control* on guard. Aircraft squawking emergency, 129 miles west of Saigon, state your problem."

"Paris, this is *Red Marker* two-seven. I am in the soup, requesting vector to nearest runway."

There was no reply, so I exhaled and transmitted again, and then a third time and fourth time. A bolt of lightning, less than ten yards in front, filled my windscreen and momentarily blinded me. I banked the airplane hard left.

"*Red Marker* two-seven, this is *Paris control*. We copy and are working it. Squawk 3247." I dialed it in.

"*Red Marker* is squawking 3247."

"*Paris* has a good paint. Come up channel 362.5 and stand by for a controller."

"Roger, going 362.5." I dialed it in.

"*Paris, Red Marker* two-seven. How copy?"

"We read you loud and clear. State intentions."

"I'd like a vector for a G.C.A. to Bien Hoa, if possible."

"Roger, turn to a heading of 082."

"Turning to 082 now."

I exhaled. I was now under radar control. But when he ordered me to descend, that old feeling—a feeling that lived deep in my gut, a feeling of an immediate and violent death, a feeling that I was about to crash into something: A mountain, a tower, a building, a tree—that old feeling surfaced. Now I needed faith: Faith in the competence of another human, a human being I had never met, to survive. It was easy to give up control when I felt terror. But as I got closer to my destination and the clouds became not so ominous, I wanted it back. But for now, my balls were in his hands.

"*Red Marker* has the runway in sight. Thank you."

"Roger, *Red Marker*," he said. "Can I call this a *save*?"

"Save? Come up to Bien Hoa, and I will give you a kiss on the lips."

"Ah, I think I will skip that. Contact Bien Hoa tower."

"Roger that." I dropped the gear and landed.

That evening we listened to Hanoi Hannah as she described a shooting at Kent State University. Four students killed, nine wounded, protesting illegal actions by Yankee war criminals against the people of the Democratic Republic of Viet Nam. A sullen FAC stood and snapped the radio off.

"They should have killed all those hippie motherfuckers," the FAC said. "Four K.I.A., hell I had more *crispy critters* than that yesterday with one fucking bomb."

The FAC had a brother who was a P.O.W. He spent all of his downtime trying to figure out how he could get further north—closer to his brother—so somehow he might be able to spring him. He was possessed with this thought. He discovered and volunteered for a program code-named Steve Canyon, after the colonel in the comic strip "Terry and the Pirates." I was familiar with the strip. As a young lad, I practiced drawing Col. Steve Canyon, Dick Tracy, Dagwood Bumstead, and several other comic strip characters. "It's a six-month commitment," he said. "Flying O-1s, in civilian clothes, out of *country X*." He smirked. "That's Laos, you know. A C.I.A. operation in a country we're not supposed to be in, working the Ho Chi Minh trail and supporting friendly Laotians."

"Hell, they got guns on the trail that can put up more lead in a minute than my airplane weighs," an O-1 driver added. We all laughed. I had heard that line before. It seemed to be a badge of courage for the pilots who flew that old and slow tail-dragger. But then I heard the FAC say: "Choice of assignments after completion of tour." I sat up and calculated. *Six months*; I would have to extend for two. This was not only a way out of my SAC assignment; it also meant flying more dangerous missions, more prestige, more respect, and hopefully better efficiency reports. And maybe, just maybe, a chance to stay in the Air Force. I listened as the discussion returned to Kent State.

"Fucking assholes!"

"Bunch of Jane Fonda-loving chicken shits!"

"Kill them all and let us fight this fucking war!"

"Yeah, call in an airstrike on those long-haired, pill-popping dopeheads." The FAC chugged the rest of his beer.

I snickered. *Dopeheads*. I could hear Joey saying, "Circumcise the boy; give him a clear head for business."

Our ALO spoke, which was unusual.

"I got orders for Kent State R.O.T.C. department yesterday."

"No shit?"

"What the fuck?"

"No way!" And we were all laughing.

"Well, be sure and take your steel pot and flak vest along with you." And in the end, even our ALO was giggling, the first time I had ever witnessed a delightful feeling ripple through his body.

A beat-up grunt walked up. "There's gonna be a *mad minute* tonight, 1800 hours."

"Question," I said.

"Yes sir," he replied.

"Is the position of town crier an elected or appointed position?" Everybody laughed.

"Hey," the grunt replied. "I'm just telling you all." As he walked away, I heard him add: "Jesus Christ! Ain't no sweat off my balls."

"What the fuck is a mad minute?" an F.N.G. asked.

The Strummer answered: "At 1800 hours, every gun inside the perimeter is going to fire for exactly sixty seconds. Shotguns are loaded with *fleshettes*. Sounds petite, effeminate, and harmless, doesn't it? But they are like nails with fins. An anti-personnel weapon that will punch lots of holes in the bad guys' T-shirts. Even the artillery tubes are lowered to about chest high and loaded with *beehive* rounds, similar but smaller than fleshettes but even more lethal and intimidating because they are traveling at supersonic speeds. They sound like bees buzzing as they rip through foliage and people; thus the term *beehive*. The grunts particularly like to do a mad minute when the weather is bad. Charlie likes to take advantage of bad weather to launch sapper attacks. The mad minute lets Charlie know that we are wise to his little games, and we will blast his ass into permanent retirement if he has the gonads to try anything. One minute seems like an hour once the guns are a blazing."

As the Strummer spoke, I studied the facial expressions on our two F.N.G.s. Expressions didn't betray their natural internal fear, but the draining of blood from their faces did. I hit the release button on my survival knife, and when the *blade* sprang open I threw it into the ground, sticking it firmly.

Three days later, I received orders to bomb "military structures." I plotted the coordinates on my map: A village on the Cambodia side of the border, ironically positioned just inside the Angel Wing. I was to hit it with four sets of F-100s carrying *snake and nape*; *snake* to blow holes and *nape* to burn it to the ground. I walked to my aircraft and then around it, checking all the surfaces and making sure the rudder, elevator, and ailerons moved freely. I crawled in and made a circle with my right index finger, alerting the crew chief that I would be cranking my front engine. I started it and then brought the throttle to idle, checked to make sure all my instrument indicators were *in the green*, and then I cranked my rear engine. The crew chief pulled the chocks, and I taxied to the end of the runway, again checking that my control surfaces were functioning properly—right and left ailerons controlled by the yoke, right and left rudder controlled by foot pedals, and horizontal stabilizer controlled by pulling and pushing the yoke. Then I checked the weather: mostly overcast but the clouds were white and puffy and unthreatening. I drove to the target area, located an opening where I could take my fighters down, spiraled down through it, and flew over the target. It was a village, a village not unlike my bucolic retreat on the banks of a river. I felt sick to my stomach.

"*Blackdog, Red Marker* two-seven."

"Go ahead, *Red Marker*."

"There must be some mistakes on this target. Recheck coordinates, please." I was flying in and out of low scud, holding to the south of the village. Blackdog came back with coded coordinates and I rechecked them on my map. They were still targeting the village.

"Say nature of target, *Blackdog*."

"Roger, *military structures*."

"Military structures, my ass!" I said out loud to myself. But there was a large part of me that was excited to hit it: A target out in the open, one we could actually see, one where we could measure our effectiveness and accuracy instead of dropping a bomb in the deep recesses of a jungle and hoping to hit something. A target where we could report positive, accurate, and meaningful bomb damage assessment data to the intel types and maybe, just maybe, shorten the war because of it. A strategic target instead of one based on WAGs (wild ass guesses). No more bombs on top of bombs, bunkers on top of bunkers, lies on top of lies. "*Looks like you got a couple of bunkers and, oh my, what's this? That swinging bamboo fucking bridge we have been trying to hit for the last five years? Yeah, you got it, man!*" Most often, all we did was drop a few bombs that dropped a few trees and loosened the soil so that it was easier for Charlie to plant another surreptitious vegetable garden. No man, this time they had given me a real target! But there was another part of me that asked: How could I destroy a family's home, in a country that was claiming neutrality, in a war that was only going to last thirty-some days? I decided I was not going to hit it. But why not? My mind argued with my soul. If I didn't hit it, somebody else would get this *cherry* target. It was going to be destroyed one way or another, so why not by me? I studied the target. There was no movement—no people, no animals, nobody—not even a breeze. Nobody that I could see, but probably a whole bunch of gooks hidden behind .50 cal. machine guns ready to take potshots at a rookie FAC. I decided to chance it, but I needed to work up some anger first. So I dropped down on the deck daring Charlie, or whoever the fuck was down there, to shoot at me.

There would be plenty of anger if the gooks decided to hose me. I flew below the eaves of the hootches. I could look in the doorways. Nobody, nothing, not a round was fired. I climbed back up to 8,000 feet, on the tops of the white clouds, where I could see blue sky.

"*Red Marker* twenty-seven, *Outlaw* eighteen, over."

"Roger *Outlaw*, *Red Marker* copies."

"Roger that, pardner. I've got my sidekick with me. We are a couple of foxy 100s carrying snake and nape. We like to work with smoke, and our guns are loaded and holstered. So tell us a little bit about the shootout down there."

"Lots of overcast. I will lead you down through a hole. Base of the clouds, 5 to 700 feet. Target is military structures. Hard stuff first, right-hand turns, expect ground fire, bailout heading 090."

"*Red Marker*, *Outlaw*. Rock your wings."

"Rocking."

"We have a tally-ho, pardner." I not only could see his airplane; I got a mental visual of him in it: an older man, wearing a cowboy hat instead of a helmet, cowboy boots instead of combat boots, and probably smoking a cigar.

"See the hole, *Outlaw*?"

"Roger."

"Pull the power back and I'll join on your wing."

"Well, how slow do I have to go, *Red Marker*?"

"About 100 miles an hour."

"I'll fall out of the sky at 100 miles an hour, pardner."

When the fighters leveled off, lead saw the objective: military structures.

"Oh, no," he said. "Tell me that's not the target." But his sidekick was young, like me, and excited to see such a *juicy* target.

"Shit-hot!" he said.

"That's affirmative," I responded, one answer for both of their comments.

I left the military structures cratered and in flames. I had done my job. I was a good soldier, but I didn't feel so good. I banked my airplane angrily back and forth, as if I could shake off the feeling in my gut. But the feeling stuck to me, withstanding G forces and logic. Nor could I outrun it. Shame, I felt shame. I was angry at myself for allowing . . . allowing whom? Allowing what? The system? My highers? Our government? I felt rage . . . angry at myself for letting *them* chip away at my soul, compromise my principles . . . until I arrived at a point where I was able to destroy a man's home. How am I helping this man and his family? How would I feel if I went out in the fields in the morning to tend to my crops, and returned home to a bombed-out and burning house? I would hate me. I would go over to the side of the enemy. I would fight forever. I would never forget this injustice . . . What was I doing here? I should be home with my family . . . I banked sharply, bleeding my airspeed, turned on final approach, and landed.

That evening, I sat on my bunk and tried again to write a letter home. I had not written since we met in Hawaii. I didn't know what to say, or how to say it. But now I had a reason to write.

> *I've been traveling a bit. The Viet Namese are taking over our mission, so I guess my last few months will be boring, lots of time sitting around working on my tan, learning a few new chords on the guitar and bull-shitting with the boys.*
> *How are our boys? Did they miss you when you were in Hawaii? Did I tell you I got a SAC assignment? I found out there is a way to get out of it, but I will have to extend for two months. That wouldn't be so bad, would it?*
> *Give the kiddies a kiss and a hug and let me know about the two-month extension. Counting the days until I rotate home.*
> *Hugs and Kisses,*
> *Sky King*

I addressed an envelope, sealed it, and dropped it in the mailbag. Then I walked out of the bunker and joined the circle of FACs.

"Tempers are getting short up there," the Strummer said. "I had a set of F-4s . . . probably some colonel pushing for a promotion. He wanted better B.D.A. Can you imagine? He couldn't hit shit, yet he wanted better bomb damage assessment."

"Probably getting nervous that the war is going to end before he gets his Congressional Medal of Honor."

"I've had fighter jocks like that," another FAC offered. "I've told them to try to hit Viet Nam today. The motherfuckers!"

"You should have sent the son of a bitch home with a full load of bombs. Let him explain that."

The Strummer ran through the four chords he knew. "I told him, 'Negative B.D.A. due to *smoliage*.'

"And he asked: 'What's *smoliage*?'

"'Smoke and *foliage*,' I said.

"'What do you mean, negative B.D.A.?' he said. 'Go down and take a better look.'

"Well, fuck him, I'm thinking. So I said: 'You got it, man. The illusive

COSVN headquarters, three dead monkeys, and a golden statue of Ho Chi Mihn. Now get off my push.'"

We all laughed. And when the laughter ceased, the Strummer said it again, "The COSVN headquarters. The commie's Central Office for South Viet Nam. The war's over, boys." And we all laughed again.

"It's probably one fucking mimeograph machine." And we laughed again. And when we finally got all the good cheer we could from the Strummer's story, another FAC spoke.

"I heard the 1st Air Cav discovered a complex seven stories deep. Point man got shot. Fell in a spider hole that led to it. If he didn't get shot, they would have never found it." I got up and started pacing, back and forth in a straight line at first, and then I walked in circles.

"Who wants to head down to the village?" I asked.

"Are you crazy? This is the Iron Triangle," the Strummer answered.

I did not answer.

"You can't do that. The base is locked down," another FAC said.

"We can bribe the Ar-vin guard," I replied. Sergeant Trung, our South Viet Namese soldier and houseboy, stood and walked into the bunker. He returned with a beer, handed it to me, and said: "We should join with the N.V.A. and kill Khmers."

"What? You've got your friends and enemies confused," the Strummer said.

"That what I think," Trung replied.

I pawed at the dirt with a well-worn combat boot.

"Trung, let's go into the village," I said.

"Not safe. V.C. everywhere!" he replied.

I crushed my empty beer can and walked back inside our bunker, strapped on my sidearm, and placed my red A.R.V.N. Airborne beret on my head, canting it just so. There was no mirrors, but I knew I looked real snazzy. Then, I *di di maued* along a road until I reached a Viet Namese checkpoint. I pulled ten M.P.C.s from my pocket and motioned for the guard to let me pass. He stepped back, and I walked out. I scurried—half walked, half ran—along the trail that led to the village. It was dark. I heard rustling on my left. I stopped and listened. Several young men—barely teenagers—appeared, rifles ready. They wore dark clothes, like black pajamas, the standard V.C. uniform. I thought of my vow: Death before capture, but realized that if I made a move, it would be certain death. If I held still, there might be a better opportunity to escape. I raised my arms slowly. A boy-soldier closest to me walked cautiously toward me, and when the barrel of his M-16 and my belly button were touching, he stopped. His comrades encircled me.

"You American GI?" the boy-soldier asked. I knew the book answer was name, rank, and serial number and nothing else, but I felt compelled to answer.

"Yes."

With his gun barrel, he pointed to the wings over my breast pocket. "You fly for A.R.V.N. Airborne?"

"Yes."

"Not many American GIs around at night."

I did not answer.

"Dangerous," he said. "Many V.C."

I did not answer, nor did I move.

He lowered his rifle. "When I am old enough . . ." He pointed to my beret. "I want to fight with ARVN Airborne."

I was confused. I thought maybe I heard him wrong. "You want beer and woman?" he asked.

A beer and a broad, I thought to myself, as opposed to instant death. Why not? I nodded yes.

"Come. I show you. You will be safe."

We walked into the village. The boy-soldier stopped at a table with two chairs and motioned for me to sit. Then he positioned his men, moving them into the shadows where they were invisible. He sat. A woman arrived carrying two Viet Namese beers called *Ba-ma-ba*, the number thirty-three for them; *tiger piss* for us. The Viet Namese believe number one is good, ten is bad; therefore the beer was appropriately named and numbered. She walked to a washtub that held a large chunk of dripping ice. Several flies flew cover above it; several more shot touch-and-goes on it. She shooed the flies away, chipped off several pieces into two glasses, placed them on the table, and disappeared through a doorway. There were several black specs on the ice. I wondered if it might be fly shit. I poured my beer into the glass.

"My mother and father killed by V.C.," the boy-soldier said. "I kill V.C. every night."

I raised my glass in a half-salute.

When we had finished our beers, he stood. "Come," he said. He led me down a narrow hallway, the sides cardboard, the roof a rusted Coca-Cola sign, the floor dirt. It reminded me of a simpler time when I was a young boy. I would cull the bin behind a department store for cardboard boxes. I would drag them home and create a house in our basement, complete with a long hallway low and narrow so that an adult could not fit through it. The hallway opened to my largest room, constructed from a box for a TV set. On the walls, I glued baseball cards. My bedroom was a box for a refrigerator. For my bed, I swiped a small rug from the floor of our bathroom, and then denied having done so. Here, the boys with automatic weapons were not much older than I was when I lived in my cardboard box, and the cardboard I was now walking down was where they actually lived. The air here was non-existent, stagnant. It smelled of rotting fish. The hallway opened into what seemed like a room. It was dark.

"Wait here," the boy-soldier said; then he departed. I squinted, trying to adjust to the darkness. There was motion at the doorway. I heard the unmistakable sound of a Zippo lighter snap open. The flint flashed and then a flame moved to light two candles, which in turn lit the face of a withered mamasan. She moved to a corner and sat on what looked like a pile of gunnysacks. She started to sing or chant. It sounded like an American Indian war dance I had heard as a young boy in my hometown movie theater. Her intonations rose from low to high and then back down again. My ears hurt. Then a younger Viet Namese woman appeared. She was perhaps in her forties or fifties, maybe even sixty; it was difficult to tell. She was emaciated. She wore a towel around her waist, her breasts non-existent. She grabbed my hands with hers. Her hands were rough, scaly, with variations in the pigments. She pulled me over to a mat, then tried to pull me down. I resisted. I tapped my temples. I wanted to say, "Headache" but I knew the words were meaningless. Instead, I said, "No" as firmly and graciously as I could. Then I reached into my billfold and pulled out another $10 M.P.C. but she would not accept it. I pointed to the chanting lady; "for mamasan," I said. She nodded and crumpled the script into the palm of her hand. I felt my way back out of the room, motioned for another beer, and sat down at the table. The boy-soldier emerged from the shadows and joined me. He was thirteen. I finished my beer, stood, and then he escorted me back to the base. We shook hands first; then I saluted him, took off my beret, and gave it to him. I watched as he disappeared into the shadows.

Flying now became a series of ups and downs, lefts and rights to evade thunder-bumpers with a few airstrikes mixed in. I flew by *the seat of my pants*, pilot speak for flying instinctively, flying without thought or the use of instruments. I flew without emotion, neither scared nor excited. I flew every day because I preferred it to baking in the sun, listening to bad guitar playing, and waiting for a cooling afternoon monsoon rain. I would be promoted to captain one week from today. I planned for a party in Bien Hoa.

The next day, after a mission, I diverted into Bien Hoa. I stopped by the FAC hootch to check on my gear and left a message for Joey to R.O.N. (remain overnight) at the hootch, six days hence, to celebrate my promotion compliments of the United States Army. I said Army because so many company commanders had been and were being killed that the Army had to shorten the time in-grade between promotion from 1st lieutenant to captain from four years, to three and one-half years, to three years. Promotions up to captain were automatic unless you were a super fuck-up. Even I didn't qualify as a super fuck-up.

"Hey, you got a letter at the bar," a TWAT pilot said just as I was about to depart. I followed him to the bar. He went behind it and rifled through some papers. "Here it is," he said. He tossed an envelope on the bar. It was from my wife. I turned it over and ripped the envelope flap open. The letter was folded in thirds, but only the top third had words.

If you extend, I will divorce you! I stopped reading. I ripped the letter to shreds. There would be no Steve Canyon program for me. I was stuck with the SAC assignment. I thought about her words as I flew back north. At first, I was angry. Then as I entered the landing pattern, I decided she might have saved my life. A guy could get killed working the trail—especially a guy like me who could not follow orders and who no longer cared if he lived or died. Even my reoccurring dream of crashing into a tree now seemed normal. I just wanted to know what happened, why I put in left aileron and rudder instead of right. I dropped the gear, turned on final, and landed.

The next six days droned slowly by: every day the same, every night the same. When I finally landed back at Bien Hoa, Joey was waiting for me. He was sitting in a jeep along with Earl, the Walrus, and Frick. He drove me back to our hootch where I showered. I scrubbed vigorously trying to extricate the baked-in red clay embedded in my pores, and I now understood why the mamasans used rocks to clean clothes. When finished, we sucked down a couple of beers at the bar, where I greeted Miss Sam. She looked terrific. Joey requested a kiss from her in between swallows, only to be rebuffed every time with the words, "Never happen, GI," which prompted the Walrus to ask if anybody knew what the Houston Oilers called their cheerleaders. When we admitted to being stumped, he answered: "The LubriCunts!" We all laughed.

Hee, hee! Hee, hee, hee!

One piece of paper and I was a captain in the Air Force. I placed my orders on the bar. My name was underlined along with a bunch of other names: nothing formal, just a sheet a paper. "Can you believe it? They promoted me to captain."

"Every officer makes captain after they have been in the service for three years! Big fucking deal!" the Walrus said.

"Guess you're right," I replied. "Even Puff made captain."

"How about a kiss for the new captain, eh Miss Sam?"

"Never happen. You want more beer?"

"Fucking A."

"*Numbah* ten! You speak *numbah* ten all the time."

By 1730, the bar was filled with staff-weenies, TWAT pilots, and other desk-flying pilots. It was time to leave. We loaded a jeep and headed for the officers club, where I walked into the kitchen and told two gomers to get me a washtub and fill it with ice. When I turned to leave, the club officer—a captain—stood before me. I moved left; he moved right. I moved left; he moved right, blocking my path each time. "What are you doing?" he asked.

"How many bottles of Chianti do you have?" I asked.

"Ten, twelve, maybe more," he answered.

"Good, I will take them all and these two Viet Namese."

"You can't do that!" he said.

I could feel the red heat rising from my gut, up into and through my neck, and then quickly exploding across my face. No non-combatant asshole was going to tell me what I could or couldn't do. I said nothing, nor did I move a muscle. I just let the anger radiate from my body. My eyes were fixed on his eyes, and they stayed fixed until he stepped back.

"Get the tub and the wine," he said to his two Viet Namese busboys. When they returned, one carried the tub, and the other cradled six bottles of wine. I pulled forty M.P.C.s—two twenties—from my billfold, a particularly disgusting denomination for U.S. *grunts*. The image on it was a soldier with a tin pot; the disgusting part was the soldier looked Asian. I gave them to the club officer. "For the wine." Then I pulled out an additional two twenties and gave one to each of the gomers and said: "Follow me with that washtub. Wherever I go I want you to be no more than one arm's length away." I held out my arm. "Do you understand?"

"Can do, easy," they both said, bobbing their grinning heads.

I walked back out and into the main bar area. Then I stopped abruptly in the center of the room and held out my arm, never once looking at the gomers who I assumed were following me. I felt the neck of a wine bottle being placed in the palm of my hand. I wrapped my fingers around it. "Excellent," I said. "But next time make sure the bottle is opened."

We resumed our little parade until we reached a booth in the far corner of the barroom. And we all sat down—Joey, Earl, the Walrus, and I. Frick pulled up a barstool and sat on it. The gomers sat on the floor.

"We are on for Hong Kong, right mate?" Joey asked.

"Fucking A! The last week in June," I answered.

Hee, hee! Hee, hee, hee!

I passed a bottle of wine to the Walrus. He examined it. "Two bucks!" he said. "Can't beat that!"

"What about the stamps?" Frick asked.

"What about the stamps?" the Walrus asked, shrugging his shoulders.

"They are free!" Frick replied. There was silence.

"You don't have to put a stamp on an envelope if you are sending it to the States," Frick explained. There was silence.

"That's a pretty good deal!" Frick said.

"S – H – I – T !" the Walrus said. He started the word while he was sitting and finished it as he walked away.

Later in the evening, when I had to take a piss, the two gomers stood, grabbed the washtub, followed me into the pisser, and stood behind me while I *drained me dragon*, as Joey would have said. When we returned to our hootch, the two gomers placed the tub in the back of the jeep. They then sat and grabbed hold of the side bars on the jeep. Their legs dangled inches from the rear tires. With Joey driving, mostly on the shoulder and sometimes on the road, they bounced each time the surface changed. They bounced so high I could see the horizon between their asses and the jeep. Poetic justice, I figured, for the terrorizing jitney rides other gomers had given me. We parked and walked in down the hallway on the staff-weenie side of the hootch. Just before we reached the main barroom, I saw for the first time a fire extinguisher hanging on the wall. I lifted it off and proceeded to spray the backs of TWAT pilots and disgruntled desk jockeys and staff-weenies who were quietly quaffing their drinks at the bar.

Hee, hee! Hee, hee, hee!

I heard a weenie yell, "I just spent the entire afternoon filling those extinguishers." I heard him just before he tackled me.

Hee, hee! Hee, hee, hee!

I think I was laughing, too, as we wrestled, but I was also thinking I've got a reputation to uphold so maybe I should pop him a couple of times. But the thought was fleeting and moot since I never got into a position of dominance where I could rain him with *a bunch of fives*. Eventually, we were separated with no punches thrown. Several shots and beer chasers later, I was dragged to my room and deposited on my bed, now one rank higher in my quest for Air Force excellence.

I felt a hand on my shoulder. "Wake up!" a major I did not know repeated once, twice, three times, four times. He was now shaking me. And had it not been for the stupor that engulfed me—and the fact that I did not have a loaded pistol under my pillow—I might have shot him dead. I sat up slowly. I let my poncho liner fall to the floor. I was still dressed in wine-soaked fatigues; my boots were still connected to my feet. "What the fuck?" I mumbled, rubbing both sides of my head. He allowed me time to open my eyes, and I assumed he figured if my eyes were open so might be my ears.

"You are going to Hong Kong, correct?" I did not answer. I couldn't even if I had wanted to. A team of horses had taken a shit in my mouth. "Here are three opals I bought in Australia." He held an envelope with the flap open. "I want you to take them to a jeweler, T. Lee Wang; the name and address are on a paper in here." He shook the envelope and I could hear the rocks roll to one corner. "I want him to set these stones in a ring." He paused after each sentence, like he was talking to some desk-flying weenie instead of a combat-tested U.S. Air Force captain. "There are six hundred dollars in here." He moved the paper, and I could see several greenbacks. "No more than $200 per setting." He paused; then he began anew, talking to me like I was some kind of washtub-carrying gomer. "Bring the rings back." I could feel gravity pulling my head back onto the bed. "I will get them from you." I don't remember him saying anything else. He studied me for a long time, and then he placed the envelope in my hand, stood, turned, and walked out of my room. My head crashed back on the bed as soon as he closed the door.

I awoke again several hours after my early morning visitor had departed. I felt no better than I had during our one-sided conversation. I looked in the envelope. One stone, two stones . . . but I could not locate the third opal. I rose, hitting my head on the top bunk, but it didn't put a dent in my head or the pain I was experiencing there. I passed the palm of my hand slowly over the top blanket. Nothing! Then I looked under my pillow, and there it was. Had the tooth fairy placed it there? Had I lost a tooth in my mini-rumble last night? I tried to remember. I thought about challenging the weenie to a real fight: fisticuffs in the parking lot. I was sure I could take him, and I felt the need to demonstrate that to my fans individually and to all weenies in general. I didn't want any of them to think I was a pussy. Besides, my head already hurt because I had picked a fight with several bottles of cheap wine. I picked the stone up, tossed it in the air, and caught it in the open envelope. I sealed the envelope and jammed it in my fatigue pocket.

I walked to the shitter. Joey was barfing in a toilet bowl. "Did we have fun?" I asked. He answered with another upchuck. I yelled at the mamasans. "Get the fuck out of the shower!" And when they complied, I turned it on.

Then I stood under it still in my fatigues with my combat boots still connected to my feet. When the temperature of the water dropped, I got out. The mamasans pointed at me, cackling and laughing. I removed my fatigue jacket and began to wring it out, only then remembering I had placed the envelope in my pocket. I ran back to my room, opened the soggy envelope, and spread the sheet of paper with the addresses on the table. The ink had bled, but names and addresses were still legible. I copied the information on a dry piece of paper, replaced the envelope, and wondered what I should do with it. What kind of idiot would entrust me, a slobbering wino, with such an important mission? And what kind of idiot would accept such a mission? I couldn't take it with me, could I? Maybe, I could . . . I could use the stones to negotiate my release if captured. I decided this strategy was unsound. I looked around the room, slowly moving my head from left to right, searching for a place to hide the envelope. Hey, why not inside my locked locker? I smiled. Now that I was a captain, I was already making good decisions. I changed into a stone-washed flight suit, wrapped the envelope in some dirty underwear, placed the dirty underwear inside my locker, snapped the padlock shut, walked to my jeep, unlocked the jeep padlock, and drove to the flight line.

We continued to pound military structures, bunker complexes, and a base camp in Cambodia so large U.S. grunts called it *The City*. But we never found the COSVN headquarters—our search and destroy objective—and the justification for invading Cambodia. And, oh yeah, did I mention that we also did it to buy time for the South Viet Namese to take over the war? After five years of war, we now had sixty days to achieve these objectives. On June 1, Congress cut off funds and all friendly troops had to retreat back across the border and several U.S. units were headed home. We had rushed in, and then rushed back out, creating a vacuum soon filled by the bad guys. The South Viet Namese were supposed to fill it, but they didn't because they couldn't. We had never taught them how to fight. We taught them to look good: boots and helmets polished, dickeys around their necks. We did their fighting for them; otherwise their county would fall into the hands of the communists. We did the fighting so that our generals wouldn't look like the fools they were, so that they could lie to our government, and so that our government could lie to the people with statements like: "Victory is just around the corner." But what did I care? For me, the *incursion* was over. I would spend the next week living in a *Red Marker* FAC villa on Tudor Street in Saigon, the capital city of the Republic of South Viet Nam. After that, I would be headed to Hong Kong with Joey. And after that, I would be headed home.

Chapter 7
ANOTHER CLUSTER FUCK

I arrived in Saigon just after dark. "Dinner will be served at 2000 hours," the Strummer said. He showed me my room on the second floor. An overhead fan whirled. The closet doors were louvered. A window overlooked Tudor Street. I opened the window and listened to the street noises: motorcycles accelerating or screeching to a stop, vendors cackling, blasting truck horns answered by the *beep, beeps* of overloaded scooters, MPs blowing their whistles. Neon lights flashed, illuminating bunkered checkpoints manned by yellow men in green uniforms. White and black men walked the streets in separate groups of three or four. Men, both Asian and Caucasian, dressed in *civvies* ogled Viet Namese whores dressed in traditional and Western attire. Buddhist monks in saffron robes strolled or sat yogi-style and prayed. I showered, dressed, and reported to the dining room for dinner. They sat me at the head of the table. Viet Namese waitresses poured water, waiters displayed bottles of wine, silverware bracketed china, and an elder Viet Namese woman sat at the far end of the table and gave orders. I suspected she may have owned the villa. I unfolded the linen napkin and placed it in my lap.

"Ready to hit the town after dinner?" the Strummer asked.

"Not tonight," I replied. "I plan to sleep for twelve to fourteen hours, then do it up right for the next six days and nights." He nodded, and we spooned soup, munched salad, cut and chewed meat, savored sweets in silence. At the end of the meal, I rose and nodded to the hostess. She nodded back. I placed my napkin on the table and walked to my room. I undressed down to my skivvies, crawled under crisp white sheets, and fell into a deep slumber.

"Wake up, wake up!" The voice of the Strummer was accompanied by pushes against my shoulder. I swatted his arm away and sat up.

"Two guys in your unit had a midair. They want you back in Bien Hoa immediately."

"Motherfucker. Who was it? Did they say?"

"No."

"Goddammit! Another cluster fuck. When will they end?" I said as I sat up on the edge of my bed. The Strummer did not answer my question.

"I'll fly you back," he said.

Was it Earl? The Walrus? I wondered. I doubt it. It had to be Frick and Frack. "Goddamn those weenie assholes!" I shouted. I slipped into a flight suit, and packed my few belongings. "Were they killed?"

"Don't know. Are you ready?"

I surveyed the room. Neon lights flickering through the limbs of trees danced on the walls. I checked my watch; the big hand was on one, the little one pointed to seven. When the big hand hit seven, we launched. Earl and the Walrus were waiting for me when we landed.

"Yeah, it was Frick and Frack," the Walrus said.

"They were flying formation," Earl added. "Frack was on the wing and he clipped Frick's wing. Fortunately, they were right over the strip. Frick managed to land his airplane. Frack bailed out . . . he's got burns on his arms and face. He's in the hospital in Saigon."

"That asshole should have never gotten through pilot training," the Walrus mumbled.

"General's kid," Earl offered.

"Ask me what I like about this place," the Walrus said. I was befuddled. My head snapped back like I was slipping a right hook.

"Okay," I said. "What do you like about this place?"

"Nothing! Not one fucking thing!" the Walrus answered. No one laughed.

They briefed me on the way to our hootch. "You gotta help with the mission," Earl said. "That's why I sent for you. It's a boring as hell mission, but we are tasked with it. There is going to be an inquiry." And I wondered how many different languages you could say *fuck* in.

The next day I flew the mission—right-hand orbits for fifteen minutes, then left-hand orbits for fifteen minutes—for three and one-half hours. Charlie never once fired a shot. And I got to wishing he would.

"I can't fly that mission, Earl," I said upon landing. "Get a TWAT pilot to fly it."

"Okay, I'll see what I can do. You take the Rome plow mission."

"Thanks Earl; three bags full."

"Let's go see what *Crash* has to say," he replied. I laughed. Frack had earned a new name.

We jumped in a jeep, and Earl set a course for Saigon. We drove in silence. I liked the stillness of the countryside. When the horns started honking, Earl began to talk.

"They say he got one swing on the chute before he hit the ground. The dumb fuck!" Earl looked at me and continued talking. "Frick is a good guy, and the general's kid almost took him out."

We pulled into the hospital parking lot, and Earl chained and padlocked the jeep. We walked through double doors. Earl led. I followed. We moved through the hospital at a fast pace—as if Earl knew exactly where we were going—down a long hallway and into a large dormitory. I tried not to look at the wounded soldiers. They were the lucky ones. The severe cases were immediately medevaced to the Philippines. Nurses hovered over maimed soldiers. "They are in combat every day," I said to Earl.

"Who's that?" he asked.

"Nurses," I replied.

Earl looked respectable in a clean flight suit, boots black but not polished, and a fresh buzz cut. I did not. My cammies were faded and frayed, victimized by too many stone washings. Any signs of polish had left my boots long ago. My hair was shaggy, bleached, and stuck straight out when I scratched just above my left ear. The hospital was spotless and colorless: White tiles on the floor, white walls—like the scrubbed tires on a cherry '57 Chevy—and white ceiling. The nurses dressed the same, all wearing white uniforms. Several wore glasses, and because of that they stood out. I thought I detected sneers from the most immaculate ones. Instead of rage, I felt like a sinner sated with guilt and shame standing before his Maker, completely helpless and unworthy. Earl slowed. He was now looking at individual beds. He stopped abruptly, and I rear-ended him.

"Hey man," Earl said, offering his hand to Frack, and I wondered if he knew the general's kid name since I surmised it wasn't Frack.

"How's it going?" I said.

He was sitting up in bed, reading *Playboy* magazines. No, I decided; he was just looking at the photos. I thought of Fast Freddie, Fighter Pilot, and his quest for finding a photo of one of his conquests.

"My right wing clipped his left wing," Frack said. "And caught fire . . . the airplane went into a right-hand spin. I tried to pull to the door, so I could jump out . . . that's when I burned my arms." He held them out. They were bandaged. "Centrifugal force wouldn't let me get to the door. When I let go, my helmet hit the side window. I don't know if it broke the window or not, but I figured it was my only way out. I remember pushing hard with my legs and I popped free of the airplane. I pulled the D-ring, got a chute, and hit the ground. They figured I got a chute at about 250 feet." He seemed remarkably composed, and I couldn't help but think ignorance had something to do with it.

"Funny thing," he laughed. "When I got back to Bien Hoa, the flying safety boys wanted me to show them how I did it. They thought it might make for a good alternate escape hatch. They had an O-2 with the window already knocked out. They strapped a parachute on me and told me to squeeze through the window." He laughed again. "I couldn't do it! I tried and tried; they even tried to pull me through—nothing doing."

Three thoughts hit me all at once. The first, accompanied by a visual of Big Al's bare ass shooting out from under the crapper door, made me smile. Big Al couldn't re-create it either, which proved that fear is a powerful motivator. Then I thought about how calloused the fly-safe officers were. Here was a pilot who had just cheated the grim reaper—a pilot with burned arms—and they had him out on the ramp playing games. And third: Why in the fuck hadn't they put a door on the pilot's side of the aircraft in the first place? The answer was probably money. I heard once that every gook we killed cost the United States $325,000. Guess there wasn't anything left over for us.

Earl wrapped up his conversation with Frack, and we walked back out the way we came in. Only this time, rage allowed me to hold my head high. I walked with my hand wrapped around the handle of my .38, index finger pointed down, and my head on a swivel. Fuck these righteous bastards!

"There is a reception for a general. Let's go," Earl said. I like how he used the words "Let's" instead of Captain Puff's words: "We are."

"Like this?" I said, using my hands to draw attention to my attire.

"Hell yes! They put their pants on the same way we do."

The reception was in a large room. A room that was full of fuck-up and move-up people. Brass of all sorts were running around burying their heads up other higher brass's assholes, and it didn't seem to matter if they were U.S. troops or Viet Namese. Anglo civilians—I assumed reporters or political hacks—munched, yacked, and drank. Viet Namese civilians—either politicians or spies, or both—cackled and smoked. My skin crawled and my stomach growled, and I realized I hadn't eaten since yesterday. A waiter wandered by with a tray full of what looked like tiny sandwiches filled with *pate* or what should be a mandatory entrée in every box of C-rations. I took three, popped them into my mouth, and immediately sent them down to appease my stomach. They hit bottom with a bounce and I was positive they were coming right back up. I grabbed a post. I leaned against it and squeezed it, maybe even humped it, for my body was rejecting the food or whatever it was that I had tossed down. Without the post, I would have heaved all over anyone within a ten-feet radius. Words such as *putrid, rancid,* or *fetid* best described it. I had never been much of an upchuck man, either drunk or sober, although there were times when I wanted to spray the contents of my stomach, and this was one of them—blast it out like buckshot from a scatter gun—but I could never make it happen. The Walrus once said we should puke with our teeth clenched so we wouldn't lose the big pieces. Eventually, my stomach stopped convulsing, and I was sure that whatever I had eaten was going to stay down. I loosened my grip on the post. Who eats this shit? I wondered. And what was it? It tasted like a chemistry lab smelled. There would be no seconds for me. I lit a cigarette, looked at my watch, and waited for Earl. I hoped he wasn't planning on attending *the five o'clock follies*—the time each day when our generals told lies to our reporters—although it might have been interesting to listen in. Instead, I walked to the bar.

"I'll take a Jack Daniels."

"Jack Daniels and what?" the bartender asked. I thought for a minute.

"Jack Daniels and Jack Daniels," I replied.

"Double shot of Jack Daniels?"

"That's right." He poured it and I drank it. Earl found me at the bar.

"Want something?" I asked.

"Yeah, I want to get the fuck out of here."

"Where to?" I asked.

"Home," he said.

The Rome plow mission was a lot like our Kontum mission: We sat in our Cessnas, the grunts sat on their Caterpillar, and we both endured hours of endless circles. Our mission was to put bombs into the encircled jungle before the plows started their endless left turns, wait for something to happen when they dozed, and then put in airstrikes after they finished. It would have been nice if we both could have dozed at the same time.

On my fourth day back, Earl stopped me after my morning piss. "Got one for you," he said. "I want you to come along. We take off at 1300."

"Three bags full." Every time I said those three words, in that order, Earl laughed. It was good to see him laugh. He was a leader who valued my opinion, and a man I could trust. So I didn't ask what he had going, and he didn't offer. I returned to my room, cranked some music, and checked the days on my short-timer's calendar. I was zeroing in on the tits and twat. I closed my eyes and waited for Earl to roust me.

We launched at 1300 hours. Earl took up a heading two, seven, zero, give or take a few degrees to dodge thunder bumpers. Out of my side window, I noticed a big "1" cut into the jungle. I pointed. Earl turned the aircraft for a better look. "The Big Red One," I said. He nodded. The 1st Infantry Division had marked its territory.

"Impressive," he said. And I wondered if *first* really meant *first*; and if it did then how many wars had it fought in. Did it go back to the Revolutionary War? Earl returned the airplane to its westerly heading. We crossed the border into Cambodian. We *violated* their airspace. I had *incurred* and now I had *violated*.

"We are looking for an island off of the west coast of Cambodia," Earl said.

"I thought we were done with Cambodia."

"So did I," Earl replied. "They told me we are on our own if we get shot down. They would deny they knew us, *and* they would not lift a finger to help us."

"Well, ain't that a goddamn good deal! Is that why you never told me where we were going?"

"No. You didn't ask, I didn't offer."

We drove on in silence until Earl spotted a small airstrip, which looked vacated, in the middle of Cambodia. He turned the airplane to line up with it and then chopped the power. "Want to do a touch-and-go?"

"Are you nuts? What if the bad guys own it?"

"We could give them the finger." He laughed and brought the power back in, but I knew he would have landed if I had said yes. We flew on—out the other side of Cambodia. We were feet wet. "There it is," Earl said. He pointed out the front windshield.

"Now what?"

"There's a small strip on the south end. Six Army types live there."

Earl turned the bird south. It began to drizzle. He spotted the airstrip. It was narrow, short, and made of P.S.P.

"Perfect for slippery landings on a rainy day," Earl said. He laughed; I did not.

I studied the airstrip. I figured the strip had a pucker factor of about ten. Pucker factor rates the tightness your asshole gets just before the shit hits the fan.

"Whoa, whoa. Wait a minute. What's that?"

"What? Where?" Earl asked.

"Down there," I pointed. "Drop down."

There was a cleared area between the airstrip and the jungle with what looked like a slew of bunkers. Earl circled over it, descending with each turn until he was about ten feet off the deck. He banked right and left so we both could see. There were poles or bars across the tops of the bunkers. Confined Asian men were looking up at us. They wore what looked like extra-large diapers. The men were stooped, so the depth of the bunkers must have been five feet or less.

"Behold the *tiger cages* our government vows we don't have."

"Wow!" Earl said.

"Must be a motherfucker in there when the sun is beating down, or when it rains."

"And at night! They must freeze their balls off!" Earl said.

"You gotta be shitting me!"

Earl banked the airplane and followed the coast going beyond the island; then he turned back and we were on final approach. A rain shower guarded the runway.

"Just a drizzle," Earl said. And I wondered who he was trying to convince.

I was glad he was driving. He had tons of experience driving light airplanes. He told me his father owned a Piper Cub. He kept it in a barn on their farm.

"I started flying before I drove a car," Earl bragged. "It was great on dates!" He said it with a huge grin. He had landed on cornfields, pastures, and dirt roads; and he did it for fun and not because he lost power. He was the nerdiest-looking *Daredevil* I ever knew. He put the plane gently down on what pilots call the *first brick*; a hell of a feat since there was maybe a foot between ocean and the beginning of the runway . . . and he managed to stop the airplane before we skidded off the end of the runway.

"Well done!" I said. And he laughed again.

He taxied back so the bird would be in position to take off. I got out and chocked the aircraft.

"Let's go talk to them," Earl said.

"You go talk to them; I'll wait here." The drizzle cooled me off. I rubbed my scalp and face. Is there anything better than a drizzle on a sizzling tropical afternoon? I couldn't think of anything. I walked around the airplane. I checked the tires and all the control surfaces. I inspected both propellers. And then I sat under the wing. I leaned back against rubber wheel and thought about Cambodia. I decided Sihanouk was a great leader. He got the French out without firing a shot, and he kept his country out of this war—Cambodia was officially declared *neutral*—despite what must have been extreme pressure from the United States to get involved. To keep his people safe, he had to look the other way while North Viet Namese troops used eastern Cambodia as a sanctuary for stockpiling supplies, massing troops, and staging raids into South Viet Nam. But when the prince left his country for a weekend, his military staged a coup. Our guy General Lon Nol took control, and shortly thereafter I was putting in airstrikes on a Cambodian village. I was all for the invasion—pardon me, *incursion*—at first. I smelled blood and I was excited.

The invasion had objectives and targets I could actually see, front lines, and real estate to be taken, secured, and held. We could measure progress in miles conquered. It felt like a real war, a war we could actually win. But now, we were again back to taking land and then giving it back to the enemy. We were back to pounding a random coordinate, a coordinate where some pencil pusher in Saigon thought a group of gooks might be hiding. Then they would send me and thousands of other GIs to locate and kill the poor bastards: men who had few options. One of which was to live in a tiger cage.

I began to imagine how a man would end up in one of our tiger cages.

A farmer kissed his children good night and reclined beside his wife on a thatched mat after a hard day of work in the field. That night the V.C. decided to pay his village a visit.

"Come fight with us," the V.C. ordered.

"But I just want to plant and cultivate my rice," the farmer replied.

"I will kill you, your wife, and your children," a V.C. soldier said as he pointed his AK-47 at a village elder, the farmer's father. BANG! The farmer's father fell dead.

The farmer joined the Viet Cong. Now, the V.C. had a gun in his back, and the U.S. had a gun in his gut. Soon, the farmer decided to switch sides. He surrendered to a U.S. Army unit. They immediately made him a Kit Carson scout. He was ordered to lead U.S. troops to V.C. base camps. "If you choose not to, we will throw you out of a helicopter without a parachute," a friendly U.S. Army officer said to the farmer. Because he was helping the U.S., the farmer feared for the lives of his wife and children. He rejoined the Viet Cong. He now had two options. He could get killed, or he could allow himself to be captured by U.S. forces and live the rest of his life in a tiger cage—a tiger cage the U.S. government insists isn't there.

Earl wasn't long.

"They love it here," he said. "They want to know if we would like some fresh lobster before we head back." He laughed. "They dive for lobster every day." I held my hand like a salute—just over my eyes—to shield the sun, so I could see him when he spoke. "There is a downside to their life of leisure," Earl continued. "There are twelve hundred V.C. and N.V.A. prisoners in those tiger cages. The bad guys are on the north end of the island and trying to spring them. That's why we are here, to put in a bunch of airstrikes on the invading gook camps." I did not answer.

"We got a whole bunch of A-37s to put in, call signs: *Rap* and *Dice*; *Dice* from the Pair of Dice Squadron that dates back to World War I. How does it feel to be a part of history?"

I still did not answer. I just shook my head and said, "Let's do it!"

And that is what we did until we ran out of bombs, and daylight, and nearly fuel. We skipped the lobster dinner and flew back to Viet Nam. "Hopefully, that will hold them," Earl said. They were the only words spoken between us until we were back at our hootch.

I continued to put in airstrikes south of Bien Hoa, around the area the Rome plows had recently cleared. The dirt was chalky white and looked like it was prepped for a future housing project. It was bordered on one side by the road running to Vung Tau, on another by the muddy river delta, and a third by a narrow strip of jungle—maybe twenty meters wide—sandwiched between the scraped-clean area and the Saigon River. My target for today was in the middle of that twenty-meter strip of jungle. Naturally, I wondered what *genius* had decided to leave that strip of vegetation. Was it to lure Charlie in there? No. I didn't believe our pencil-pushers were smart enough to plan such an elaborate strategy. Was it for protection against soil erosion? No. Protection of any kind had long ceased to be a priority; destruction was the word of the day, month, and year. There were signs Charlie had moved into that strip, so maybe it was genius. We could smack him good. All we had to do was place bombs in that twenty-meter strip.

"*Smoky* four-four, *Shark* two-niner."

"Roger, *Shark*. I copy you loud and clear."

"We are a couple of *Fox* fours."

F-4s, and I had the perfect target for them. F-4s had a difficult time with accuracy. Maybe it was because they were used to hitting *hot* targets in the north or on the trail. Targets with lots of heavy and large-caliber ground fire. These targets required *jinking*—high-speed, high-G maneuvering—around the target instead of lining up and coming straight in. Or maybe it was because of aircraft deficiencies, using aircrafts designed for air-to-air as bombers. For whatever reason, it certainly wasn't the pilots. They were shit-hot and tits up. Most targets were missed long or short—north and south, not east and west. That is why all bombing runs were made perpendicular to our ground troops. This reduced the chances of a *short round* exploding on top of our troops, resulting in deaths by friendly fire. There were no friendlies in the area on this target. Ground fire would be at a minimum, if any, and it was no biggie if they dropped short or long. I cleared each aircraft through for one pass. The bombs were close, within five meters of my mark.

"*Shark, Smoky*. Hold high and dry while I drop down and check for B.D.A."

"Roger I copy, hold high and dry."

"Two copies."

I buzzed around trying to find a bunker, or a trail, or something that might indicate enemy presence but discovered nothing. We just created two more craters in the middle of some trees. I climbed and rolled in for another mark. Lead rolled in and splashed napalm. Two dropped hard stuff. Lead's bomb was on target. Two's was not. He had dropped wide. I mean way wide—thirty meters wide, out in scraped-clean-earth wide. When the smoke cleared, I was stunned to see he had uncovered bunkers and trench lines; bunkers in the middle of nothing, bunkers in the middle of nowhere, bunkers with no overhead cover anywhere within thirty meters. Charlie—in this case *Mister Charles*—was a fox. He had already moved back into the area scraped clean by our Rome plows, into an area no one would have ever thought to look for him, into an area where he would have never been discovered had it not been for one errant bomb. Who was the genius now? I wondered. I continued to hit the open area with additional sets of air when available. When there was none, I pounded it with artillery. I registered a battery of guns. They would fire a tube; I would observe where it landed. I would give a correction. They would make an adjustment and fire again. And when we had all the tubes dialed in, I told them to "*close sheath* and *fire for effect.*" I was fascinated with Charlie's ingenuity as I watched the shells landing, so fascinated that I forgot to keep an eye on the weather.

"*Smoky* four-four, *Smoky* forty. Be advised, Bien Hoa airfield is closed due to weather. State intentions."

Intentions? Well, I intended to land. Get this bird on the ground. Find a nest. But where? I was being pushed into the South China Sea. I tried to get around the storm, over it, under it; no dice.

Vung Tau was my only option. I drove toward the coastal town.

"Vung Tau tower, *Smoky* four-four."

"*Smoky* four-four, Vung Tau, go ahead."

"Roger, requesting landing instructions."

"*Smoky* four-four. Vung Tau airfield is closed due to high winds."

"How high?"

"*Smoky* four-four, Vung Tau. We have a direct crosswind at 30 knots, gusting to 45 with sporadic rain."

I pulled out my checklist and ran my finger over the graph. My aircraft could take 27 knots of direct crosswind. I figured they had at least a 10 percent fudge factor, so I could push that up to 30. Still, it didn't sound too appetizing: crosswind, rain, P.S.P. matting for a slippery landing surface . . . maybe there was a better option.

"*Paris Control, Smoky* four-four."

"This is *Paris Control*. How can I help?"

Polite son of a bitch. *You can help me by landing my fucking airplane*, I mumbled while still driving toward Vung Tau. Now the base of the clouds had pushed me down to 500 feet.

"Paris, *Smoky* four-four. I am an Oscar Deuce, ten west of Vung Tau. The airstrip is closed. Do I have any other options?"

There was no response.

"*Paris Control, Smoky* four-four." And again.

"*Paris Control, Smoky* four-four."

"Stand by *Smoky*. We are checking."

"Roger."

Two days before Joey and I were scheduled for R&R to Hong Kong, and I get my ass in this crack. Always some kind of death-defying bullshit before this shithole country could release me. As if it was saying: "*I've got you now, you little fucker. And you are not going to get away!*"

"Fuck!" I yelled inside my passengerless aircraft. "Fuck! Fuck! Fuck!"

"*Smoky, Paris Control*. All airstrips are closed in your vicinity. We are working on a solution."

"Can you vector me to Bien Hoa?"

"That's a negative. Expect extreme turbulence in the thunderstorms, and once again, all airstrips are closed."

I could see Vung Tau's runways. I could also see that the storm was moving in fast, and soon I would not be able to see those runways.

"*Smoky, Paris Control.*"

"Paris, *Smoky.*"

"*Smoky*, Paris. We have a Navy ship standing by. We suggest you fly to it and jump out."

"Obviously, you have never seen me swim."

"The Navy is confident they can fish you out."

"If I was a fish, I might consider it. I'm going into Vung Tau."

"Be advised, *Smoky*. That strip is closed!"

"Vung Tau tower. *Smoky* four-four. I am going to land. I plan to fly initial and pitch out."

"*Smoky* four-four, Vung Tau tower. Be advised our airfield is closed due to high winds."

I was done with radio calls. I reckoned the ocean would always be there, and I could always jump into it. Hell, I didn't even have to worry about missing it. Swimming terrified me; flying an airplane did not. And right now I had my hands full of airplane.

I would fly down the runway to get a feel for the winds; then I would bank back around for a turn on final. I planned to carry every extra knot of airspeed I could using my 10 percent fudge factor; I planned to carry all the extra airspeed I could and then plant the airplane on the runway. I would fly initial and pitch out to get a feel for the winds. I lined up the airplane with the runway. It felt like the airplane was flying perpendicular to the wind instead of straight into it. I cross-controlled the airplane using rudder and aileron. I had a slow-motion visual of my ALO doing just that several months earlier. Then I began to whistle. I was whistling just as my former flight instructor the Judge had done back in pilot training. I pitched into the wind, slowed the aircraft, and watched the airspeed bleed until I was able to drop the gear.

When I looked back outside, I could not see the runway. I looked over my left shoulder. "There it is." The wind had pushed me well past the runway. I had not planned for this. I continued my circle to the left while maintaining altitude until I was back where I could turn onto final. This time I started my turn early to compensate for wind. This time I would not *overshoot*. I turned on final and held her there carrying lots of extra speed and drove her onto the runway. I was shocked. *Ker-thud!* The front prop remained intact; I remained intact. Even on the ground, I had to use aileron to hold the wing down. Several gusts tried to tip my airplane. I taxied to the *Smoky* revetment and shut her down. I unstrapped and got out. I patted the bird's aluminum body. She had served me well. I had survived another scare just before R & R. I was getting reckless, getting cocky, feeling immortal, and not paying attention to what was important. Jefferson's voice echoed inside my head: "This war is not worth it. Your job is to stay alive." I needed a beer. While drinking it and several more, I wrote a letter home.

> I made captain. Joey and I are heading
> to Hong Kong. He has been an incredible
> mate. Earl is an excellent boss. The Walrus
> is funny. I have been working on my tan.
> Some of the guys wanted me to go for
> a swim, but I declined. I am safe,
> and in a short time I will be home,
> holding you and the boys in my arms.
> Sky King

The next morning, I flew directly back to Bien Hoa, parked the airplane, and announced that I would not be flying until I returned from Hong Kong. "Relax," Earl said, "and when you get to Hong Kong, stay as long as you want. We will cover for you."

Chapter 8
MY FRIEND JACK

Joey was barfing into the sink. "Today's the day, mate." I said.

Bar- ruff! He looked at me and nodded.

"Want to get some food before we get on the airplane?"

Bar-ruff!

When he was finished, I unlocked the door on the staff-weenie side, released the mamasans, and walked back to my room. I finished packing. I was traveling light. I reckoned I would shit-can everything once I got settled in Hong Kong and buy all new stuff. I counted my money from my gambling stash. Then I added in the stoned major's money. He must have been stoned to give it to me. I had $2,800. I put the envelope with his opals in my right sock, stuffed $2,500 in my left sock, the rest in my billfold, and waited for Joey.

"Ready, mate?" he asked when he appeared in the doorway.

"Damn tooting!"

Frick drove us to the Saigon terminal where we mingled with a gaggle of other GIs, all of us scrubbed and most of us primed to get our rocks off in the exotic Oriental city of Hong Kong. The flight seemed long—I was excited; and short—and the final approach looked menacing. There was a ten-story building just before the end of the runway. Our commercial pilot had to clear it by chopping the power and dropping us in: a landing with a pucker factor of eight or more. His technique was flawless.

The airplane door swung open and we ran out like kids at recess. We ran across the macadam, through the terminal, and out the double doors where we caught a cab that took us to our hotel. Once there, I threw my stuff in a drawer, showered, and met Joey in the hotel bar where we had a couple of bumps and chased them with beer.

"Got an errand to run," I said to Joey. He stood without answering or questioning me, and we departed, leaving a healthy tip for our waitress. We giggled. We could stay until our money was gone; then it was back to crazy land where people I never met or knew tried to kill me. Funny, I never thought about me killing them, just them killing me. We walked to the jewelry store noted on my paper, bypassing many pleading merchants trying to separate us from our dollars. Several were so aggressive, I had to dislodge their hand from my arm. We entered the jewelry store and were immediately offered drinks. If it was liquid, they had it. Joey and I both opted for beer: American beer. My goal was simple. Get the opals into someone else's hands and get them back before I left Hong Kong.

"Mister Wang here?" I asked.

"One minute please. You want more beer?" a gorgeous Chinese girl with red silk wrapped tightly around her body asked. We accepted. She swished her way through a baubles-on-strings doorway and disappeared, then reappeared with the beer followed by a slender Asian man with a wispy mustache. They looked very much like a pimp and prostitute, or maybe I just had screwing on my mind.

"How can I help you?" he asked.

I stooped and pulled the envelope from my sock. Three opals spilled out on the glass display case. I pulled a pack of cigarettes from my pocket, took one out, and shoved the pack into my now-opalless right sock. The jeweler placed the stones on a black pad. The colors—blues, yellows, greens, and reds—sparkled under the bright lights in the store. The jeweler spun the stones, pausing periodically to study them with a loupe. The gorgeous woman stepped in to light my cigarette. I drew in the smoke and then exhaled what was left of it.

"I need these set in rings," I said. "I have two hundred dollars for each ring."

"No, no, no," he replied while shaking his head from side to side. "These stones are much too beautiful to spend only two hundred American dollars to set them. You will not be satisfied. I will not do this." I silently studied the Asian. At first I was angry. I thought that he was trying to hustle me. Then I was angry at the major for putting me in this predicament. "How much?" I asked.

"Maybe six hundred dollars per ring . . ." He rolled the stone with his nicotine-stained thumb and index finger . . . "no less than four hundred." I moved down the display cases. I spotted an elegant set of black sapphires surrounded by gold: necklace and earrings. "How much?"

He slid a door open and reached for the case. "This one?"

"Yes."

"Three hundred fifty dollars."

"How much for just the settings?"

"Three hundred and fifty dollars."

The price seemed fair. The man seemed fair. The woman was gorgeous.

"I'll take it. And this one with the emeralds," I said, pointing. "One for my wife, one for my mother."

"Special deal. Eight hundred for both."

I didn't care. What was money? Besides, it was money I had won, not earned.

"And this ring for my father." I pointed again.

"How about one for yourself?"

I smiled. "Yeah, and I'll take another beer. And another one for my friend." I figured if I drank enough beer, I could cut into his profit. My deal would be better. And I didn't have to negotiate. I hated to negotiate. I always felt I was getting screwed or that I was stealing food from the mouths of the jeweler's children.

"What about the settings?"

"Same, same as I told you."

"Can I pick them up in five days?"

"No, I will mail them."

Again, I felt like I was being hustled, maybe even swindled. I felt for the hand grip of my pistol, but it wasn't there.

"We do all the time for GIs," the jeweler said. "Here is my card. I will take the two hundred for each now. I will set them beautifully for four hundred. You send me the rest of the money later. Then I will mail the rings. They will be insured."

I studied his gorgeous assistant. She was the only bright spot in this cluster fuck I was in. Eventually, I came to the conclusion that the jeweler could be trusted, but maybe it was just that I had reached the point where I no longer gave a shit. I had spent enough time worrying about some major I had never seen before and who could have gone to Hong Kong but went to Bangkok instead to shack up in a whorehouse. Fuck him!

"Okay," I said.

I chugged my beer while the gorgeous one wrapped my purchases, and I gave her the addresses of where to send everything. I told her to hurry. I was anxious to get on with my R & R.

We walked back the way we came. Only this time we stopped at an electronic shop and I bought a Super 8 camera and projector, another reel-to-reel, two large Pioneer speakers, and a Seiko watch. I wore the watch and had the other stuff shipped to the U.S. Then, an Indian tailor grabbed me and pulled me in his store where I bought seven suits, all custom-fitted, a half-dozen frilly shirts with cloth-covered buttons, and a buckskin jacket complete with fringes under the arms and around the back. I browsed through a fashion magazine and ordered two leather capes for my wife. Then we stopped at a shoe store and I bought two pair of boots made from elephant skin and wallets with an engraved map of Southeast Asia for every male I knew. And finally the work was done, and it was time to play.

That evening Joey and I put on sport coats we had purchased. We wound up in a bar inside the Hong Kong Hilton. There was some kind of black-tie affair going on. The bar was full of men in bow ties and women in sequined gowns.

"I'm not sure we should be here, Joey."

"In a pig's eye," he replied. He walked up to a large black man who was playing mood music—it wasn't our kind of mood or music—on a piano. Joey dropped a ten-dollar bill into the piano player's tip jar.

"Do you know 'Throw a Nickel on the Grass, Save a Fighter Pilot's Ass'?" Joey asked. I expected the piano player to say, "Know it? I wrote it!" but he didn't. Instead he smiled and said, "I've been dreaming of a night like this." The tempo changed and the piano player sang: "Halleluiah, halleluiah. Throw . . ."

Joey sang right along with him. He picked up the tip jar and walked to each table, singing and waving the jar under the noses of the patrons. Most dropped money into the jar. Half got up to leave, and the other half began to remove their ties.

Hee, hee! Hee, hee, hee!

When they finished the song, Joey started right in on another: "*The night that Paddy Murphy died, I never shall forget. Everyone got stinking drunk and some ain't sober yet . . .*" Between the chorus and the verse, Joey took the mike from the piano player, walked to the bar, removed his boot, and placed it on the bar. "Fill it up with beer," he said to the bartender, who smiled and did just that. Joey raised the boot and downed the contents while the crowd shouted encouragement.

Hee, hee! Hee, hee, hee!

Joey was working his magic. He had the whole room singing and laughing.

"... *On the night—old Paddy—died!*"

Joey raised the mike to his lips and shouted: "Any goddamn Kiwis in the house?" A young man walked over from the far corner of the bar and nervously said to Joey, "I'm a Scotsman. Will I do?"

"Fucking A!" Joey replied. And the crowd roared.

That night Joey put on a performance extraordinaire, and I had a front-row seat. When the bar closed, patrons stood in line to slap his back and shake his hand. They told him jokes, and he would top them with one of his own.

Hee, hee! Hee, hee, hee!

We walked out of the bar with our sport coats slung over our shoulders, like sloppy flyboys after a raucous twelve hours in the stag bar. A starry-eyed young lassie followed Joey, and before we arrived at our hotel she took Joey's hand. He walked directly to the elevator. I followed. We got off at the same floor. They entered Joey's room; I entered mine.

The next afternoon Joey hosted a couple of his mates who were now flying for Cathay Pacific. Two stews accompanied the pilots, and they handed them off to Joey and me. My God, mine was a beautiful creature: half Portuguese, half Brit; coal-black hair and pupils, ivory irises; long slender arms, fingers, and legs; short skirt; cool demeanor, warm, passionate voice; concave breasts, convex belly button, which was displayed beneath her half blouse. Joey asked them to walk in front of us so "we could perve on their ass and calves," and they did.

"Let's go bowling," Joey suggested.

"Go bowling?"

"Yeah," Joey replied. "Can you think of a better way to perve on their asses?" He tapped his right index finger to his right temple.

Hee, hee! Hee, hee, hee!

At the bowling alley, I discovered my lady packed her ass in camouflaged undies. She sat on my lap when Joey was bowling. We shared a cigar, and it may have been sweeter than the one Thumper and I shared on the mountaintop in the State of Washington. I was happy, maybe even ecstatic, but uncomfortable, and it wasn't because she was sitting on my lap. She was too beautiful, too lovely, too gracious, too tender, too loving, too pure: pure because she was unsoiled, unlike me. She talked about how we were going to spend the night together. I began tossing down straight shots, flashing money, buying drinks for everybody in the alley, and making a big deal out of it. I cut her down with demeaning and caustic remarks. Once again, I became the *Ugly American*, the person I hated most. The four of us then dined at a fancy restaurant on the top floor of our hotel, where I pressed on with my impersonation of a perfect asshole. I wanted her to hate me like I hated me.

"Let's go to my place," she whispered after the meal. "It's cozier."

I picked up the bill, paid it, and we rode the elevator. Joey got off with his lady on our floor; I continued on to the ground floor. We walked through the lobby and out the revolving door. I hailed a taxi. I opened the door to the backseat for my lady and watched her swing her legs in, which she did, making no attempt to hide the number-one square on a short-timer's calendar. Her thighs were firm and inviting. She smiled and hesitated, offering one last longing look. I closed the back door and opened the front door. "Move over," I said to the stunned cab driver. "I'm driving." I waved a wad of money. "Okeydokey. Can do! Can do!" he said as he moved to the passenger side. I smiled. My lady giggled. "Give me directions," I said to her. She did, and the cabbie told me when to turn, stop, and go. I was submissive and silent driving the cab, as I was sometimes while driving my airplane. I was confused, conflicted, and felt cornered. And for some reason, perhaps because I did not know what was happening with me, I could not verbalize it. Which made me even angrier, more agitated, more detached, meaner.

"Get out!" I ordered.

She laughed.

"Get out!" I shouted louder.

She began to cry.

"Get out!" I roared.

"I don't understand," she said.

I did not answer.

"Is it because you are married?" she asked.

"I don't think so."

"Is it something I did or said?"

"Absolutely not. You are perfect. Too perfect."

"Then why?"

"I don't know. Just get out."

She opened the cab door, stepped out slowly, closed the door, and without looking back she walked to her front door and out of my life.

"Where to?" I asked the cabbie.

"You make big mistake," he said.

I squeezed the steering wheel and stared straight ahead.

He gave me directions back to the hotel. When I spotted it, I pulled a Jefferson. I shut off the engine and coasted in. The meter read $6.20. I held out my hand, palm up, my eyes fixed on the cabbie's, like a rocket on a V.C.

bunker. "That will be twenty dollars," I said. I did not laugh, but he did. I stared at him. He began to fidget. He turned to look both left and right, and then to the rear. We were alone. When he looked back at me, I saw fear in his eyes and on his face. He was a little like me, a cornered animal. Finally, I laughed and handed him a twenty. He smiled and with renewed confidence he said: "You make big mistake." I knew that I had, but I wasn't sure what it was.

I staggered to my room where I had a quart of Jack Daniels stashed. I took a drink, followed by a long, scalding-hot shower. I scrubbed my skin until it was cherry red, and then I scrubbed it some more. Whatever it was, it was not coming off. I stepped out, grabbed a towel, and rubbed it against my skin. I rubbed until I noticed I had rubbed the hair off of my left forearm. I dressed and picked up my jug of Jack Daniels. Jack and I walked hand in hand out into the streets.

The sky had lightened, just a wee bit of dawn peeking through. I wandered the streets, stumbling occasionally on a high curb. I thought about the possibilities of being mugged, but I did not care. In fact, I may have wanted it. I peered down an alley; a Chinese vendor cooked food on a homemade grill. People sat nearby on their haunches. All were Asian with the exception of one white woman who sat on a garbage can lid and gnawed at her food. She looked doped up. Her hair was matted. There was no way she could resist me. I sat down beside her.

"What are you doing here?" I asked. She did not answer. She did not even look at me. "Are you American?" I asked. Again she did not answer nor did she look at me. Instead she rose, picked up her lid, and moved to the other side of the alley. Rejected. I felt dejected, neglected, disconnected. I rose and walked back down the alley. I stumbled and bounced off the walls. When I fell, I checked my six o'clock. Where was the enemy? It felt like they were everywhere. Once I turned and fired—*Ratty-Tat-Tat*—even though I had no weapon, even though there was no one behind me. I laughed and took a long swig from my bottle.

When I reached the main road, I spotted an elderly, skinny woman wearing a conical hat and black pajamas. She was sweeping the street with a broom made from a palm frond. I approached her, flashed a $100 bill, and motioned for her to follow me. She dropped her broom and we walked in tandem back to my hotel. I led, she followed: several paces behind. I opened the door and we moved across the lobby. A voice from behind the counter shouted something in Chinese. The old woman stopped.

"She's with me!" I shouted back. I stared at the man and he went back to his paperwork.

We continued to my room, where I slouched in an easy chair. She tugged at my boots with cigarette-stained and gnarly hands. When she pulled them off, she placed them neatly side by side. I let what little liquor that was left in my bottle drip into my mouth, swirled it around, and swallowed. The room began to spin. Taut muscles relaxed. My body was limp and lifeless. I struggled to keep my eyes open. I dropped the bottle as she opened my belt buckle, unzipped my fly, and began rolling my jeans down. *What am I doing?* I asked myself.

I awoke in the very same position. The old woman was gone. And so was my $100 bill. I pulled my jeans up and zipped and buttoned them shut. I tried to recall what had happened, but I was stuck on a story I had once heard . . .

A prostitute approached a baby-faced GI. "Would you like to sleep with me for one hundred dollars?" she asked.

"Well, I'm not tired, but I could use the one hundred dollars," he replied . . .

I stood and placed a hand on the back of the chair to steady myself. I kicked the empty booze bottle under the bed. And then I fell on the bed, facedown, arms outstretched. I was compliant and broken. Soon thereafter *Ralph the Rack Monster* took me to a safe place.

I awoke with a massive hangover. I showered, dressed, and walked to the hotel bar for a jolt of the *dog that bit me*. Joey was sitting with his lady and two other round-eyed women; one older, one younger. They were sitting on a soft sofa and drinking Bloody Marys. I whistled for a waitress, and when she finally arrived she said: "You no whistle. I am not a dog!" The group laughed; I did not. I ordered a Bloody Mary and bought a round for Joey and the ladies. The older one was Australian and married to an airline pilot; the younger one was a grade-school teacher from San Diego. She was plump but pleasant.

Joey wanted to order some food. "Wait, let me do it," I said. He opened his hands and pushed them toward me, like he was offering me center stage. I waited till the room was quiet, and then I yelled, "Heel!"

I laughed heartily. Joey laughed half-heartily—only one hee, hee! The ladies did not laugh. I did not like myself, but yet again, I could not stop.

We snacked, and at around four o'clock Joey and I bid adieu to the ladies and adjourned to an Australian bar. Joey had another scheduled rendezvous with his Aussie buddies: dinner and drinks.

"You will be alright here, mate?" he asked.

"Hell, yeah," I replied boldly.

He left and I drank. When he returned, I was getting bounced out on my ass by two burly Australian blokes. "You see these buttons?" I yelled, holding my shirt buttons away from my chest. "They are bombs, and I'm going to tear one off and blow this place up. *Boooom!*"

Hee, hee! Hee, hee, hee!

The blokes turned, walked back into the bar. Joey picked me up off the sidewalk.

"What did you say, mate?"

"I don't know." And I honestly didn't know.

We returned to our hotel, and the sofa in the bar. The grade-school teacher walked in and looked around. When she spotted Joey and me, she came over and sat next to me. Around eleven o'clock, I crashed.

"I've got to spin in, mate."

"Alrighty," he replied, "I'll see you in the morning."

I stood, turned, walked to the elevator, punched in my floor, walked from the elevator to my room, closed the door, and collapsed fully clothed on the bed.

Sometime, in the middle of the night, I awoke and the schoolteacher was sleeping beside me.

"How did you get in here?" I asked.

"I told them I was your wife and I lost my key."

I shut my eyes. Using my eyelid muscles, I squeezed them tight until I saw iridescent blues, yellows, and greens. Then I began to shake, an uncontrollable and unwanted shake. I curled up with my knees pulled tight to my chest. I was sobbing and sweating and still shaking. I could not stop. From behind, the grade-school teacher wrapped her arms around and held me close. I shook for hours. I tried to shake out all the fear I had buried and the pain and loss of innocence and the shame and the guilt . . . When that was finished I shook for Billy, and Doggie, and each one of Buddha's boys who had died. I shook for Lucky Larry; the muscular one and the skinny one, whose bodies had been cut in half. I shook for hours for everyone I knew who had been killed in this fucked-up war, and then I shook because I was alive. They were dead, I wasn't. They found peace, and I hadn't. I wondered if I had done enough, been brave enough. And then I shook because I had done too much, like when I took out that village. I shook all morning and through the afternoon.

I shook while the sun set and the room turned black again with only Hong Kong's neon lights twinkling in a variety of colors. And she held me, all through this; sometimes she squeezed tight; at other times she cradled me. Neither of us spoke a word. Hour after hour I shook. Sometimes I broke out in sweat, and sometimes I shivered with my teeth clinking. I shook for all the times I should have and could not; times of stress when I was at death's doorstep; times when the grim reaper was standing over me smiling; times when the devil was grinning over me; times when I needed to think and act instead of shaking and dying; a time when an F-100 nearly crushed my tiny O-2; a time when an M-16 was shoved in my gut and a round was chambered; a time when a fellow pilot wanted to kill me and I didn't know why; times when my airplane took hits and I didn't know it; a time when my airplane pitched up because I was trying to stop the maps from flying out the back window; times when I lost an engine and limped home; a time when my gear wouldn't come up or go down; times when weather engulfed and trapped me; a time when they wanted me to jump in the ocean; and a time when I should have crashed against a tree trunk and didn't and still don't know what happened or why I was spared . . . And somewhere in there I must have fallen asleep for a while, and when I awoke I was still shaking and she was still holding me. I could feel the contours of her body, the warmth it generated, and I shook for all the times I had failed in my marriage. I shook until the sun rose. A new day was beginning, and suddenly I felt strong and angry that I shook like a baby. I rose and ordered her out of my room. She cried, but left. I showered, walked downstairs, ordered and ate a breakfast, and downed a straight shot.

"Where were you, mate?" Joey asked.

"I'm not sure," I answered.

"Well, let's go raise some hell."

"Why not?" I replied.

We didn't raise much hell the last days we were in Hong Kong. Mostly we just lounged, drank beer, told jokes, and enjoyed our freedom and each other's company. I think we both knew our time together was coming to an end, and we were in some sort of mourning. I felt sadness. I wanted to be mates, comrades, brothers-in-arms, compadres, friends, pardners—forever. I wanted to be within walking distance of Joey for the rest of my life; a man I could trust, a man who would put his life on the line for me and I for him. A man I could go back-to-back with in a bar fight. A man I could laugh and cry with. And now it was going to end. He would disappear, drop out of my life like Doggie, Billy, and Thumper; and Buddha, Father William, and Jefferson. And it was sad. Then I thought: Hey, Captain Puff, Colonel Buzz Cut, and a whole host of other assholes had also left my life, and that was good. I smiled. But it didn't feel like it balanced out. I could tolerate the assholes; I could even replace them; but I couldn't replace Joey. And then I felt guilty. He had extended his tour to be with me, but I would be leaving him behind. It wasn't Joey who was walking out of my life; it was me walking away from him. I wondered if I would have extended for him, and I decided I wouldn't. Not because I was married with two sons, but because I just couldn't stand another minute in this Viet Nam shithole. And I felt guilt—even shame—maybe because the sadness I felt inside for leaving Joey hurt more than the joy I was supposed to feel for rejoining my family.

"Hey mate, I am running out of money. We'd better get back, eh?"

"Yeah," I replied. I reached into my sock and pulled out the few dollars that were left and tossed them on the table.

"Might as well drink it up."

And then both Joey and I pulled all our dollars out from our billfolds. I counted our funds, and then I subtracted our bills. When my calculations were complete, I realized we would have to leave Hong Kong tomorrow. We had managed to stay nine nights and ten days.

We arrived at the ticket counter and stacked our bags and packages on the floor beside us. A line formed behind us.

"As broke as we are, it's a good thing we bought round-trip tickets," I said to Joey.

"Are all these extra packages yours?" a round-eyed woman behind the counter made up to look like a doll asked. Her hair was wound like cotton candy then sprayed with starch. Her glued-on false eyelashes were nearly as long as her glued-on fingernails. A circle of rose-colored gunk was applied to each of her cheeks. Her mouth was caked in lipstick so thick that only the bottom half of her mouth moved when she spoke, but she cackled like a mamasan.

"Yes, they are ours," I replied.

"Put them on the scale, please."

Joey picked up each bag and placed them on the scale, and I thought I heard him mumble *cow* or *cunt* or something akin to that when he did.

"That will be an extra $25 for the additional luggage."

Joey and I emptied our pockets, including change. I counted it.

"We have three dollars . . ." I counted the change again . . . "and sixty-seven cents."

"Here take it all," I said as I pushed it forward. "It's all we have."

"Hey, hurry up, up there!" I turned to see a man in line behind us pointing to his wristwatch. I noticed a slight forward motion by Joey. I grabbed his right bicep but his mouth still worked. "Shut the fuck up!" Joey said. The man's head and eyes dropped. If he had a tail, it would have been between his legs.

"That's not very nice language," the painted lady said.

"Yeah, I know. I speak *number ten* all the time."

"Pardon me?"

"I said, I speak *number fucking ten* all the time! Look lady, we are going to Viet Nam. Can't you just waive the fee?"

"Well, I must ask my supervisor."

She opened a door and vanished. The man behind us tapped his watch again. The painted lady returned in time to hear Joey ask the watch tapper if he was going to hell or something to that effect. She tied tags to our bags and parcels, and waved us on to the delight of a cheering and applauding crowd. Joey bowed. And when the ticket taker said: "It's okay to get *on* the airplane," Joey replied, "I'd much rather get in the airplane if you don't mind lady."

Hee, hee! Hee, hee, hee!

Part 3
The Verdict

Chapter 1
FINI FLIGHT

We arrived safely in Saigon. Joey found a *lima lina* (land line) and contacted his TOC. A *Daredevil* FAC agreed to fire up an OV-10 and fly down and pick him up. I called the *Smoky* FAC hootch.

"*Smoky* FACs," the voice on the other end said. I did not recognize the voice.

"Is Earl there?" I asked.

"That's a negative."

"Are you a *Smoky* FAC?"

"That's a Charlie."

"Well, jump in an O-2, and pick me up at Tan Son Nhat."

"I can't do that. It's against the regs."

"What? You gotta be shitting me!"

"No sir."

"What's your call sign?" I asked.

"I'm *Smoky* forty-four."

"The fuck you are! I'm *Smoky* forty-four." I hung up. I called the *Red Marker* villa and the Strummer answered.

"Hey Strummer, I need a ride to Bien Hoa."

"I'll be right there," he replied.

The Strummer dropped me off at our FAC revetment in Bien Hoa. From there, I bummed a ride back to our hootch. I was tired and angry; I just wanted to flop in my bunk and sleep for a day or two. I opened the door to my room.

There was a guy sleeping on my bunk, and all of my belongings—including my reel-to-reel tape deck, speakers, and guitar—were stashed in a corner.

I put my foot on the neck of the sleeping guy and applied pressure until he stirred and gagged.

"Where the fuck is Earl?"

"He is down at Binh Thuy flying missions back into Cambodia." I was befuddled.

"Keep talking."

"That's all I know, honest."

The Walrus appeared in the doorway.

"Man, some limp-dick full-bull colonel in the DASC hates your ass," he said. "You are going down there too. Earl and the Vung Tau ALO argued for you—saying you were *short* and shouldn't have to go—but the asshole was insistent," he said. "He said he wanted to see your ass killed."

I tried to visualize all the full bulls I had pissed off since I'd been in-country and stopped at that prick in the O club, the one the Ranger lieutenant confronted and warned that no one would find any of his body parts if he came after me. Where was that Ranger now? I wondered.

"Are you going down there, Walrus?"

"Nope. Just the O-2 drivers."

"Motherfucker! There is just no end to the bullshit, is there? It's not just three bags full, it's three thousand bags full!"

"No end that I can see," the Walrus replied.

"What about Frick and Frack?" I asked.

"Both grounded, fined, and frozen in rank." I shook my head.

"I kind of liked Frick," I said. "His only mistake was that he trusted the general's kid."

"That's a big fucking mistake over here. *Know thy enemy*," the Walrus replied.

That night Joey, the Walrus, and I got roaring drunk. I told everyone else who wanted to hang around to "Fuck off!" Our conversation was limited and not to be interrupted by our drinking. The session ended abruptly. We each just got up and went our separate ways. I stumbled into my room. The weenie had again parked his ass in my bunk. He obviously wasn't very smart. "Hey asshole," I said, "do you know Captain Puff?"

"Huh? What? Who?" he replied.

"Get the fuck out of my bunk!"

I helped him up, flopped on my bunk, and passed out.

I dreamt I was shaking in the arms of the Hong Kong schoolmarm until I awoke and realized it was someone shaking me.

"Where are my rings?" the shaker said. The words echoed from left to right, in one ear, then across my brain—or what was left of it—and out the other ear.

"Where are my ringssssss?" he said again. I saw a blurred outline of a face, which was connected by a neck to a body with arms that continued to shake me.

"Where are my ringssss? I should have never trusted a drunkkkkk!"

"Fuck youuuuuuu!" I wanted to shout back, but my tongue was set in concrete. I sat up holding my head with both hands. I pressed my tongue against the roof and sides of my mouth searching for saliva. Finding none, I wagged it back and forth in an attempt to manufacture some, for a chance to express myself.

"I left them in Hong Kong." The words came out slowly and were no more than a whisper. I hoped the shaker did not mistake the volume for intimidation, for I was not intimidated. My words were followed by a barrage of words, some profane, some not; but the gist was that he was not happy with me. When there was a lull—he needed to breathe—I started.

"Listen, asshole! You were the one who gave me the stones. So be pissed at yourself!"

"I am, I am," he said. He appeared to be calming down.

"The stones are with the jeweler . . ."

He began shouting again. And I decided, based on his word choice and intonation, that it was the first time he had ever used the words "fuck," "fucker," "fucked," or "fucking" in the same sentence. And when I began laughing, he seemed to become even more agitated and began to stammer. "You, ou, ou . . . f-ff-fff ucker!" When he again took a breath, I told him it would cost him an additional $200 per stone to get his rings back. He stood and began walking in circles while flapping his arms like a drunken mallard in a small pond. When he gathered enough speed, he flew out my room and I returned to my comatose state upon my bunk.

I departed for Binh Thuy—immediately after sobering up—for three reasons. First: I wanted to confront my new ALO, who had promised me that no one would dick with me if I took the first mission into Cambodia. Second: I did not want to run into the stone collector again, for he might try to kill me. And third: I did not want to run into the colonel who banished me to Binh Thuy, for I might kill him.

Earl and our division ALO met my plane when I landed at Binh Thuy, the southernmost significant air base in Viet Nam. They were sitting in a jeep. Earl was in the driver's seat. He stuck out his hand and a big grin monopolized his face. The sun glinted off his front teeth and the shaved sidewalls of what he called a haircut. Our new ALO wore gold oak leafs on his fatigues, signifying the rank of major. He was smiling, but it was a forced smile.

"I know, I know," he said before I could say anything. "I promised that no one would fuck with you after Cambodia but I was outgunned. I did, however, get you a three-week drop. You will be heading home in three weeks instead of six."

He was a hard man to stay angry at because I knew he spoke the truth, with no bullshit and no agenda. I shook his hand, too, and Earl drove us to our quarters: A trailer with Earl residing on one side and me on the other.

"Not bad," I said as I inspected it.

"I filed your O.E.R.," Earl said as he handed me a sheet of paper. I studied the officer efficiency report. In every category he graded me all the way to the right: the highest score possible. At the bottom he wrote a glowing endorsement, recommending me for regular Air Force status and future promotions. Under his signature there was an additional blurb by the colonel who hated me. It read: ". . . his performance in the air was exceptional," followed by the dreaded *however:* ". . . his conduct on the ground was not conducive to that of an Air Force Officer." Whatever that meant. And then he downgraded me in all of the above categories. I shook Earl's hand once again and told him I appreciated his glowing report, and then he briefed me on our A.O., which was everything south of the highway running west out of Phnom Penh to the port city of Sihanoukville.

"You might fly with a Cambode or a French-speaking American in the right seat."

I nodded. Then he showed me the schedule. I would be flying solo tomorrow with a noon launch. That evening at the O club, Earl introduced me to the rest of the guys in our unit. I was too *short* to give a shit, too short to remember names or faces. I just wanted to do my three weeks and get the fuck out of Viet Nam.

At 1200 hours the next day, I cranked my front engine. I launched and headed west. At the border, I transmitted: "Crossing the fence, red rabbit." I was back into Cambodia. I remembered Earl's words: "We are not supposed to be here. If you get shot down, we have never heard of you. Then I remembered another thing he told me. He said he got a letter from his wife and she said their hometown newspaper ran a story about eighteen seniors from the class of 1965 who had made a pact that when they graduated, they would all enlist in the Marines. Apparently the Marines had some weird program: fourteen months in the Marines, as opposed to a minimum of two years in the Army, in return for thirteen months in Viet Nam. Obviously, the Marines needed a "few (more) good men." Nine of the graduates were dead before their twentieth birthdays. I wondered why anyone back in the world would write a letter like that to a loved one who was in battle in Viet Nam. Was that her way of saying: "Be careful!" or was she just insensitive? All I could say when I heard the story was "What a waste!" I smiled as I *synced* my two props. Hell, I was getting a really good deal. I got Viet Nam and Cambodia too.

I flew over Phnom Penh, the capital of Cambodia. Looking down my left wing, I spotted a bi-wing aircraft painted bright yellow, and I wondered if the pilot was yellow too—or was he red. I joined on his right wing. He was wearing a leather helmet. Perhaps I had entered a time warp when I crossed the border. The pilot gave me a smile and I gave him a thumbs-up before peeling off.

On the runway I saw MiG-17s. There was no mistaking the bright red star on their upper wing. And when my fighters checked in, they, too, were flying MiGs. "What a fucked-up war!" I shouted to no one in particular. "I'm putting in MiGs against the commies."

It was becoming more and more difficult to discern who were the good guys and who were the bad guys. The grunts' motto of "Kill them all and let God sort them out" seemed to make some sense. Sometimes I even wondered if I was a good guy.

After the fighters departed, I flew to the coast, pulled the power back, and began descending with silky-smooth *clearing* turns, both looking for right and left, and looking for anything that might be flying in this uncontrolled airspace. Without the turns, I might let down on top of an airplane flying below me. I spotted a white gull and mimicked its moves; gliding and soaring, turning and floating. I used variation in altitude and turns to keep it in sight. Was he a good guy? I wondered. We both leveled off, maybe six or eight inches above the water, where the slightest miscalculation on my part would result in a belly-landing or a flip of my airplane. I fed the power back in by moving the throttles forward and aimed the nose of my craft at fishermen in their sampans. I flew so low that several of them jumped into the water. I felt all-powerful and immortal.

I spotted an all-white villa on the top of a cliff overlooking the ocean. I aimed my airplane for the front door. I wanted to fly right through the front door with my throttles firewalled and then down the hallway bisecting the villa. Just before impact, I pulled the nose of my bird up into a gentle right turn so I could keep the villa in my line of sight. I soared upward until my airspeed slowed to where it could no longer sustain the climb. I pulled the throttles back to idle and fed in right rudder as my angle of attack diminished and eventually my nose dropped through the horizon. I descended gracefully, picking up speed like a roller coaster heading down the rails after it had reached its apex. I was filled with exhilaration. I was immortal and in control of my destiny. Up and down I swooped, climbing and turning, falling and turning until I finished it off with a full roll, 360 degrees with the nose of my aircraft fixed on the imaginary head of a pin. I did this effortlessly and without forethought: man as a machine, a machine as man, united and working with one mind, body, and soul. I was joyous and free even though I was *across the fence, red rabbit.*

The days crawled by, each one the same: reconnaissance, airstrikes, free flying; always ending with a near dip in the ocean to test my immortality before re-crossing the fence. Only one day was different. I was listening to Paul Harvey on Armed Forces Radio over my A.D.F. He was talking about how Cambodian peasants were defending a cement factory. It was spooky, for I happened to be flying over the factory as he talked. He implied the peasants were using pitchforks, scythes, and rakes to hold off the enemy. I wanted to call him up, tell him to *stay tuned for the rest of the story.* The siege had ended five days ago. The pitchforks were rockets; the scythes were bombs with daisy cutters; the rakes were tiny pistols on A-37s. Yes indeed, we did rake the target area. But what did I know? According to the Air Force I wasn't even here, so why would he listen to me? Why would anyone listen to me? I had to be lying. Trust your government. I did. That's how I got over here. Listen to your government. They will give you the straight skinny. Yes sir, yes sir, three bags full of straight skinny.

After ten days, Bien Hoa sent word that I should return for processing as my DEROS had been moved up. I ignored the orders. I would fly till my very last day. After several days, they sent somebody to retrieve me. But I was advised of all incoming traffic from Bien Hoa. When I got the call, I would jump in an airplane and cross the fence. Each day they tried; each day I jumped across the border and stayed there until the pencil-pushers departed.

"Where is he?" they asked. And Earl and my ALO would just shrug their shoulders.

"Are you sure he isn't here?"

"Positive."

"Well, then where is he?"

"Sorry, that's classified information."

"Have him ready tomorrow!"

"We will try."

But the strain of actually finishing a tour unharmed was destroying my nervous system. I could not sleep. I could not eat. And my innate cast-iron stomach was crumbling under the pressure. I began to throw up, several times a day and several times at night. My weight dropped until I weighed less than I did as a freshman in high school.

"You're too sick," Earl said. "Let me take your flight."

And I was, so I acquiesced. That day Earl got his wing stitched with .50 cal bullets, and I vowed no one would fly my mission no matter how sick I was. I could not live with the guilt if someone flying my mission got maimed, killed, or captured. I could return to Bien Hoa and be safe, but that didn't feel right either. "Fuck 'em! I'd come out of the boonies when I was good and ready."

One night, toward the very end of my tour, our guys were raising hell: Lots of hell. Lots of drinking and loud music; music that rocked the walls of our trailer; music that drowned out the fears that lay trapped inside our young bodies. Fully grown men, officers and gentlemen on the outside; kids on the inside. Man-boys playing grab-ass and dousing each other with beer while laughing and trying to out-swear each other. Two FACs had swiped two six-foot folding tables and a gallon of cooking oil from the O club. They stretched the tables end to end and then oiled them down. They stripped down to their shorts and combat boots and then practiced carrier landings. They would back up to get a run at the tables and then swan dive onto them—skidding along on just their bellies, back arched, head and feet elevated—and crash off either the sides or the end; crash into spectacular balls of laughter, flesh and bone, while the onlookers cheered and hooted. A FAC decided we should score the landings. He produced paper on which he wrote numbers from 1 to 10 with a black grease pencil.

"Should ten be good as it is in the world, or bad as it is in the Nam?" a FAC asked. A discussion ensued and we were forced to vote on that also. "The number ten will be shit-hot!" a FAC announced after the scores were tabulated. We were ready to go. *Thump! Thump! Thump!* A FAC raced to the edge of the table. Splat! He planted his belly firmly on the runway, arms outstretched. Suddenly, he was hydroplaning, skidding out of control. He veered hard left like he was going off the edge, but corrected with differential breaking. But wait, he overcorrected and now he was heading off the other side. "O-oo-h!" the crowd roared. He straightened it out and somersaulted off the end of the runway. Darn near a spectacular landing. He landed on his feet, but he was too drunk to hold it and he fell back on his ass.

"And now for the scores. Let's see, a seven, an eight, a nine. For an overall average of . . . of . . . of . . . let's see . . ."

"Eight, you dumb fuck!" another FAC yelled.

"No fucking way!" the landing pilot argued. "That was a fucking ten for sure!"

"Well, let's ask one of the judges.

"He was carrying too much speed and he overshot the runway. He must be a REMF (rear-echelon motherfucker)!" The crowd hooted.

"Ah, what the fuck happened there, lieutenant?" the interviewer asked the dejected pilot.

"Hey, fuckstick," the pilot answered. "Any landing you can walk away from is a good landing!"

"Spoken like a real Navy pilot," the interviewer summarized. And everybody cheered. "And now for a commercial." Another FAC stepped up.

"You know folks, nothing tastes better than sucking down some real honest-to-goodness Tiger Piss while you are watching a war unfold before your very eyes. So put your feet up, pull your head out of your boss's ass, and pop a can of Tiger Piss. That's right, folks. Remember, be sure to pop a Tiger Piss before you get popped!"

"Fucking A!" the crowd chanted.

I watched with a smile, like a grandfather rocking in his chair, puffing nicotine through a pipe, and observing at a distance a follow-on generation. I was an old-timer, a short-time FAC observing F.N.G.s acting out their primal and well-earned rite of passage: Young men trying to screw up their courage and assuage their conscience and fears through the use of alcohol and silly games so they, too, could kill with the giddiness of schoolboys winning a championship football game.

A major, who was not wearing any pilot wings, appeared. "Turn down that music!" he shouted, but the celebration continued. "Captain," he said to me, "control these men; people are trying to sleep."

I stood. "I can't," I replied.

"What do you mean, you can't?"

"I can't!" I said again. "The guy whose reel-to-reel is playing that music is on R & R. It would be wrong for me to touch his personal effects without his permission. We will have to wait until he returns."

The major stared at me in disbelief, I believed. Then, disgusted, he turned and departed. Our young FACs cheered like they had defeated the enemy, beat him at his own game. This was their turf. They were calling the shots here. In the jungle, he who held the ground had home field advantage. In the jungle, the young and the fit made and enforced the rules.

And then it finally happened. The day of my finis flight—my last mission. My ALO scheduled another man to fly with me. He was a large lieutenant. I'm sure he sent him along so that I would not kill myself by doing something stupid: like flying too low, like trying to tear the wings off the airplane, like trying one last time to avenge the deaths of many friends, like trying to do a victory roll over the field before I landed. End-of-tour show-off *whifferdills* were forbidden ever since a pilot *augered in*. He killed himself while celebrating the fact that he had lived through his tour.

Sending another man up with me may have worked. It may have saved my life. If I was flying solo, I probably would have tried to do all those things I wasn't supposed to do. But I couldn't now. I had another life in my hands. My life didn't count, but his did. I was aircraft commander on this flight. And I would make sure he lived to fly and fight another day. But I felt like I had to do something. I felt I had a reputation to uphold, and I was determined to go out in style. I thought about doing an aileron roll or maybe a loop over the runway, both illegal maneuvers, both maneuvers the airplane was not designed to withstand, but both maneuvers I had done before under Jefferson's tutelage. But I knew the maneuvers would be forced, pre-calculated, not in the natural flow of flying, and therefore dangerous. I was also concerned the man in my right seat might find the maneuvers cool and decide to try them on his own with possibly fatal consequences. Therefore, I ruled them out. But I did fly low over the water. I did it with trepidation. We did not speak, the man in the right seat and I.

Three hours and we did not speak. I thought about passing along Jefferson's advice: "Your job, lieutenant, is to live through your tour and return home to your loved ones in one piece." But it would be a lie. We didn't return in one piece. We returned in thousands of pieces, and many of those were scattered throughout this land: in rice paddies, in jungles, in villages, in bomb craters, in the souls of those who had died. I thought about all these things until it was time to land.

I requested a pitchout and it was granted. As I flew *initial*, I could see a fire truck waiting to hose me down at the end of the runway. At our revetment, a small contingent of men—Earl, my ALO, and several other pilots I did not want to know—waited for me. Joey, Father William, Jefferson, Carlos, Buddha and his men, the Walrus, Billy, Moondoggie, Lucky Larry—would not be waiting for me. They were scattered throughout this world and the next. Several of the men below pointed, several used their hands to shield their eyes from the sun, several waved. They were waiting with champagne to spray, toast, and drink. They were waiting for me: the rule breaker, the combative one, the rebel. They were waiting to see what I would do, hoping I would put on a little air show as a final act of defiance. I was nervous, but I felt I had to give them something. I was nervous in my airplane for the first time since my first solo mission when I may have taken a hit.

Halfway down the runway I pitched by snap rolling the airplane 90 degrees. I held my wings perpendicular to the earth, maintaining altitude until I reached the *perch*—the point where I would normally bleed airspeed until I could drop my gear and start my descending turn to line up with the runway. I snap rolled back to wings level, and instead of dropping the gear, I dropped the nose and brought power in until my airspeed was redlined.

"Ah, Binh Thuy tower, I don't think I will be able to land out of this one. Requesting a closed pattern."

"Roger, you are cleared for a closed pattern."

I descended until I was at the end of the runway and ten feet or so off the ground. Then I banked sharply left and aimed the nose of my airplane at the small crowd, once assembled but now scattering. Just before I reached the point where they were standing, I reversed my turn, rolling from perpendicular left to perpendicular right, and began climbing while rolling the aircraft slowly back to wings level—a *chandelle*. I was in charge, in control, invincible. I pulled the power to idle and let the airplane climb. I watched as the hands on the altimeter spun. The V.V.I. (vertical velocity indicator) quivered then dropped to zero. The ball, indicating rudder position was centered. And when my forward motion slowed to a speed where I could safely drop the gear, I dropped the gear and pointed the nose of my airplane at the end of the runway. I was off the perch and heading down the chute when I heard the gear doors open, the gear drop down and lock in place, and the gear doors close. I checked for green lights. "I'm in the green," I said to no one in particular.

"Binh Thuy tower, final turn, full stop."

"Roger, you are cleared to land."

"Roger, I copy."

I landed on the first brick and jumped on the binders. The tires belched blue smoke and farted burnt rubber. I turned off on the first taxiway while the fire trucks waiting at the end of the runway now scurried to catch up. I screeched to a full stop. It was over. I was drenched by sweat, water hoses, and fizzy champagne—a girly drink that I hated. I took a sip out of respect for Earl—whose grin exposed his upper and lower rows of choppers—and the

ALO who said: "I have never seen an O-2 with so many degrees of bank, so close to the ground!"

This was followed by a host of handshaking—shakes of congratulations as opposed to shakes of welcoming—and backslapping. We soon adjourned to the officers club where I ate a steak—the first food I was able to consume in many a day—and drank many rounds of beer, told war stories, and listened to random bullshit. On the ceiling of the officers club, there were messages and signatures of those who had arrived and departed before me. I walked around, head up, Adam's apple protruding, and read them all. Earl approached, still grinning. He handed me his grease pencil. I paused—trying to think of something clever, something original, something humorous, and maybe even memorable to write, but my brain was mush. Eventually, I realized clever, original, and humorous were lost somewhere in the bottom of a beer glass, so I borrowed a phrase from General MacArthur, only I bastardized it. I wrote: "I shall NOT return!" Then I signed my name. How could I return, I wondered, when parts of me would never leave? I handed the grease pencil to a still-grinning Earl. He slapped my back for maybe the twentieth time in the last hour. And he would do it many more times before I departed for Bien Hoa early the next morning.

The Walrus was waiting for me when I landed back in Bien Hoa. He stroked his bushy mustache while I loaded my gear into his jeep.

"Big party for you tonight," he said. "Joey and everybody will be there. Even Father William is in town."

I nodded. "Out processing first," I replied.

He stopped in front of the headquarters hootch, and we both got out and walked inside. The colonel who hated me stood in the doorway to his office. He stood on one foot; the other was crossed over it at the ankle. He stood, blocking the entrance. He held a coffee cup in one hand, his other hand held a clipboard. His chin and gut were exposed. A fist to either would have probably dropped him. My confusion was which one to crush first: belly or jaw? I felt the rage building inside me. Boiling blood bloated my face. I wiped sweat from my forehead.

"'bout time you came in," he said.

"You didn't get me, did you, you asshole?"

His right arm dropped first; then he uncrossed his feet. He made one step toward me, stopped, smiled, pivoted, and returned to his desk. A sergeant stacked papers in front of me. He licked his index finger and began reviewing each sheet, stopping periodically and pointing to where I should sign this form and that form. And when I did, he placed the sheet facedown until one pile dissolved into another pile. He handed me my travel pay voucher, and then he picked up the completed pile and tapped the ends of the papers on the counter until they were all aligned. He placed them into a file.

"That ought to do it, captain. Your flight leaves tomorrow at 1530. Here's your ticket." He handed it to me and held out his hand for me to shake.

"Good luck to you," he said.

Good luck? I thought. Good luck is something you should say to someone who is setting foot in-country for the first time. I had good luck. Lucky Larry did not. I nodded. The awards and decorations officer approached.

"One last thing," he said. "You need to write up your end-of-tour Distinguished Flying Cross." He handed me a blank sheet of paper.

"I need to write up my own decoration?"

"Yeah, just put down some facts. I will dress it up—you know, put all the right buzzwords in—and get it signed." I looked through the empty doorway into the colonel's office, the one who had denied my D.F.C. for my first mission. He sat with his feet up on his desk. I shoved the blank sheet of paper off the counter and onto the floor.

"Fuck that!" I said. I gathered up my documents, and the Walrus and I walked back to the jeep.

"Let me drive."

He tossed me the keys, and when I hit the perimeter road I goosed her up to full speed. I drove to the roach coach, munched a scrawny chicken, tossed the bones, and restarted the jeep. Small stones pinged against the rusted sides of the trailer as I fishtailed out of the parking lot and back onto the perimeter road. There, I revved her up to full speed, hesitating only to pop the clutch and change gears, like Billy used to do in his 442 Olds. When I passed the BX, I shut her down, like Jefferson used to do, and we coasted into the hootch parking lot. We were traveling so slow I could count the tire tread as it turned. I rocked my body—hinged at the waist—forward and back . . . once . . . twice . . . seven times . . . until I could not coax another inch out of her. We stopped: two feet short. Not bad for a short-timer, I thought. If it were a bomb, I would have called it a *shack*. I was not going to restart that jeep. This mission had come to a successful conclusion. What was one little lie in a shithole of deceit? I smiled, grabbed the chain, wound it around the steering wheel, and closed the padlock.

Joey, Father William, and several Army men stood at the bar. They cleared a spot for me. F.N.G.s, TWAT pilots, a smattering of REMFs (rear-Echelon motherfuckers), and Frick stood behind them. Miss Sam, tending bar, stood in front of me.

"Good to see you, *dai uy*," she said. She turned to look at a weenie who was sitting on my stool. "You move!" she ordered. He got up and the Army men picked me up and planted me on my stool.

"Well, the war hero returns!" Father William said. He stared straight ahead. "You get a drop and I get another three weeks of enemas! That frosts my ass, peasant." I smiled.

"Does this mean I am not going to get your blessing?" I asked.

"I give you a blessing right here, numb nuts!" he replied as he grabbed his balls.

Hee, hee! Hee, hee, hee!

"What a ripper!" Joey yelled as he slapped Father William's back just as he was about to take a drink. Father William spit the beer. A fine mist moved forward from his mouth. Bigger drops dribbled from his nose, and then he began to cough. And every time he coughed, Joey would slap his back again.

Hee, hee! Hee, hee, hee!

We all laughed: hearty laughs that covered several octaves from Joey's bass line to Miss Sam's falsetto. Ha, ha, ha! We laughed for more than a minute; but it seemed longer: laughter that would have to last a lifetime for me. It felt like I was already home.

"To the peasant!" the Walrus yelled.

"No," Father William said. He waited for silence. Then the devout and pious Father William turned toward several F.N.G.s who were still talking and yelled: "Shut the fuck up, you weenie, scumbag dildos!" Father William then stood with his head bowed and his hands on the bar, like a priest at the altar waiting for the choir to finish. He waited patiently until all movement and chatter inside the barroom ceased. He waited so long the silence became uncomfortable, almost painful. He turned and raised his beer can. "To Sky King," he said, "the fucking peasant . . . pacifist . . . pussy." I smiled. And we all clanged beer cans—all except Miss Sam. She clanged a Coca-Cola can. It may not have been an actual blessing, but I felt blessed.

"Hey, Father William," I said when things had settled down. "Where did you get that Sky King bullshit?"

"Oh," he replied. "Women talk: Or didn't you know that, doo-fuck? Your wife told my wife a long time ago."

"You gotta be shitting me?"

"I wouldn't shit you, you big turd!" he replied.

It was like flipping a switch. Chaos in the barroom for hours, and then it was over. Chaos on the battlefield, and then it was over. Oh, a few TWAT pilots tried to impress us with some shouting, mostly vulgarities, but they were amateurs. Then they tried to jump-start the party by dousing each other with beer, but that too fizzled for lack of authenticity and commitment. We—Father William, Joey, the Walrus, and I— did not say much of anything. Joey did not even tell a joke. And soon the crowd thinned. Some slapped me on the back and wished me good luck on their way out the door; others just disappeared, disappointed I reckon. They had heard stories. They were expecting a huge blowout, maybe a fistfight or two, for sure a confrontation of some sort. Instead they got solace, inactivity, borderline depression. And now it was time for Miss Sam to leave, to get her beautiful ass off of the base. A TWAT pilot stood by, ready to drive her to the front gate. We watched as she mopped the bar, once, twice, three times. Finally, she threw her bar rag on the back counter and emerged from behind the bar. She walked over and stood beside me. Then she leaned in and kissed me on the cheek.

"I hope you never have to return to Viet Nam," she whispered. A few weenies, those who were still in attendance, began to hoot and bang their beer cans on the helicopter blade that was our bar. Miss Sam turned, and without looking back, she walked toward the door. I studied her intently, and I thought I detected an extra swing of her ass just before the door closed.

I do not remember Father William leaving, nor do I remember Joey leaving. The hootch was quiet now. Only the Walrus and I sat at the bar, sipping beers.

"Where is everybody?" I asked. "It's my going-away party. Where are they?" The Walrus did not reply. "Couldn't they stay with me till the end?" Still he did not answer. "It was a lousy going-away party!"

"Are you kidding me?" the Walrus said. "It was the greatest going-away party I have ever seen!" He got off of his stool. The stool tipped and clanged as it bounced off the floor. I thought he was going to walk out on me too. "It was shit-hot!" he hollered. "Look at all the people that were here! Nobody has a party like that!" He grabbed the back of his stool and slammed it down on its four legs; then he sat on it; then he got off of it and walked behind the bar. He chugged his beer and cracked open two more: one for him, one for me. "It's never enough for you!" the Walrus yelled. "You're an asshole!" We drank the beers in silence. Then he stood, turned to me, and said: "I'll see you tomorrow."

And I was alone, all alone, and scared; just like my first night in-country.

Chapter 2
MEMORIES

When the sun rose, I gathered my things. A staff-weenie entered the bar. "You still here?" he asked.

I shouldered my duffle. "Can you drop me off at the terminal?"

"Here, let me take that," he said as he grabbed my duffle and tossed it over his shoulder.

I walked into the terminal and was funneled into a holding area. I looked for a position in a corner but all four were filled. I sat down in the middle of the terminal and waited for my number to be called. It looked like any terminal in the U.S., except there were no civilians, only gaunt GIs dressed in pressed khaki uniforms instead of grubby fatigues. They sat slouched in chairs or wandered aimlessly. Those who sat tapped their fingers or feet. Several grunts carried blaring boom boxes on their shoulders, eliciting thumbs-up or thumbs-down depending who was listening. One GI was singing a solo version of the Temptations' "My Girl."

Others paced. Nearly all were smoking. Nobody was sleeping. There were no groups, just individuals. Sappers like to target groups. Periodically, someone would shout, "I'm *short*!" Others yelled back, "Fucking A, baby!" or "Right on, brother!" This was followed by a period of silence until someone shouted, "I'm *short*!" echoed by, "Fucking A, baby!"

My fifteen-o-fives—a tan summer uniform—sported white embroidered rank, wings, and name tag. I ran my finger over the stitching. I felt my name, perhaps to make sure I was who it said I was. I smiled as I remembered the story of Jefferson getting yelled at by a colonel: "Lieutenant, where is your name tag?" And Jefferson answered: "Name tag? Oh, I memorized it and destroyed it."

I would receive no more shit from colonels. My white embroidered rank and wings would ensure that. Only those who had been in combat wore white embroidered rank, wings, and name tag; everyone else went with metal rank and plastic name tags, and when a senior ranking officer noticed the elaborate stitching, he would show me respect: The kind of respect that a combat vet deserved, a respect based on performance under fire rather than *outstanding performance* for pushing a pencil *above and beyond the call of duty*.

One GI shouted: "Ten more days and the fucking Army can kiss the pimples on my ass!"

"Fucking A, baby!"

"Right on, brother!"

I held my boarding papers in my left hand. It was shaking so I used my right hand to steady it. I looked right and left to see if anybody had noticed. No one had. They were alone with their thoughts. I stood and paced the perimeter of my roped-off pen. A GI walked up to me. "Ask me what I like about this place, captain."

"What do you like about this place, sarge?"

"Nothing! Not one fucking thing!" He laughed and then walked up to another GI.

"Ask me what I like about this place?" he said.

A brief cheer stirred the room. I walked to the window and tried to look out. GIs were lined up in front of me. I rose up on my tiptoes and stretched my neck. I spotted a freedom bird taxiing in. It stopped in front of the terminal. Raindrops bounced off of its wings and I started to mouth the words to the song "Early Morning Rain" . . .

Now, I'm a long way from home and I miss my loved ones so . . .

I walked to an open spot inside the holding pen . . .

. . . Out on runway number nine big 707 set to go

I had caught myself singing this song often in the last several days.

. . . This old airport's got me down. It's no earthly good to me . . .

'cause I'm stuck here on the ground, cold and drunk as I can be.

You can't jump a jet plane like you can a freight train.

So, I'd best be on my way in the early morning rain . . .

"Okay, line up!" a man with a clipboard shouted. Two other GIs moved the stands that held the ropes holding us in. They pushed the stands close together so that the pen now became a chute. I followed in tandem like a passive lamb not wanting to attract attention, not wanting anyone to recognize me, not wanting anyone to say, "There's been a mistake! You will have to stay here!" Yeah, I thought, stay here another day, another month, another year, another lifetime. I scrunched up so I was small: small like I was on the receiving end of a mortar attack, or sapper attack, or rocket attack, or getting shot at; so small that I was invisible to the man with the clipboard. I huddled, existing on short breaths. Drums pounded in my head, sweat streams formed in my armpits and crotch, staining my uniform. I stood: frozen, hiding, hyperventilating. I squeezed my shaking hands into fists.

I watched as the F.N.G.s disembarked. They were walking into the terminal in a line parallel to mine. More men with clipboards were milling. I looked at my feet. My black elephant-skin boots were shined with spit from my mouth. I had chosen boots, instead of the dress-code low-quarter shoes, to complete my statement, so there would be no doubt: I was a combat vet. We shuffled forward now in baby steps. When the line stopped suddenly, my heart stopped with it. I looked up to see what had happened. I looked into the eyes of the men facing me, the men entering the terminal, the men who would call the Nam home for the next year of their lives. I saw fear in their eyes, and I wondered if they saw fear in mine, for I was terrified—terrified that I was not going to make it out of here, that I would be trapped in this shithole for the rest of my life. And then I saw a man from my high school class. He was moving toward me, walking into this shithole.

"Hey Zimmerman," I yelled.

He looked at me—canted his head like a dog that maybe knew something but was not quite sure what it was and figured a different angle might provide more clues. Then his eyes went blank, and his head realigned with his body. "Man, get back on that airplane," I whispered. I could see he did not recognize me, nor did he understand what I was trying to tell him. Was it because I had lost so much weight? I wondered. Was it because nothing was registering with him? The lines moved forward and the distance between us grew.

The shuffle of feet continued onto the airplane, down the aisle about halfway in, to a window seat. I sat and cinched the seatbelt tight—then tightened it some more—for the tighter I was cinched to the airplane, the more difficult it would be to remove me from it. I thought about the story I had heard, about the man who was waiting to board a freedom bird when the bad guys decided to lob a few rockets into the base. He was led to a bunker to outwait the attack when a 122 rocket penetrated the roof of the bunker, but his luck held because the rocket was a dud. It did not explode! No, it did not explode; it stabbed him in the heart—killed him—just minutes from getting out. I shivered. The man sitting next to me noticed it. I sucked in my gut and pulled the seatbelt one notch tighter. I felt the airplane moving, straight ahead at first, then swinging right and left as it maneuvered along the taxiways until it stopped abruptly. Had the brakes locked? I looked out the window. I could see the tower, and in my head I could hear the instructions, ending with, "You are cleared for takeoff." I felt the power come in. I heard the engines roar as fuel was dumped into the burner basket. Then I heard the shrill hum of turbines turning. And then my trained ears went on high alert—listening for any unusual noise that might indicate trouble. I grabbed the armrests and squeezed them. My hands changed from the color of Caucasian flesh to albino white. I looked around as I and several hundred GIs braced for takeoff. I saw terror in the eyes of those around me, so much terror that I had to look down. I felt the airplane gather speed. I felt it rotate, and several hundred-thousand pounds of mass suddenly felt lighter. I heard the gear start up and fold into the belly of the airplane, and then I heard the gear doors close. One door lagged behind the others before it banged shut. Then a spontaneous and simultaneous clapping of hands began. Not an exuberant applause but a refined acknowledgment of the ending of a show. No one told us to clap. No one ordered it. If they had, we would not have done it. We did not rehearse it. Nor did it originate in a certain section of the airplane where it might have been preplanned and spread outward. It just happened. Officers and enlisted men from four branches of the service—on land, at sea, and in the air—with ages spanning five decades, with urban and rural roots, with a variety of skin colors representing scores of ethnic backgrounds—atheists, agnostics, warlocks, Buddhists, Muslims, Jews, Christians; some lax, some Bible thumpers—each having experienced war differently felt compelled to bring their palms together precisely at the same time while otherwise maintaining silence. No one cheered or hooted. There was only a steady and prolonged applause. Individuals sucked up by a random vortex that carried them halfway around the world, and spewed them out in the southern half of a small Asian country, now expressed themselves as one.

When it ended, I was able to grin; not an Earl-sized grin, not a smile; but just a slight upward opening of the lips. I could feel the grin. My eyelids seemed to open wider; objects were crisper, colors more radiant. Now I exhaled. I had made it. We had made it. The war was over for me. I had done my duty; killed many, but saved many lives also, including my own. I was on my way home. We were on our way home. I peered out the window to make sure.

My God, it was beautiful: the jungles lush from monsoon rains, and then the stretches of golden sand bleached by centuries of searing sun. And finally, the seamless blue of sea and sky. It did not look like I was leaving a shithole. So, what made it a shithole? I wondered, for it clearly was. Inland, the country looked like it was dying from leprosy: pockmarked with bomb craters ugly in color and content, now cesspools with rotting carcasses, a place where only disease could live. A country with smells so awful that retching was a reasonable response. A country with dioxin-destroyed foliage and Rome-plowed lunar landscapes: kill zones that would last for generations. If any human managed to live in this environment, we searched him out, using helicopters to dispense death rather than rescue; and when that didn't suffice, we threw big stuff at him—barrages of artillery shells launched from land and sea, and antipersonnel bombs from the air: bombs that would fuck up your whole day. We did all this to save lives. We did all this to save the country.

Could Asian people cause a country to be labeled a shithole? Certainly not the young women who were double- and triple-take beautiful, particularly when attired in their traditional, colorful silk clothing, clothing designed to emphasize their innately slim and graceful bodies. Women with long, shiny ebony-colored hair, dark eyes, ivory-white teeth, and seducing smiles who sometimes managed to keep a safe distance away from horny American males because of the food they ate. Their foul-smelling breath extended farther than outstretched searching hands. Was it then the men? The men were of good humor. Their pilots were dashing and brave. But many other young men—much like in all cultures—were obnoxious, corrupt, shifty, listless, and resentful when we wanted them to be grateful for what we were doing for them. Worst of all, they were not willing to pay the price for the policies we thought their country should follow. We called them gooks and gomers, zipperheads and slopes—so we could kill them with a clear conscience. So it wasn't the land or the people that made this county a shithole; it was the policies: our policies. Policies that destroyed long-standing traditions of strong family unity, respect of elders, and hard work; policies that killed off a generation; policies that destroyed their homeland.

I felt exhausted now, both mentally and physically. It was over. Why worry about it? Why think about it? Why try and make sense of it? I was done with it all. I had survived. I would never have to think about the Nam again. I fell asleep . . .

Bodine appeared and flipped a cigarette from his hand to his mouth and then he disappeared. Thumper sauntered by, flipped me the bird, and then he faded into the ether. FOD arrived, showed me something he held in his hand, and then Sandy strolled in, removed FOD's hat, and tossed it to the ground. They were replaced by Father William. "Fucking peasants!" he said. And then he turned and walked away, and with his back to me, he flipped me the bird before he, too, disappeared. Jefferson stood with his arm around Carlos. They both waved, then disappeared. The PAC AF Junior Officer of the Year with his gas mask on walked by, followed by the Kiwi in flak vest and steel pot, Doc, Major Personovich, and Big Al, the Kiddies' Pal. Buddha appeared, lifted his fatigue shirt, and said: "Rub my belly for good luck," and then he turned and walked away until he dissolved into a dot. There was a brilliant flash on a white background and when I drew back away from it, I could see it emanated from Earl's front teeth. And as I pulled back farther, I noticed his right boot stood on a prone Captain Puff, and then they both were gone. The Walrus appeared, his eyes scanning the ground around him like he was flying low bird on a trolling mission.

"What are you looking for?" I asked.

"I'm looking for a whorehouse," he replied and then he disappeared.

Miss Sam blew me a kiss and then she, too, disappeared.

And then Joey appeared. I reached out for him, but I could not touch him. "Hey matey!" he said. "I'm wearing the digger hat you gave me," I replied. We looked at each other for a long time; neither of us could think of anything else to say. And then he started to fade.

"Hey, where you going?" I hollered. I tried to run after him but I couldn't catch him.

"I've got to drain me one-eyed dragon," he answered.

Hee hee! Hee, hee, hee . . .

I awoke sucking air and unsure of my location. Was I in my hootch? The man sitting beside me stared at me. My head was heavy and began to wobble. My eyes closed. I was anxious to get back to my friends . . .

I was flying my airplane. People were shooting at me. Weather had me boxed in. I could feel myself squirming. An F-100 came out of the clouds and its underbelly filled my windshield, millions of rivets the size of flat screws that held it together. What was going to hold me together? I felt my arm go up to cover my face. "Got to get below these clouds! Got to break out to where I can see!" I descended. Explosion! My airplane is inverted. I'm going to crash into a tree . . .

I jammed my left foot into the seat in front of me and swung my arms until my left arm crossed my right. There was a hand on my shoulder. "You are all right," a voice whispered. "You had a bad dream."

I stirred, sucked in a huge amount of air; my lungs swelled. My chest rose to accommodate my lungs. I held the air in until it swirled through my body, relaxing my muscles. "Sorry," I said.

"It's okay. I have them all the time myself," the man sitting beside me said.

I rubbed my eyes, then my cheeks. "Sorry," I mumbled. And I fell back asleep . . .

Billy was there. "Where you been?" he asked. "We are all waiting for you. Look, Moondoggie is here." He pointed. There was a group of men standing behind him. All were dressed in flight suits or fatigues. Their boots were devoid of color. They hadn't seen the inside of a can of Shinola in years. I recognized the others: Lucky Larry, Mike in the Jungle, the two men I ate breakfast with before they died, a bunch of Buddha's boys, and more behind them. I nodded. They were all smiling. I was not. I started to cry. "Why all of you and not me?" I asked. There was no answer. "I miss you guys terribly."

"Have a beer," Moondoggie said.

"We're always here," he added.

My crying continued. It turned into sobs. "I feel like I have let you down."

"No! No!" they replied in unison.

"I hate it when I cry," I said. "I feel like a baby. You all are soldiers, grown men. I should be with you."

"No! No!" they replied in unison.

"But I'm weak. I need you. Why couldn't it have been me instead?" I continued to sob. "Are you still mooning people?" I asked Moondoggie.

"Yeah," he said. "I think I'm the only one up here who does it."

I tried to smile. "I want to join you."

"No! No!" they replied in unison.

"Not yet, my friend," Billy added.

Their images began to fade, and when they disappeared, I reached out to them, still sobbing...

The hand was back on my shoulder. Again I had to suck in air. "Another dream," the man beside me said. I wiped the tears rolling down my checks. *God, I hated crying. I've got to suck it up and stop that.* "You scared me," the man said. "You stopped breathing."

"I remember feeling like I was suffocating," I replied. I waited until my breathing returned to normal.

What is normal? I wondered.

"What are you going to do when you get Stateside?" I asked.

He paused, then answered. "I have one week until I am discharged. Then I am going to burn my uniform and head for a deserted beach . . . Let the sun, surf, and sand clean my body."

What about the part that is seared in my brain? I wondered: *The part that won't let me sleep through the night unless I have a dozen beers in my body.*

"Sounds like a good plan," I said. I unbuckled, made sure there were no more tears, and walked back to the galley. "Got any coffee?"

"Sure," she answered as she pulled a cup from a stack and then pulled a spigot on a container. "Cream and sugar?"

"No, black."

"Damn, I should have known. I was briefed: GIs drink their coffee black.

Sorry," she said with a smile, and I wondered how people could talk and smile at the same time. I couldn't do that, could I?

"Yeah, Marine coffee," I replied. "Coffee so black you can't see the bottom of the cup." She smiled again.

I leaned back against the bulkhead and took a sip.

"Bet you are glad to be going home?" she continued.

It was a simple question. One I should have been able to answer without thought. One I should have laughed and said, "Are you kidding? You betcha!" But I didn't. I couldn't. I thought about seeing my wife in Hawaii and how I did not recognize her. I thought about how soon we ran out of things to say to each other. I thought about the distance between us when I departed. I looked down at my arms and legs. How could I tell somebody that I was maimed when all my limbs were there? I had no wounds, no visible scars. I appeared unharmed, but I was no longer whole. I left body parts in Viet Nam. I didn't know which parts, but I knew something was missing and the remains were on their way home.

"You married?" she asked. I nodded.

"Kids?"

This time my response was rapid and I was laughing. "Yup! Two sons." I took another sip. This time I thought about how much I wanted to hold them, roughhouse with them, laugh with them, kiss them, teach them everything I knew. "God, it's going to be great!" I said as I headed back to my seat.

On my way back, a hand that belonged to a major grabbed my arm just above the elbow. I had to curl my body into an S to avoid spilling my coffee.

"Captain," the man said. "Do you remember me?" I wasn't sure so I did not answer. "I'm the guy with the opals. The ones you were supposed to get set while you were in Hong Kong." I tensed. "Just wanted you to know my girls loved them. The guy did an outstanding job." And that was it. No thank you. No acknowledgment that I did an outstanding job. No apology for yelling at me when I was asleep and hung over. I wanted to say, "Fuck you!" but I couldn't since I was in a good mood. So as I removed his hand from my bicep, I said, "Three bags full, major!" He cocked his head to one side, then scrunched, contorted, and distorted his face, looking very much like the *doofus* he was. I tried to copy his look with my own, but I was not sure I captured it completely. I walked away. I studied the young men who occupied the belly of this airplane. I wondered if these hundreds of GIs were feeling the same as I. These GIs returning to *the world*; reborn after a baptism of fire, now alone with just thoughts. GIs excited yet cautious about our eventual homecoming, fearful of the anger—the juice that boiled in our bellies— and the violence we now knew we were capable of. Slowly, I walked toward my seat, excused myself as the man on the aisle stood and made way for me to pass. I let gravity pull my tired ass into my assigned seat and cinched the belt tight around my shrunken waist, where it remained for the rest of the flight.

I had a short stopover in Anchorage while the plane was serviced before continuing on to the East Coast of the United States. I sat seething with anger as GI prisoners deplaned first; those who served with honor superseded by those who hadn't. I followed them into the terminal where they were confined while I was allowed to walk around. I stared at the clocks on the wall. What day was it? I wondered, knowing that I had crossed the International Date Line. I couldn't figure it out. I laughed; it was just like Viet Nam where I never knew what day it was either by number or title. Was it Wednesday? Or was it Thursday? "Ah, fuck it! Who cares?" I mumbled.

I began my *reccy* mission: walking around, checking things out, making sure no one was following me. I stopped at a few shops, purchased several gifts, and then enjoyed the change left over from my purchases. It jingled in my pocket—a sound, feeling, and touch I had long forgotten. I cupped my hand in my pocket, like a teenager trying to cover up an inadvertent hard-on, and shook the change as I walked from shop to shop. A strange thought surfaced. Change in my pocket was so pleasurable that a real hard-on might be the end result. I smiled at my silly thoughts. I noticed a T-shirt in a store window. It read: Southeast Asia War Games, Second Place! I felt anger but laughed: anger and laughter, my only two emotional responses. I noticed a woman: young, stylish, and beautiful. She walked by me and glanced back. She was not wearing a bra, and now I actually felt a surge as my member signaled for more blood. God it was exciting. I followed her up a flight of stairs and into and out of mezzanine shops. She peered back at me, and when she did my nostrils instinctively opened, like thrust attenuators on a jet engine, as the aroma of an exotic perfume fanned out inside my head and throughout my brain. It staggered me. I grabbed onto a post to steady myself. She smiled. I wanted to study her forever, but an announcement interrupted, an announcement calling for the re-boarding of my freedom bird. The prisoners boarded first, and this time I did not complain. I wanted to linger under her spell until I was forced to move on.

The announcement to re-board seemed unusually loud. I had a vague recollection that this may have been the third or fourth time the order was issued. It was like this one was meant just for me, that it took repetition and an increase in volume to turn my head away from the woman and turn it toward my wife and family. I sat down and cinched my lap belt, and then fell asleep.

I awoke to cheering. I looked at the man in the seat next to me. I, too, must have canted my head like a puzzled dog. "We have crossed into the forty-eight contiguous United States," he said. It was official now. I was on my way home and nothing—not a change in orders, nor an amendment to the rules of engagement, nor an act of Congress, nor a desk-flying colonel—could muck it up. I smiled as I mentally wrestled with my sons on the floor of my house. My oldest had fashioned a cape from a bath towel. It was the only fight I had ever been in where all the combatants were giggling. Suddenly, the action and laughter stopped. My oldest son had farted. We paused for only a moment to assess the damage, and then, just as suddenly, we were right back into it.

My plan was to overfly our home in North Dakota, land in New Jersey, and catch a flight to New York where I could sign in and then take thirty days' leave. By signing in, as opposed to taking leave en route, I could get my name on the base housing list. I wanted to live on base. I began to imagine all the things I loved about military service . . .

I loved wearing the uniform with an impeccable gig line—a straight line running down the middle of my body aligning the edge of my shirt with the end of my belt buckle and continuing down along the edge of my fly. I loved it when the guard at the gate saluted my car as he waved me through. I loved getting out of my car and standing at attention, holding a perfect salute while our flag was lowered at the end of the day. I heard a bugle play "Day Is Done" over the base loudspeakers. I stooped to straighten the salute of my sons. I couldn't wait to get on the base and show off my embroidered rank and wings, a tolerated but unwritten infringement of dress regulations, but necessary to identify those who had been to war from those who had not . . .

We landed at McGuire A.F.B.—a civilian plane landing at a military installation. I caught a cab downtown, for I had several hours to kill before I boarded a regional airplane for my stop in New York. I walked into a neighborhood bar attired in my summer khaki uniform with my embroidered wings and rank, fully expecting to be greeted warmly by the patrons within, fully expecting to drink free compliments of all the grateful men and women. There were no women in this bar, just working-class men sitting in booths and on barstools. I stopped just inside the doorway and let my eyes adjust to the smoke and darkness. All heads turned toward me, but no one said anything.

Perhaps they were waiting for someone else. I picked out a stool in the middle of the bar and sat down with a man immediately on my left and another two stools down on my right.

"What'll you have, captain?" the bartender asked.

"Just a tap beer," I answered. I was impressed that he recognized my rank. He returned with a glass with an inch of beer foam on top.

"Four bits," he said. I pulled a dollar from my pocket and tossed it on the bar. He returned with change, then took his place leaning against the back bar. Miss Sam had a much nicer ass, but their tits were about the same size and he looked as though he might be five or six months pregnant.

"Fucking hippies!" the man next to me said. I was tired. I hadn't slept, except for dozing, for thirty-six hours.

"Now they want to give the eighteen-year-olds the right to vote! Ain't that a bunch of shit, captain?" He struck my shoulder with the back of his hand. Several other men nodded in agreement. "I mean, what the hell is the world coming to?" he continued, and at the end of every sentence he struck my shoulder and said, "Ain't that a bunch of shit, captain?" I wrapped my hands around my beer glass. I couldn't tell if he was trying to include me or antagonize me with his slaps. All I knew was that I didn't like it. He got off his stool. He was taller than me, maybe five years older. "Eighteen-year-olds! Why their noses are still dripping. What the fuck do they know?" I turned toward him. "Don't hit me again," I said. I lit a cigarette and dropped the pack on the bar.

"Why, they are barely out of diapers! They don't pay any taxes! Now they want to let them vote. It's a goddamn disgrace."

"That's right!" several others at the bar said.

"What do you think about that, captain?" the man asked after he hit me on the shoulder again, this time perhaps to get my attention.

"Where I just came from *beaucoup* eighteen-year-olds gave up their lives and limbs so you can sit here and drink in peace. I reckon they should be able to vote."

"Oh, you're one of those baby killers." He looked around the room. "Hey, we got ourselves a baby killer here!" Then he turned toward me. "I suppose that makes you feel like a big man, killing women and children."

I am not sure who threw the first punch. Chances are I did. I just know I got a few in before I was wrapped up by a bunch of arms and tossed out on the sidewalk. I heard one man shout that I was a loser. Had I landed in the wrong country? I wondered. I stood and brushed myself off. "Why, the fuckers even kept my change!" I thought about going back in, not just to get my change, but to teach them a lesson about respect: respect for the uniform, respect for our country, and respect for the men who wore the uniform and fought for our country; a uniform that now had a little of my spilled blood on it. Using "discretion is better than valor" as an excuse, I retreated to fight again another day, even though I was never known for using discretion. I needed to plant my feet on a military base where my service would be valued and—by extension—I would be validated.

I boarded the regional airplane, a prop job, which stopped en route at every city with a runway long enough to accommodate it. It was the U.S. version of TWATS (Viet Nam's Teeny Weenie Air Transport Service). Only this bird was larger, the pilots were older, and I was the spare part being transported. At most stops, an honor guard met the airplane and a casket was unloaded. GIs deplaned and knelt to kiss the tarmac before passing through the checkpoint where family and friends waited. I watched as I smoked a cigarette, and when I ground the butt out and shredded it, I got back on the airplane. When I reached my destination, there was a car waiting for me with an airman second class as a driver. "Thanks for picking me up," I said. "Oh, we meet every plane, captain," he replied.

He drove me to squadron headquarters. I entered and spotted a fellow captain. "Where's the squadron commander's office?" I asked. The captain looked around. We were the only ones in the hallway. He leaned in so that his mouth was inches away from my ear and said: "Oh, you mean Colonel Maytag's office?"

I checked my orders. "That's not his name."

"Yes it is. It's a derivation of Wishy-Washy." I laughed. He pointed right. "All the way to the end," he said.

At the end of the hallway, I turned right again and into an office where I spotted the sign-in and sign-out book. A sergeant stood and checked my embroidered name as I checked his name tag. His name was Blaine. "Sign in," he ordered. And I did. "Then sign out on leave." And I did. I was allowed thirty days' leave after a combat tour. I would spend them at home. After thirty days, I would again depart without family, T.D.Y. (temporary duty), for a base in California for four months' training in the art of flying B-52s where twenty degrees of bank constituted a steep turn.

"Here are your leave papers and a set of instructions, captain," Sergeant Blaine said. He pointed to the top sheet. "This is your tentative class date. We will call you with the specifics as soon as we have confirmation. I will then mail out your orders. Is this a phone number and address where we can contact you?" I nodded. "Okay," he said and then added, "The squadron commander wants to meet you." I nodded again. He got up and walked to an open door. "Colonel, the new pilot is here." I frowned at the label new pilot. I didn't feel new. I didn't feel like a F.N.G. I felt like a veteran, a combat veteran. "Send him in!" came the response. I moved toward the door and then through it. I stopped in front of his desk, snapped to attention, and saluted. He did not acknowledge me, or my salute. He continued to peruse his paperwork. I dropped my salute. His hair was grey and coiffed ala Johnny Unitas. His only color belonged to the blue uniform he wore and the ribbons beneath his wings. I spotted his longevity ribbon and counted back the years. He had been in the Air Force for the end of WWII, all through Korea, and now Viet Nam, but there were no combat ribbons: no air medals, no campaign ribbons, no Foreign Service ribbons, and I wondered how he could have been in the Air Force for more than twenty-five years yet managed to miss participating in three wars. Colonel Wishy-Washy finally looked up. He scanned me vertically—once, twice, three times—and then he said: "I'm gonna tear all that Southeast Asia shit off your uniform and make a combat soldier out of you." He said it with a sneer. I did not answer. I could feel the heat rising from somewhere in my gut. I could feel my skin as it turned the color of a live lobster dumped in a boiling pot, and it happened just as fast too. I could feel steam radiating from my face.

"I want all that embroidered rank shit off your uniform the next time I see you. Do you hear me, captain?"

"Three bags full," I said softly.

"What did you say, captain?" He stood, placed his palms on his desk, like a cat ready to pounce. I wished he had, but this cat turned pussy when we met eyeball to eyeball. He sat back down and began shuffling his papers. I glared down at him. This non-combatant puke was going to make a combat soldier out of me? *I got news for you, motherfucker.* I thought it but did not say it. I wanted to punch his lights out. I wanted to tear his heart out and eat it. I wanted to jam an M-16 in his gut and pull the trigger. But I also wanted to get home, play with my sons, hug my wife, so I said nothing. "Get the hell out of here! I'll deal with you later," he said and I did.

I landed in Minnesota, for a night of visiting with my brothers and parents before heading to my final destination, North Dakota. My brother met me at the airport. "God, you are skinny," he said. "The little woman is cooking up a big meal for you. Something special. She's been scurrying around all day. I'll bet you are dying for a home-cooked meal." No, I thought to myself, dying would not be a word I would use.

We entered his home, where my mother hugged me and my father shook my hand, as did my other brother. "God, you're skinny. Didn't they feed you over there?"

"Come on everybody. Dinner is served," my brother's wife said, and we all sat down at the table. My father said grace, as he always did, and thanked God for my safe return. "I prayed the Rosary for you every day," my mother said. "That's why you made it back." I smiled and nodded my appreciation, but inside I felt confused. Did that mean those who died did not have a mother praying for them?

"Eat up!" my brother's wife said. "We have got to get some weight back on you."

She dumped a heaping pile of food on my plate: Chow mein over white rice. "Have you got a beer?" I asked.

"Hell yeah," my brother said, and he left the table and returned with a can of Hamm's. I nursed it while others ate. "You've hardly touched your food," my mother said.

"I'm not too hungry." I could see the disappointment on my sister-in-law's face. So I shoved another couple of forks full into my mouth and asked for another beer.

"Okay, let those dishes go. Everyone in the living room. I want to hear everything about what it was like over there," my brother's wife said. We rose on cue and adjourned to the living room, where everyone sat staring at me—the women with their hands folded on their laps, the men lighting up cigarettes.

"We could beat those guys if the politicians stayed out of it," one of my brothers started.

"The war is wrong," my other brother replied.

"Isn't that right?" my first brother said. "Give the military a free hand, and the war would be over in weeks."

"Yeah, we've been holding back," I heard myself say.

"Is it true that everybody is on drugs over there?" my brother's wife asked.

"A lot of beer. Can I have another?"

"I think you have had too many already," my mother said. "You didn't eat much for dinner." My brother left to get me another beer. I popped it open.

"I've heard," he said, "the V.C. chain guys to trees so they have to stay and fight."

"It's hard to tell what's real and what isn't over there," I said, then added, "I heard the V.C. and N.V.A. wrapped tourniquets around their arms and legs, then shot them up with heroin, and got up on line, and every time their left foot hit the ground, they fired. They couldn't bleed, and they couldn't feel pain so they just keep on coming."

"See, how can you fight fanatics like that? They are not like us. Life doesn't mean anything to them. We should nuke them all!"

"No," my other brother said. "We should just get out of there."

"What about the Negroes?" my father asked.

"They bleed red just like we do," I replied.

"What about massacres? Like My Lai," my brother's wife asked. "Did you kill women and children?" I ignored the question.

"We should march right up to Hanoi," my brother declared.

"We'd lose a lot of men," I replied.

"We haven't lost that many men," my brother said. "Hell, we lose more people on the highway every year than we have in this entire war."

"I think we ought to salute the draft resisters," my other brother said. "We are murderers. They are the patriots." He looked at me, and then asked, "How could you do that? How could you bomb villages?"

I took a mouthful of beer and swallowed. He rose. "We need to stop this war. Stop this killing of innocent people."

"Stop it!" my mother yelled. "No more talk of war. He is home now. The war is over for him. Let's just enjoy life."

I stood. "I have to use the bathroom." My brother's wife pointed.

"See, it's all that beer," my mother said.

I walked to the bathroom, locked the door, sat down, and cried.

The next morning I flew to North Dakota. The plane taxied to the terminal and stopped. I sat in my seat and watched as two coffins were unloaded. All passengers stood, those under the luggage racks stooped, and then they filed out. I stayed seated, staring out the window; immobilized, stoic, seeing nothing. A stewardess walked down the aisle. She placed the palms of her hands on each aisle seat as she approached. She stopped at my row and looked down upon me.

"Sir," she said, "you have to deplane."

"I don't know if I can."

"But you have to."

The pilot appeared. "It's time to get off, buddy," he said. I rose slowly and walked to the door, stopping at the top of the stairs. There were cheers when they—my wife and her family and my two sons—saw me. There was a huge "Welcome Home" sign. I moved down the stairs, holding on to each side rail. My oldest son ran to me yelling: "Daddy! Daddy! Daddy!" I scooped him up and squeezed him against my chest. I had arrived home. I was exhausted.

Several days later, I was sitting in my living room, reading. My boys were running back and forth, hiding behind chairs. My oldest was shouting, "Bang! Bang! Gotcha. You're dead!" I called for my wife.

"What is it, hon?" she asked.

"I want you to discipline those boys. And take those guns away. I never want to see another gun in this house."

"Come on, boys," she said. "Daddy's tired. Go play in your room."

I stood. "I'm not tired," then I added, "I need to get away for a while."

On my twenty-ninth day of leave, I walked to the mailbox, opened it, and studied the contents one by one. "Where the hell are my orders?" I asked my wife.

"I haven't seen them."

"I need to call the squadron." I picked up the telephone and tried to place a collect call. "They will not accept the charges," the operator said.

"Okay, I'll pay."

"329th Bomb Squadron."

"Sergeant Blaine?"

"Yes."

"I haven't received my orders."

"Just a minute; the colonel wants to talk to you."

My wife stood in the doorway with her arms folded, as Captain Puff did so often. I felt the hot flames of anger shoot through my body as I waited for the colonel to pick up.

"Captain, is that you?"

"Yes."

The phone fell from my hand. I pulled it back up by the curled cord and slammed the receiver down on the cradle.

"What did he say?" my wife asked.

"He said I was AWOL!"

Epilogue

The night we smoked a cigar on a hilltop in the State of Washington was the last time I saw or talked to Thumper. I heard he had stayed in the Air Force, was promoted to the rank of general, and died shortly after retiring from the Air Force while on an operating table where he was undergoing a routine procedure.

My son visited Joey in Australia, nearly forty years after I left Joey in Viet Nam. Joey, the Kiwi, and I reunited shortly thereafter—the first time we were together since 1970. After my tour in Viet Nam, Father William joined me for training in California. We stayed in touch ever since. I have never heard from nor contacted any of the other characters in this memoir.

View full color map at https://en.wikipedia.org/wiki/File:Usaf-vietnam-map.jpg

Map of major U.S Air Force Bases in South Vietnam during the Vietnam War — 1965-1973

Glossary

A-1Es: airplane

A.C.: Aircraft commander

A.D.F.: automatic direction finder

A.G.L.: above ground level

ALO: air liaison officer

A.O.: area of operation

A.P.: air policeman or ape

A.P.C.: armored personnel carrier

A.R.V.N.: Armed Forces, Republic of Viet Nam

A.T.C.: air training command

B.D.A.: bomb damage assessment

B.O.Q.: bachelor officer quarters

BUFF: Big Ugly Fat Fucker

BX: base exchange

C.B.U.: cluster bomb units

CONUS: Continental United States

COSVN: Central Office for South Viet Nam

DASC: Direct Air Support Center

DD: Department of Defense

DEROS: date estimated to return from overseas

D.F.C.: Distinguished Flying Cross

D.M.Z.: Demilitarized Zone

DNIF: duty not including flying

E.O.D.: explosive ordinance disposal

EWO: electric warfare officer

FAC: forward air controller

FIGMO: Fuck It, Got My Orders

FM: frequency modulation, or *fox mike*

F.N.G.: fucking new guy

F.O.B.: forward operating bases

FOD: foreign object damage

FUBAR: fucked up beyond any recognition, or fuck it up beyond all recognition

G.C.A.: ground-controlled approach

GIB: guy in back

H.E.: high explosive

I.F.R.: instrument flight rules

I.L.S.: instrument landing system

I.P.s: Instructor Pilot

K.B.A.: killed by air

L.B.J.: Long Binh Jail

L.D.S.: Latter-day Saint

LERPs: Long-range reconnaissance patrols

LOACH: light observation helicopter

L.Z.: landing zone

M(i)F/Miffwick: motherfucker what's in charge

MiG: Russian jet fighter

MPC: military pay certificates

N.C.O.I.C.: non-commissioned officer in charge

November Delta Papas: night defensive positions

N.V.A.: North Vietnamese Army

O.E.R.: officer efficiency report

OV: type of aircraft (OV-10)

PAC AF: Pacific Air Force

P.B.R.s: patrol, boat, river

P.E.: personal equipment

P.I.: Phillipine Islands

pitot-boom: impale

P.L.F.: parachute landing fall

P.O.L.: petroleum, oil, lubricant
pommies: prisoners of Mother England
P.O.W.: Prisoner of War
P.S.P: pierced steel planking
PX: Post exchange
PSYOPS: psychological operations
RAF SOB: regular Air Force son of a bitch
REMFs: rear-echelon motherfuckers
R.O.E.: rules of engagement
ROKs: Republic of Korea soldiers
R.O.N: remain overnight
ROTC: Reserve Officer Training Corp
R.P.G.: rocket-propelled grenade
R.S.V.N.: Republic of South Viet Nam
R.T.B.: return to base
R.T.O.: radiotelephone operators
SAC: Strategic Air Command
SAM: surface-to-air missile
SAR: search and rescue
SEA: Southeast Asia
SEATO: Southeast Asia Treaty Organization
S.F.: Special Forces
S.I.E.: self-initiated elimination
S.R.O.: senior ranking officer
STOL: short takeoff and landing
studs: students
TAC: Tactical Air Command
TACAN: tactical air navigation system
TASS: Tactical Air Support Squadron
T.D.Y.: temporary duty pay

Thud: F-105, Thunderchief

T.I.C.: troops in contact

TOC: Tactical Operations Center

T.O.T.: time on target

TWATS: Teeny Weenie Air Transport Service

UHF: ultra-high frequency

U.P.T.: undergraduate pilot training

U.S.A.F.: U.S. Air Force

V.C.: Viet cong or Victor Charles

VHF: very high frequency (sometimes called victor)

V.F.R.: visual flight rules

VNAF: Viet Namese Air Force

V.V.I: vertical velocity indicator

WACS: Women's Army Corps

WAG: wild ass guess

weenies: new trainees

WIC: what's in charge

Wilco: will comply

Willy Peters: white phosphorous rockets

Y.G.B.S.M.: You Gotta Be Shitting Me

zoomies: Air Force Academy grads

Z.P.U.: Russian anti-aircraft gun

About the Author

One year after my tour in Viet Nam ended in August of 1970, I was ordered to Thailand for 120 days of flying combat missions as a copilot in B-52s. When I told my squadron commander that I did not have to return since I had already served a one-year tour in Viet Nam, he replied that my orders read TDY, or temporary duty, and the rules allowed them to send me back for 90 days.

"But the orders read 120 days," I protested.

"At 90 days we will call you in, and you will sign a waiver, and we will give you an attaboy."

"But I am not going to sign a waiver."

"We don't care if you do or don't. We will rotate you to Guam, which is considered CONUS or Continental United States, for one day and then we will rotate you back to Thailand for 90 more days."

Two additional involuntarily six-month tours in B-52s from Guam to Viet Nam (14- to 16-hour missions) in 1972 and 1973 were tacked on to my career. I flew in the middle B-52 on the last bombing mission of the war. TOT, or time over target, was 1,159 on August 15, 1973, months after our POWs were safely home. The war officially ended at noon on that day. I wore a large patch on my flight jacket that read: SAC— *just one good deal after another*. Total combat missions flown in O-2s and B-52s: 350, give or take.

In 1974, the Air Force asked me to hang up my blue suit under a program called RIF (Reduction in Force). If I chose not to leave, I would be reduced in rank to staff sergeant, four stripes instead of dual silver bars. Some choice! I knew I could never again wear *any* uniform, which ruled out flying for the airlines, or what we called *bus driving*. I bought a small farm in the foothills of the Adirondacks, isolating and essentially becoming a survivalist. My departing words to the Air Force were, "I'd rather shovel shit than eat it." I hated everyone. If I could have, I would have put quad 50s on each corner of my property, to keep humans out. Animals affected me differently. I had been a hunter since high school, but now I could no longer pull the trigger with a bird or a deer in my sights. I lost several cows and calves to a brutal winter and buried two of our family's German shepherds. I shuddered when I had to butcher chickens and rabbits. It seemed like death was everywhere. I had to move. In 1976, I interviewed for a job with a major international corporation back in the town of my youth.

"We like you," the personnel manager said as he rocked back on his chair with his arms behind his head, "but you have no management experience."

"No management experience?" I replied. "When I made a good decision, bad guys died. When I made a bad decision, good guys died. Now you tell me about your management experience." All four legs of his chair returned to earth. "I've never met anyone like you," he said. And he offered me the job. I signed on, working with and under men who had stayed out of the war with college deferments. I needed to augment my income, so I decided to fly once again and add "instructor pilot" to my ratings. A young kid, my instructor pilot, walked up to my briefing table.

"How many hours do you have?" he asked.

"I am not sure," I replied, "maybe 2,100 or 2,300 hours."

"Oh, you must be one of those military assholes," he said. And then he added, "You may know how to fly the heavies, but I know how to fly the lights." I stood.

"Pick out two airplanes," I said. "We will strap guns to them. You pick one, I'll take the other, and then we will go fly. The one who lands will be the instructor. How about that?"

He walked away, and I walked out; never to pilot an aircraft again.

In 1979, I stood crying on the steps of a VA hospital. I was about to admit that I was crazy, and they should lock me up. "I would rather go back into combat than walk through these doors," I said to my wife as I entered the hospital. "What is the number one thing wrong with you?" they asked when I finally summoned the courage to walk in. I was stunned by my answer. "I am unable to love anybody or anything," I replied.

In my gut, I knew this would be my last chance. If this did not work, I would head for Central America to become a mercenary pilot. I wanted to die, but I wanted to go out with a tinge of dignity. The VA diagnosed me as a depressed drunk. "How long is this program?" I asked one day after feeling a little bit better. "There is no time limit, but normally the program is twenty-nine days," the psychiatrist replied. "I will do it faster," I said. Four months later, they released me. They said I had a 50-50 chance of staying sober. I have been sober for thirty-five years now and still think about picking up a beer, or a shot of whisky, or a thousand shots of whisky.

Seven years after I got sober, and just shy of twenty years of marriage, my wife divorced me. "Changed her name to the plaintiff," as Joey once said. Fortunately, I rebounded into the arms of a woman who gave me "a peaceful, easy feeling," yes, just like the words from the song, and for the last twenty-nine years, with hours of tender loving care on her part, she softened me up; allowing me to open my heart just a crack. We married in 1995.

I watched the Gulf War on television and I started to have flashbacks. For no apparent reason, I would break down crying, both publicly and privately. When I started my truck, I could see a propeller rotating through my windshield as I taxied out onto the highway. In 2008, my wife insisted I get help. I was officially diagnosed with chronic PTSD (post-traumatic stress disorder) and spent another fourteen weeks in a VA hospital learning to understand my symptoms, my triggers, and how to live with them. While there, I was also diagnosed with sleep apnea.

War and geo-politics make strange bedfellows. My daughter and second son both married refugees of two longtime enemies of the United States of America, and today I am the proud grandfather of two Cuban-American grandsons and three Vietnamese-American granddaughters.

In 2011, I was diagnosed with stage 4 lung cancer. The VA decreed this disease was a direct result of my exposure to Agent Orange. I am still battling.

Editor's Note: Jerry Hall died on August 25, 2015. Just six months before the publication of *Yes Sir, Yes Sir, 3 Bags Full!*

www.ingramcontent.com/pod-product-compliance
Lightning Source LLC
Chambersburg PA
CBHW050531300426
44113CB00012B/2043